MARKETING INTELLIGENCE

DISCOVER WHAT YOUR CUSTOMERS REALLY WANT AND WHAT YOUR COMPETITORS ARE UP TO

Jack Savidge

BUSINESS ONE IRWIN
Homewood, Illinois 60430

Sponsoring editor: Cynthia A. Zigmund
Project editor: Jess Ann Ramirez
Production manager: Ann Cassady
Jacket designer: Kay Fulton
Designer: Heidi J. Baughman
Art manager: Kim Meriwether
Compositor: Eastern Composition
Typeface: 11/13 Century Schoolbook
Printer: Book Press, Inc.

Library of Congress Cataloging-in-Publication Data

Savidge, Jack.
    Marketing intelligence : discover what your customers really want
and what your competitors are up to / Jack Savidge.
        p.   cm.
    Includes index.
    ISBN 1-55623-579-8
    1. Marketing research. 2. Marketing—Management. 3. Small
business—Management. I. Title.
    HF5415.2.S28   1992
    658.8'02—dc20   92-99

Printed in the United States of America
1 2 3 4 5 6 7 8 9 0 BP 9 8 7 6 5 4 3 2

PREFACE

WHY I'VE WRITTEN THIS BOOK

On any given day, go into any office, garage, deli, or greeting card shop and ask, "How do you get good ideas to improve your business?" The answer will be "From a Kiwanis meeting," "from my brother-in-law or my uncle who knows all about business problems," or "from one-on-one conversations with other businesspeople who have faced similar business challenges." This seeking and sharing exchange goes on during every business day between retailers, restauranteurs, car and pharmaceutical company managers, and service professionals, including accountants, doctors, lawyers, and Indian chiefs. They learn from talking with mentors, teachers, Dutch uncles, friends, and coaches. Personal exchange seems to increase the absorption and adoption of sound business ideas. Why? Because these people have been down that road before. They know where the twists, turns, and potholes are that every enterprise faces sooner or later. Look, business is simple when these five realities are believed and executed:

1. Your business is managing customer value and competition.
2. Customers are constantly changing their values and demanding new products or services.
3. The competition wants your customer.
4. You must accept change, and provide the customers with what they want, or lose them.
5. Marketing intelligence helps you understand:

   - Who wants change, and why they want it.
   - What to change.

- How much the customer will pay for change.
- When change must be available.
- Where the customer wants to buy a new value.

WHO IS THIS MAN?

You're going to be learning about these business truths from someone who has walked in your shoes and knows the terrain. I'll take an extra minute to describe my experience. It all started in the early 1950s when I "hit the road" selling fresh meat as a Midwest territory salesman for Armour & Company. At 3M Company an order clerk job led to field sales in Chicago and New York City; then I was promoted to federal government sales manager officed in Washington, D.C. (incidentally, at that time I was the youngest sales manager at 3M). I moved up to product manager in the home office at St. Paul; and for the last part of my career at 3M, after I championed for and internally sold the need for a new business function, I was the first person in the company to ever hold the position of "marketing manager." If I made a contribution to 3M, it was to organize and manage the components of the customer persuasion system into an integrated marketing department and to do away with the fragmented efforts of sales, advertising, public relations, product definition, pricing, and distribution.

Well, I was itchy to be on my own, and in 1969 I convinced my wife to pack up our five children and move to California, where I would start a marketing consulting company. With no customers, a little venture capital, and lots of naivete, I hung out the shingle. Now, without the net of a big company, I had to practice what I preached. The challenge was to find customers, give them what they wanted, and forge my way into markets already being served by the competition. Twenty-three years later, I'm still here. I have been immersed in hundreds of different businesses and engaged in their struggles from just about every perspective. When you have to survive on your own, you leverage your core strengths and change your product to serve new customers. For example, on four occasions I deviated from my consulting practice for one- to two-year periods to turn around and sell, as CEO, a small industrial equipment company; join a subsidiary of Eastman Kodak, first as a consultant and then as an employee, to identify and facilitate new businesses; learn about and then become a professional venture capitalist for one of the country's largest investment firms to look for southern California companies in need of capital; and become the founding executive director of a nonprofit organization (now in its 18th year) that brought management and marketing help to minority and disadvantaged small businesses.

My clients range from raw start-ups to global Fortune 25 firms. I have served as a member of the boards of directors for nearly 30 companies, including public and private, high- and low-tech, manufacturing and service, and big and small enterprises. They all have had the same problem: giving their customers what they want and keeping ahead of the competition.

WHAT THE BOOK'S ABOUT

So, in addition to knowing how to create and build an independent small business, I've coached, mentored, instructed, led, and shown big and small company managers how to execute marketing intelligence challenges. I have watched very intelligent and trained individuals overlook or avoid critical questions that demanded answers. They've taken wrong directions in their search for answers and arrived at unsupportable market conclusions. Many large consumer product or service companies have developed market research skills and practices that are effective. But what about the millions of businesses that lack the financial resources and incentives to reach accurate market research conclusions? That's what this book is all about: to provide a set of thinking processes and practical actions that *anybody* can use. This book may only add a little to the existing body of market research methodology. My intent is to make the subject much easier to understand and use in real business life.

Marketing intelligence (or market research, as some call it) is a business tool used to discover what customers want and what competitors are doing to satisfy customer wants. It is also the only tool I know that should be used to build marketing strategy and sales programs. The methods to execute data collection and evaluation and to draw market conclusions vary in complexity. They depend on the size of the business, the sophistication of the market research practitioner, and the amount of money the business could lose by proceeding without knowledge of what the customer really wants.

I have cast this book in a workshop setting to help businesspeople better understand the ideas and proven techniques of marketing intelligence. My students are businesspeople, and the business problems we solve are based on real market information. I am their coach, guide, and mentor. We discuss marketing intelligence issues, tell stories about our experiences, challenge one another, and talk about how to improve our understanding of customers and competition.

I had considered not having narrative exchanges with the students, as some readers might find the technique distracting to the learning process. But in my years of teaching, I have found the "nonstop" transmission of concepts, guiding principles, and implementation methods is *always* interrupted by the less timid students who just aren't getting it. My objective in using narrative is to give the reader time to absorb and integrate the material.

Also, throughout the book I share my insights with the reader by putting those insights in brackets. [*I hope I'm making the point that this is a different style of business book.*] My mission is to present ideas and build confidence in you to find new ways into your customers' behavior and needs. My method of communicating with you is the same as in real life: we listen, and then we talk to each other about common business problems and solutions.

Business readers come in all shapes, sizes, and experience levels. Their decisions can cost hundreds, thousands, or millions of dollars. How did I decide who would most benefit from this book? I looked over the business landscape and saw companies of all sizes, in all industries and locations. So, I took my own advice by gathering marketing intelligence. I browsed library and bookstore shelves to understand what the competition is asking you to read. I evaluated how they were packaging marketing intelligence concepts and methods. My conclusion? You have not had the right guided tour through the marketing intelligence mystique.

MY NICHE VERSUS THE COMPETITION

How did I come to this conclusion? *First*, there is a huge and excellent selection of market research books mainly targeted to highly skilled professionals in large companies, texts for the emerging business student, and instant market research success handbooks. *Second*, while useful, these books almost always begin with the assumption that the reader understands the basics of market success. That assumption, I believe, is naive, biased, and unfounded. As you flip through the book, you may see these concepts as too fundamental and believe you understand them. Perhaps you do. But my long experience with managers and business owners indicates that you intuitively understand the basics but may not be consciously weaving them together to get the best marketing pattern or strategic design. I must assume you can benefit from a refresher on the fundamentals. *Third*, what is common knowledge to my competitive market research authors is not common knowledge to their business readers. *Fourth*, my product must be different.

So for you, my reader, this book is a package of concepts translated into practical and useful tools to help you understand your customer and your lurking competitor. My service will be (1) communicating in an easy-to-understand style that will help you remember what questions to ask, how to ask them, where to find people to answer them, and how to evaluate the collected information and (2) guiding you to make decisions to change your business and get more sales or profits.

BUSINESS CHARACTERS AND EXAMPLES USED IN THIS BOOK

Throughout my marketing career, I have used the cliche "It doesn't matter whether you're a doctor, politician, corporate executive, butcher, baker, or candlestick maker, all market questions and answers are almost the same; it's just the language of each business that's different." If that's true, then gaining an understanding of how to do marketing intelligence for any type of business should be helpful.

Market research is a dry subject. To liven it up, I use different business examples throughout the book. Each has a common focus on the customer and the competition. Your business probably has a lot of the same characteristics of one or more of the examples used throughout the book. Let me introduce the characters and their businesses:

John has his own bookkeeping/accounting practice. This business has been operating for two years, and his practice fees total about $125,000 per year. While John has all the accounting skills to serve the customer, the special skill of cash management sets his business apart from the competition.

Betsey has her own food catering business. She's been in business for seven years and has sold franchises in other localities. As the business has grown to about $450,000 in sales and the company's reputation has become well known, she wants to offer customers other nonfood products to increase the revenue for each catering sale.

Susan is the marketing manager for a wooden toy manufacturer. This successful, rather small company ($10 million annual sales) makes and sells high-quality wooden toys. Competitive materials, like plastic, are threatening the wooden toy market. The company wants Susan to identify new products to offer its customers.

Bill is sales manager of a $3 million regional janitorial supplies distributor. This old, established company is the market share leader of the region's institutional and industrial purchase of mops, brooms, and cleaning solutions, but competitors are coming into its geographic market. The management is set in its ways and reluctant to change customer policies to keep its customers.

Peter is a divisional product line manager for weighing scales. This company has sales in the billions and Peter's weighing instruments division for factory and office applications has sales of slightly over $100 million. They have charged Peter to develop marketing strategies to expand their business into foreign countries.

Anne is the manager of a local bookstore. The bookstore is struggling to increase its retail sales volume beyond $250,000 per year. While she has been in business for some time, and offers an intellectual "coffeehouse" atmosphere, competition from larger discount bookstores requires finding new ways to attract and keep customers.

Let's begin.

Jack Savidge

ACKNOWLEDGMENTS

We're always beginners, and so the challenge to put decades of marketing intelligence experience between the covers of a book was daunting. I must credit Harry Helms of HighText Publications for motivating me to mount the task. Harry led me to Cindy Zigmund, my entrepreneurial and courageous editor at Business One, who defied "business book" publishing convention by agreeing to a writing style that I believed appropriate to communicate with businesspeople. Thanks to Susan Millen for her editorial red pen and objective content organization skills. Gratitude to my wife, Clementine, for constant encouragement to meet the challenge and her tolerance in being awakened to clicking computer keys. Last, thanks to all my clients, employers, and the hundreds of small businesspeople who shared their marketing problems that we solved together.

CONTENTS

CHAPTER 1

THE IMPORTANCE OF CUSTOMER FOCUS

GOOD MORNING, CLASS—YOU'RE MY CUSTOMERS

What is a customer? Today *you* are my customers. I need to know what you are expecting to learn so I can change the workshop topics to ensure meeting your expected performance. [*Because they're the customers, they have a say in defining the product or service they are buying.*]

Now for some intelligence gathering. I'd like to know some things about my customers. So, would all of you please tell me who you are, where you work, what's your business, why you are here, and just a few comments on your business background.

Would you be first? First names will do just fine. Thanks.

JOHN

My name is John. I'm a sole proprietor who offers financial services to small companies. I want to know how I can get potential clients to understand why I'm better than my competitors.

About my background: I finished college six years ago with a degree in accounting, worked several years for a major public accounting firm here in the city, and was progressing to more responsible client assignments. I had always been drawn to small businesses, but the professional fees our firm charged were far beyond what small businesses could afford. I guess I was ready to be independent and thought, why not start my own business to provide good accounting to the small business community? It's been pretty scary, but my wife supports my independence. Is that enough?

Sure is. But tell me, John, what do you mean by financial services?

JOHN

> Accounting services to help customers manage their businesses better.

We will come back to what business you are really in and how to appear differently than your competitors to your customers. Who is next?

SUSAN

> I'm Susan, and I am a marketing director for a small manufacturer of children's toys. I want to know where and how to get information that will define new products for our company.
>
> Right after graduating from a two-year child psychology program at a junior college, I tried working with preschool children but found it too confining. I went to work for my toy company about 12 years ago. I got started in marketing as an order department clerk, then became an assistant to the advertising manager, went out selling for a few years, and now am the marketing manager.

Do you make toys or games? Just what does your company do?

SUSAN

> We only make wooden products like little wagons, blocks, and stand-up soldiers.

Thank you. How about the next person?

BILL

> My name is Bill. I work for a regional distributor of industrial and commercial cleaning supplies as their sales manager. We are trying to figure out how to expand our business to get new sales outlets, and that's what brought me here.
>
> When I was a teenager, I made extra spending money being a part-time janitor. I got to know the supplies wholesaler salesman, who said I was a natural peddler. They gave me a job right after high school. I've been there for 25 years and loved every minute. All the kids are gone, and now it's just me and my wife. I read anything I can find about new business methods so I can keep up.

Great habit. Who's next?

BETSEY

> I'm Betsey, and I own a food catering business. Let's see, my business history: I graduated with a home ec degree, got married right out of college, and have three children, 10, 12 and 14. I took a part-time cooking job for the catering office of a large hotel downtown. Gee, that's eight years ago. After a couple of years' experience, catering looked easy, so I asked a few friends if I could do their parties. One thing led to another, and here I am with franchisees. My husband says it takes too much time, but the extra money and mental challenge is worth it.

Good. Knowing the customer and competition in a service business is really important. If I can ask, how big is your business, and why are you here?

BETSEY

> We've been in business for five years. We have franchisees who operate in four states. I'm here to find the most practical and least-expensive way to understand what new services or products we can sell to our existing customers. Also, if possible, to learn how to set realistic sales forecasts for our franchisees.

That's a tall order, but I think we'll be able to do that. Now, sir, can we hear from you?

PETER

> I'm Peter, and I am the product manager for a division of a very large company, Global Instruments Ltd. We make weighing devices of all kinds for businesses and factories. I'm here to learn how to change the way we distribute our products. Also to find out about keeping track of the competition in this country and in foreign markets.
>
> I have a mechanical engineering degree and an MBA. My company also underwrites some advanced classes I'm taking at the university. I went to work for them seven years ago right after grad school. My wife is also an MBA and works for the city in the finance department. We have not decided to have children yet.

Now, is that everyone? One more? Please go ahead.

ANNE

> Yes, I'm Anne. For over 10 years I've managed a retail bookstore

that has a coffeehouse. Someone else owns the business; I don't. The owner has not been in the store for a very long time. My incentive for being the manager is that I get to keep what little profit the store generates. I am here to learn how to position our store as different from other bookstores. I want to see if there is information available to do better marketing so we can attract more customers and, hopefully, make more profit. I guess that's asking a lot.

My background: Well, I raised my family and then decided to use the librarian degree I got a long time ago. As an avid reader, I was always in bookstores. One day the owner asked whether I would manage it while he went on vacation. I really liked meeting all the customers and arranging new book displays. The owner offered me a permanent managership position, and as I said, a percentage of the profit. I talked it over at home and even though I don't have business experience, here I am.

Terrific. What a great business cross-section. [*I've had some experience in all of their product or service areas. I feel pretty comfortable that they'll walk out being able to improve their businesses.*] We should really be able to solve some problems today.

THE ALMIGHTY CUSTOMER—WHAT DOES THAT MEAN?

There are only two critical participants in the marketplace: customers and competitors. As a matter of fact, success in business depends on really knowing all about your customers and your competition. After that, the rest is doing the job right.

So, let's define a customer. Here are the four conditions that qualify a customer:

1. The customer must need the product or service.
2. The customer must be able to pay.
3. The customer must be willing to buy.
4. The customer must have the authority to buy.

Pretty simple. [*It's simple, but do they really understand that they must put the customer first in all their business thinking? I have to keep driving this point home.*]

On Being a Valued Supplier

To become and remain a valued supplier of goods and services, the customer must be the central focus of our business activity. Let me tell you why customer focus is so important.

Years ago, when I started in business, suppliers designed products or services they wanted customers to use. They constructed products and services to their standards of quality. They shipped goods and executed services to customers by using long-standing wholesaler or retailer friends. They set prices based on what it cost them to build the product or offer the service. And back then, we customers bought them. The choices were few in terms of color, size, weight, style, and most of all, customer service.

Think about how limited product and service offerings were, compared to today. There weren't as many makes of cars, in as many shapes, colors, and prices. There weren't as many selections of magazines on the shelves. By the way, do you know there are about 3,100 magazines published in our country, and 400 to 600 new ones are started each year? Imagine all the small special interest groups these magazines appeal to. How about brands of soap? And all the banks available to hold our money? Now we have too many purchasing options. What changed all that? Does anyone know?

COMPETITORS ARE LURKING

PETER

> Competition is new suppliers coming into a market with new offerings that the old established suppliers didn't have or would not supply.

Exactly. New competitors somehow understood what customers wanted: something more, something different, something cheaper, something of better quality, something they could buy faster or in more convenient places. Something the customer could perceive as a greater value.

The customers didn't scream and shout for new products or services. They didn't set up picket lines in front of stores or corporate headquarters. But they sure bought when new market entrants offered them what appeared to be better choices than what they had been using. But:

- How did the new competitors know what the customer really wanted?
- How could they tell where people wanted to buy new products?
- How did they find the right price to charge?

You guessed it; they went out to potential customers and asked good questions about their preferences. Then they:

- Compared what customers said they wanted with what the competition was offering.
- Understood what performance standard the new product had to meet.
- Made design decisions to create something new.
- Set prices the customer would pay to get that performance.
- Built the product or service to make a profit.
- Found the place where the customers said they would most like to purchase it.
- Convinced distribution to stock or represent the product or service.
- Followed up to make sure the end customer was satisfied.

Marketing intelligence is the building block to business decisions that lead to commercial actions. We don't just collect information to write a report and learn some interesting facts about customers or competitors, but to change and redirect our business efforts to gain market and profit advantage.

WIN–WIN–WIN

The perfect business causes all the players in the game to win. The customers want better product or service performance for a price lower than they now pay. The distribution outlets want to sell more, faster, and easier. The supplier wants higher revenues at greater profit. Our job is to determine the proper win-win-win questions, find their objective answers, and take steps to make this business formula happen. [*I could stop here and adjourn the class if only I believed they would all go back to their businesses and do this!*]

Discovering customer preferences and competitor positions defines new business opportunity.

JOHN

What you just said is true, I guess. But isn't that really just for companies like the one Peter works for, a big global instrument manufacturing firm? I've got a small, local service business to help little, struggling firms. Do I need all this marketing intelligence stuff? It seems too complicated and expensive. Even if I collect some information, how will I understand what to do with it?

PROFILE OF TODAY'S SMALL BUSINESS

Let's talk about what size company needs marketing intelligence, and whether there are differences between companies that market products and services to industrial or commercial customers and those that market to consumers like you and me. [*This is a key point with me because most firms believe they are too small or too big to need intelligence, and industrial and commercial companies think only the consumer product or service firms need to do marketing intelligence work.*]

There are nearly 20 million small businesses that make up the U.S. economy. Almost 75 percent, or 14 million, are owned and run by individuals and do not have any employees. These are solo, lone wolves who maybe earn a living by providing some business or professional service. My interpretation of certain government data suggests their average net or take-home revenue is less than $35,000 per year. Furthermore, only 10 to 20 percent of these owners make more on their own than they could working for somebody else. What real economic importance do these solo 13 million firms represent for suppliers of goods and services? Not much! Yes, they are the fabric of our entrepreneurial culture, but they really don't buy very much because

FIGURE 1-1
U.S. Business, 1989

Number of Employees	Percent of Firms	Cumulative Percent of Firms	Number of Firms	Average Sales ($000)
1	7%	7%	1,330,000	$ 125
1-4	45	52	8,493,000	313
5-9	23	75	4,399,212	875
10-19	12	87	2,346,912	1,875
20-49	8	95	1,503,022	4,375
50-99	3	98	497,346	9,375
100-500	2	99.6	357,530	37,500
500-999	0.2	99.8	38,000	93,750
1,000-4,999	0.2	99.97	29,112	375,000
5,000-9,999	0.02	99.99	3,945	937,500
Over 10,000	0.02	100.0	4,030	2,225,000
Total	100%		19,000,000	

Source: Adapted from U.S. government statistics.

they don't have the resources to purchase more than business survival necessities. So, as we discuss potential markets, I'll leave them, not disrespectfully, out of our equations.

Figure 1-1 illustrates the 1986 employee characteristics of businesses. The information has been derived from unpublished U.S. Small Business Administration statistics and other data taken from the *1990 Statistical Abstract of the United States.* Incidentally, this isn't old information. I have tracked small business populations here and in other countries for 20 years. Over that time, the numbers have not changed much and are not likely to change very much in the future. But here's the message: millions and millions of companies struggle to get their slice of the economic pie, but only a very few are able to grow to any significant size.

PROFILE OF U.S. BUSINESS ENTERPRISE

We all relate to business from what we usually read in the business sections of newspapers or national and regional magazines. We read that most companies are large, have lots of money, and buy expensive products and services to keep the business moving ahead. But it's not true. Our economy is dominated by small businesses. What marketing intelligence information can we draw from this rather sterile data? [*They'll see a lot more of the* Statistical Abstract. *I've chosen to use it, almost exclusively, to help them understand how to determine market conditions and customers. Many other documents would provide more detail, but I really feel the* Abstract *is the best beginning reference.*]

First, going to the cumulative percent column in Figure 1–1, the reality is that about 95 percent of all your potential business customers have less than 50 employees. Second, using my rule of thumb, each employee produces about $125,000 in sales revenue. So 98 percent of your potential customers have sales revenue of less than $6 million. Another rule: after paying production and selling expenses, there is about 5 percent of the revenue left for the business owner or distribution to the stockholders. We'll return to the American business landscape when we discuss segmenting market sectors. So, John, this kind of data begins to profile your customer base.

I have studied the business demographics of many countries and compared them to U.S. demographics to find similarities. The number of businesses operating in each country is different, but the business size percentages are about the same. Small firms dominate our world economy. As suppliers of goods and services, we are only just beginning to understand how owners and managers of these companies make purchasing decisions. More importantly, we are discovering what motivates them to buy certain goods and services.

HABITS AND ATTITUDES ARE HARD TO CHANGE

Specifically constructed market research [*I prefer to call it* marketing intelligence] only became a tool for sales or marketing decision making in the 1950s. Before that, field salespeople reported customers' preferences from what they heard from sales calls. They talked to retail store buyers and commercial or industrial purchasing agents. They learned wants and needs from distributors and occasionally from end users. They talked to anybody moving the goods from the factory back door to those who put them on the shelf. Each year the company asked the salespeople for new product or service ideas. The messages from the field were all different because each messenger had a bias or personal preference for certain products and services. Most of the information had nothing to do with what the end customer or user wanted. It wasn't until the competition offered what the customer did want that anyone said, "I wonder what our customers really need and want? We'd better find out why they are switching to our competitor by going out and asking them."

So formal marketing intelligence gathering is rather new. Do you think this idea to ask the customers what they wanted caused any problems with salespeople?

BILL

> In sales management, our tendency is to keep anybody outside the sales department in the dark about what's going on in the marketplace. Sales management tends to be very nervous about market researchers snooping around dealers and customers.

I think you're right. Tell me, have you done any market research?

BILL

> No, that's why I'm here. We are afraid to get realistic information about our market because it may prove that we have to change the way we do business. My company has been doing business its way for a long time. But now we're getting competing distributors in our region and they're offering products and services that we don't. Competitors are using new sales methods and policies and the customers are buying from them. That's why I've decided we had better find out what's going on. Unfortunately, market knowledge makes management very uncomfortable.

You bet it does! They are probably more uncomfortable about the possible need to change the way they do business than they are about getting realistic customer opinions. It may mean: a change in the product or services offered; a change in customer treatment; a change in billing or pricing practices; or a change in resellers for their products or services. Change is the threatening outcome of knowing about customers and competitors.

[This concept of change is always a hard one. Most people think about the little changes, minor details. Getting everyone to go beyond today and look at tomorrow is the problem.]
But with change comes growth, opportunity, and profit. Let's look at your businesses and consider the effects of change.

IMPACTS OF CHANGE

John, the accounting or bookkeeping business used to be based on pencils, paper, and lots of erasers. Then along came the calculator and lately a computer that a small business could afford. New software with tax templates allows the solo accountant to double the number of customers served.

- What's the next technology that will change your product performance?
- Why won't businesses do their own accounting tasks with off-the-shelf software programs?
- When will you have to do business differently because of new technology?
- Which service companies, like banks or insurance firms, may become competitors by providing easy accounting as part of their service package to the customer?
- What about do-it-yourself accounting seminars that could replace your value as a provider of professional financial services?

John, it's never too early to think about the what-ifs.
Susan, your toys are made of wood—a scarce and expensive commodity. Here are some questions you should consider:

- Why do customers still prefer wooden toys?
- When will newer plastic materials that really look, feel, and sound like wood change customers' perceived value and attitudes about higher-priced wood products?
- What, if any, distribution alternatives are available for your products that will assure your company the same or greater profit?

- When will you have to lower your prices for wooden wagons to meet the prices of lower-cost alternatives?

I guess the bottom line is, what is the selling message for wooden toys that will cause customers to pay more than for toys made of alternative materials? There's only so much they will spend for a kid's wagon.

Bill, the need to keep offices clean will not change. However, you need to address these questions:

- When will your customers begin to buy similar maintenance products from large warehouse-type stores at lower prices?
- When will chemical technology for cleaning agents and solvents become more widely available to ordinary small manufacturers who run their businesses at much lower cost?
- How much will these low-cost suppliers drive prices down?
- How will your supplier react to meet their reduced prices?
- When will pricing erode the profits of middlemen, like your company, beyond where distributing is a viable business? [*This one is critical. Most wholesalers never see the approaching end of their value in the distribution system until it is far too late to diversify either into becoming a retailer or base supplier. I don't want to bring that strategic marketing intelligence into view just yet.*]

Betsey, it's fair to say that food preferences probably won't dramatically change. We've all participated in the convenience revolution of fast food. People do spend on extras, like having social events catered in their homes. Businesses cater many holiday events for employees. The trouble is, even minor downturns in the economy change our views on what's essential and what are extras.

As I recall, you want to figure out marketing intelligence methods to discover new products that can be offered along with your catered products. I assume you believe that when you are in someone's home or business there is an opportunity to sell the customer something else. I also assume you believe they will easily change their current purchasing patterns and buy these additional products or services from you.

Let's look at your goal another way. You want to:

- Understand what the existing distribution channel is.
- Know where they buy.
- Create new programs to sell products and replace your customers' existing purchasing processes.
- Change where your customers buy these yet undiscovered products.

These are assumptions. It's essential that you know if customers will change their buying habits *before* you commit time and money for inventory, advertising, and selling of new merchandise. What key information do you need to feel comfortable in making new product and customer buying pattern decisions?

BETSEY

> I think if I ask enough existing customers what else they would buy along with our current offerings, that should be a good clue to new products.

That's true, as long as you ask the right questions in the right way to enough customers.

Peter, engineering and marketing change must be constant in the instruments business. Electronics, optics, and computer technologies all converge into instruments. Customers surely are offered wide new choices by your competition.

- How much change has the customer demanded in quality?
- What changes in product reliability are they expecting?
- How do they want after-sale service changed?
- Have your customers changed their quality, reliability, and service needs? Or are they now demanding what they want instead of accepting what you have to deliver?

But you're here about distribution, keeping track of competition and foreign business opportunities. Lots of change.

I'll bet customers want your weighing devices more integrated into overall systems. You know, tied to a computer or some other machines. The change to a systems approach is sweeping our globe. More market-based information, coupled to automation, helps define:

- Increased product quality.
- Decreased defective parts in manufacturing.
- The ability to target customers.
- Reduction of all costs.

PETER

> That's right. Last week I was looking at our sales records to see where products were being sold. An increasing percentage of our products are now bought by "systems integrators."

Just a minute, Peter. Please define a *systems integrator*.

PETER

> A systems integrator is a new class of industrial dealer or reseller who "does it all" for the customer. That is, they buy scales from us, and buy additional devices to fit with ours, and computers from someone else, until all the system pieces fit. They put it all together, test it to the customer's performance specifications, install it, and usually service it under a maintenance or service contract. These integrators are new in the industrial distribution channel. They're also called *value-added* resellers. Customers are willing to pay for the value-added service to get a total solution for their problem.
>
> My management says our business is making devices, not systems. But I'm worried about our narrow business definition. I think it will allow competition to get a stronger market position. Maybe these integrators will know more than we do about our customers because they are getting closer to the customers. They appear to be giving the customers what they need to do the whole job. Maybe if I can objectively confirm these marketplace distribution changes and customer preferences, my management will consider changing our business definition to offer more than just separate weighing devices.

So, it sounds like you have added the systems integrators as a competitor, even though they now buy scales from you. Allowing another company to add value or productivity to your product creates a serious competitor. Why? Because they step between you and the user and take control in satisfying customer needs. It's *vital* to understand why the customers have changed their perception about suppliers. Knowing this, we change the methods to solve customer problems and regain the preferred supplier position in the customer's mind.

PETER

What about understanding foreign markets?

Certainly worldwide marketing is in a state of change. Europe continues to consolidate into a purchasing giant. Southeast Asia and Pacific Rim countries have trade pacts and are erecting market barriers to outsiders. Changes in tariff rules, local and regional distribution, and warehousing represent opportunities and challenges. Companies wanting to supply foreign markets must first understand the new business rules, and then adopt marketing methods to satisfy these global customers. A supplier can no longer say, "This is the way we do business, take it or leave it!"

So, Peter, where and how to get foreign marketing intelligence—that's the information task.

Yes, John, do you want to make a point?

JOHN

Here we go again. What do foreign markets, the Pacific Rim, and Europe have to do with my problems? Is this workshop just for big-company situations?

[*This fellow is really practical. He wants instant answers. He has no time for talk about things that don't relate directly to his business. He has trouble connecting ideas and situations from other business situations to use in solving his problems. That's alright. I'll have to help him bridge these ideas.*]

Think about this. Your business serves a local market, right? There are different types of small businesses in this market. We saw the profiles of small businesses—some very small, a little bigger, large, and very large. Well, at each stage of life these businesses have different financial information and cash flow needs. Cash flow in very large firms might mean millions of dollars, in medium-sized firms it means hundreds of thousands, and in a small firm it means hundreds. The hundred dollars to a small firm is just as important as the million dollars is to a large company. Also, understanding the different business behavior of foreign firms, as we were talking about with Peter, is like understanding the different buying decision behavior of very small companies and medium-sized ones looking for financial expertise. [*I'm not sure that bridged well enough, but if he thinks about it he will see the commonality.*]

Now to Anne's bookstore and coffeeshop. I'm sure you have seen lots of change over ten years in the business of selling books. The major changes I've seen are that the big stores got bigger, and the small stores really got smaller. There is deep discounting by major bookstore chains, more cut-rate mail order, and the loss of in-store service for serious book buyers. These trends create questions for me.

- What new perceptions do book buyers have about the value of owning a good book?
- Why have paperbacks *not* replaced hardback books?
- What attitudes allow us to throw away a book or give it to charity?
- Considering the change to smaller living space, how much space is needed to build a small home book collection?
- Why aren't people collecting books any more?

Are these customer perceptions important to a small bookstore manager? Maybe knowing how the customer feels won't bring immediate sales. But, Anne, you can start understanding which types of customers may be more interested in the bookseller's services you want to offer. This way you may be able to position your store to the best customer potential.

What are the social habits of your coffee drinkers? Think about it. Today, people have fewer places where they can just sit and talk in a relaxed atmosphere where it's a bit intellectual, and off the rushed path. Your shop offers that ambiance to customers. In return, you hope they will buy a book on the way in or out. Your strategy: coffee traffic sells books. Has it worked?

ANNE

> Well, not really. The trouble is they just sit. They don't buy more than one cup of coffee and usually don't even buy a newspaper, never mind a book.

That situation is not trivial. It forces us to ask, what business are you in—the coffee or book selling business? Later, we are going to examine what we *say* our business is, compared to what business service we offer.

VITAL THOUGHTS

- Focus on customer needs and competition.
- Understand how change is constantly threatening the life of your business.
- Collect facts and opinions to create marketing intelligence.

CHAPTER 2

LOOKING AT YOUR BUSINESS

As never before, the bottom line reality for the entrepreneurial business owner, product line manager, CEO, business partner, or executive director is to really believe that, "If we don't go forward, we're going to go backward." Aggressive competition, alternative ways to achieve performance, and constantly shifting customer needs demand that management examine its position in the marketplace almost daily, and then make those business changes necessary to retain or advance the company's competitiveness.

You've got most of the answers right in your company files. Perhaps you just don't know what the questions are! I'm telling you that getting answers to questions is easy. Sorting answers into marketing intelligence is not hard. Deciding to change your business to satisfy customers and beat competition is straightforward. Developing the right questions is the most difficult work.

The three basic groups of questions that fit all businesses are strategy questions, value questions, and distribution questions. The answers tell us about our business, our customers, and our competition. So let's first look at the strategy questions.

COMMON QUESTIONS AND ACTIONS FOR ALL BUSINESSES

Below is a list of questions that every business, no matter how big or small, needs to consider. These are cornerstone questions. The answers are the tools that build tactical and strategic marketing plans and manage change. Cut them out of the book or make a copy, tack them on the wall in your office, on your dashboard, the bathroom mirror—anywhere—but make them part of your business thinking life.

- How do I understand the sales and profit elements of my own business?
- How do I find and attract new customers?
- How do I define and create products and services my customers will buy?
- How do I determine what customers will pay and set the right prices?
- How do I identify and select the best distribution channel to reach customers?
- How do I collect the data and calculate market potential?
- How do I learn about and track the competition?
- How do I position and communicate my business story?
- How do I create potential customer traffic and sales leads?
- How do I define and implement after-sale service needs?
- How do I continually monitor and measure the marketplace?
- How do I identify competitive technologies or services that may replace my performance?
- How do I locate import or export opportunities?

STRATEGIC THINKING

In my other life as a consultant, I run strategic planning sessions for small firms. My goal is to force managers and owners to objectively answer three questions: (1) where are we? (2) where do we want to go? and (3) how are we going to get there? Struggling for answers to these questions always leads management to change the business to achieve its goals of:

- More sales.
- Better market positions for price and performance.
- Lower manufacturing or marketing costs.
- Defining new products and services.

- Geographic market, warehousing, or manufacturing expansion.
- Finding ways to beat competition.
- Changes in the company business culture and practices.
- Higher profits.

BETSEY

Is strategic planning part of this workshop?

Sure, strategy is the business road map. There are two quotes I really like that capture the need for strategy:

- "If you don't know where you're going, any road will get you there." *Theodore Levitt*
- "Having misplaced our objectives, we redoubled our efforts." *Anonymous*

Today, it is futile to just randomly pursue a business direction. Competition and changing customer preferences demand that business managers be in sync with their marketing environment. Only then can they rapidly adopt new strategic directions and execute tactics.

OKAY, WHAT'S THE REAL SITUATION?

Now let's look at each of your businesses with emphasis on its current status—not where you want it to be, but where it is right now. We'll develop questions and methods to objectively determine where you are. You're going to be surprised by how many answers are buried in your own business records.

John, where are you?

JOHN

I've just started the business so there isn't much history to look at, but I have some clients.

I assume you have decided on a set of bookkeeping services or products. Your business is local, maybe regional. Your combined skills could be called a financial system or package. Finally, you have a fee schedule you assume customers will accept. Now let's look at some questions that will tell you where you are.

Do you know where your prices are:
- compared to other bookkeeping competitors?
- compared to your customers' ability to pay?

Do you know how your financial system performs:
- compared to competitive products?
- compared to nonbookkeeping services offered by the competition?
- compared to what the customers really need?

Do you know when or how often customers want the books done:
- compared to when or how often you want to do the books?
- compared to how often your competition services their customers?

Peter and Susan, these questions also apply to your businesses.

Now, Anne, you should know where you are. There are four walls in your store shelved with books. You are ready for people to grab a book, come to the counter, and pay money for the value you have provided. Just the right book, at the right price, in a store atmosphere that moved the customer to want to read something new. That's the value you have added. Simple. But what I want to know is:

- How many books did you sell today compared to yesterday?
- How many have been sold this month compared to last month?
- How many have been sold to date this year compared to this time last year?
- What percent of all the books you sold were history? romance? travel? etc.
- What was the price range of all the books sold?
- What was the average price today compared to last month? last year?
- How many were hardback? how many paperback?
- What percent were credit card versus cash sales?

- How many customers came in the store? How many bought a book?
- How much time did the typical customer spend in the store?
- How many people told you the prices for your books were too high? just right?
- How many cups of coffee did you sell?
- What percent of the coffee drinkers bought books?
- What percent of book buyers sat down for coffee? Which did they do first?
- How many bookstores are within three miles of your store?
- How many square feet do these competitors have in their stores?
- How many books do customers buy at one time in the competitors' stores?

These questions about your bookstore, when answered, will go a long way toward helping to redirect your marketing efforts.

ANNE

Are you serious? I've never thought about some of those questions.

The pressure of day-to-day business is difficult and doesn't leave much time to really think strategically. It is important to know book sale units, price levels of the books sold, and what fractions of your customer base are buying what kinds of books. Coffee sales were also an issue, so developing data to know if coffee drinkers are book buyers, or if book buyers like to drink coffee, is of interest. [*I'm afraid the coffee program is a distraction. It's hard to manage two different businesses at once. Focus is essential.*]

Collecting and studying this historical and current information will clearly illuminate your past business patterns and suggest future trends. Put in place some simple sales volume measurements to determine how quickly certain floor merchandising promotions or book subject selections sell. This will help you confirm or refute the inventory stocking recommendations proposed by publishers' representatives. Internally developed information about your business makes you more sure of your buying decisions.

Now, my hunch is that a minority of Anne's regular customers buys the majority of the books she sells. If it's true, Anne can set up promotional strategies for the heavy bookbuying customers. But she must scout up the business intelligence from her own sales records, from a competitor's store, or from the publishers' representatives to validate whether my minority–majority assumption exists for other booksellers.

Let's talk about Bill's business, distribution of maintenance and cleaning supplies. Bill, I have a few questions that I know can be answered from your business records:

- How many customers do you have?
- What percent of the customers account for 50 percent of your business? 60 percent of the business? 80 percent?
- During which part of the month do they normally reorder?
- How many units of each product make up a typical order?
- How many employees does your smallest customer have? your largest?
- How many units do big and small customers buy during a month? a year?
- How many new customers have you gained or lost in the last year?
- Who returns goods for credit?
- How many of those are large customers? small customers?
- What are the reasons they tell you for returning the merchandise?
- What percent of your sales are phone orders?
- How many calls per day do your salespeople make?
- What is the major reason your salespeople give for not getting an order?
- Who, at your large customers, specifies what to buy?
- Who acts as the purchasing agent?
- Who has the final authority to place the order?
- What is the turnover time for your inventory?
- What kinds of customers is your competition attacking?
- How many salespeople does your competition have in your territory?

- Which salesperson gets the most sales per call and why?
- How long is the average sales call?

BILL

I've got answers to some of those. But I'll add another question: where am I going to get the time to hunt for the data?

Some of the questions are vital. Bill, identify which questions they are and just take the time to find out the answers. Most of the data is right there in your sales records and invoices. The other answers come from your customers. You'll find it's not difficult or time-consuming.

Betsey's consumer service business also needs answers to questions like these to determine its status. Again, most of the data can be found in her own business records.

- What is the average size of the house where you provide catering?
- How old is your typical customer?
- Who decides to hire a caterer for the event?
- What is the price range of cars in the customers' driveways?
- What is the geographic location of your big customers? small customers?
- What percent of the catering units are residential? commercial?
- What percent of your dollar revenue is from residential business? commercial?
- What percent of your business is breakfast? lunch? cocktail time? dinner?
- How many sales dollars are generated by food and how many by beverages?
- How many sales calls does it take to get residential orders? commercial orders?
- What season or months are the highest for orders and revenue?
- How long before the catering event do you usually get customer inquiry on price?

- What reasons do potential customers give when they decline to buy?
- How many catering competitors are in the yellow pages?
- What do you purchase from non-food vendors?
- What percent of your expenses are these outside purchases?
- When you are losing to the competition, is it because of price, quality, or delivery?
- What other services or items do your customers buy to complete the event?
- How many salespeople does the competition have selling or servicing customers?
- What is the average dollar size of the catering order from residential customers? commercial customers?

Betsey, these are questions only you can answer about your business, your customers, and your competition. The answers lead to long-term strategies for repositioning your business or short-term tactical decisions to put into action now.

RANK YOUR ACTION PRIORITIES!

Think about how we execute everyday decisions to get jobs done. We usually make "to do" lists, write reminders on slips of paper or on blank three-by-five-inch index cards, or stick Post-It™ notes all over our desks, car dashboards, or mirrors. Now if we expend *equal* effort to do all those jobs it means each of those tasks has *equal* importance in our lives. Sometimes we mark them *A*, *B*, or *C*, or assign a number to those that must get done first, second, or third, and that process creates some efficiency. But there is a better way to group what we must do by using four business words. I've already mentioned some of those priority or ranking words.

PETER

You said understanding how customer preferences change was "vital."

How about another priority word?

FIGURE 2–1
Marketing Intelligence Priorities

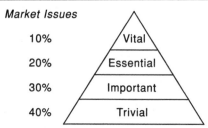

Market Issues	
10%	Vital
20%	Essential
30%	Important
40%	Trivial

In my experience, at most, 30 percent of all customer and sales decisions you make are vital or essential. Prioritize market issue questions.

BETSEY

> Knowing whether my customers would change from where they now buy to where they might buy was "essential."

I also mentioned *important* and *trivial*. We can go out and collect lots of interesting information. Can just *any* data be really worthwhile for a business decision in meeting customer needs and competitive threats? No! We must rank our marketing intelligence needs. To define the priority words:

Market Question-and-Answer Priorities

- *Vital* means to *sustain* the life of my business.
- *Essential* means of *utmost* importance.
- *Important* means needs *immediate* attention.
- *Trivial* means is of *little* importance.

All the questions or decisions that surface during your business life are defined by one of these words and the frequency of their use is illustrated in Figure 2–1, Marketing Intelligence Priorities.

Take a minute to jot down the first 10 questions or decisions about your business that come to your mind. Don't think about it too hard, and don't sort them out in your mind: write whatever

FIGURE 2–2

Jot Down 10 Quick Questions	Check Most Important
1. _____	____
2. _____	____
3. _____	____
4. _____	____
5. _____	____
6. _____	____
7. _____	____
8. _____	____
9. _____	____
10. _____	____

first comes to you. If Figure 2–2 is too small, copy it to a larger piece of paper. Now in the right-hand column, mark the questions that are vital with a *V*, mark the Essential ones with an *E*, then the Important questions with an *I*, and finally the Trivial questions with a *T*. Interesting, isn't it? There should only be one that is vital and that's the one to tackle first with the most effort. [*I know people use "to do" lists and make priority decisions all day long, but it's usually not a conscious process.*]

WHO, WHAT, WHERE, WHY, WHEN, HOW MUCH, AND HOW MANY?

The springboard to developing marketing intelligence is a set of *W* and *H* words: who, what, where, why, when, and how. By applying the priority words of vital, essential, important, and trivial to the questions that follow, we begin to identify the questions that need answers.

Before you rank each question V, E, I, or T as it applies to your business market situation, make a copy of the chart to give to your fellow workers. It will be interesting to see if they rank these customer and competitor questions with the same priority as you see them. [*This is a great way to get management consensus. I distribute the questions to each manager, tell them their ranking will be kept anonymous, and then present the results. It's amazing how disparate the priorities for knowing customer and competitor information is within a management team.*]

Who

[ ]   Is the end user?
[ ]   Is the buyer?
[ ]   Is the specifier of product/service performance?
[ ]   Is the reseller closest to the customer?
[ ]   Is the current competition?
[ ]   Is the potential competition?
[ ]   Are the competitors' major customers?
[ ]   Are the industry opinion leaders and gurus?

What

[ ]   Is currently performing to meet customer preferences?
[ ]   Product/service is needed to replace what the customer uses?
[ ]   Competitive technology or service can replace me?
[ ]   Are the customer's criteria in making a decision to buy?
[ ]   Do customers like or dislike about my store or service?
[ ]   Is the current distribution channel for products/services?
[ ]   Are the perceived good and bad points of the competition?
[ ]   Does the customer expect in after-sale support?
[ ]   Products/services give me the most revenue and profit?
[ ]   Are the periodicals that potential customers read?
[ ]   Does the customer really think about my products/services?
[ ]   Does the customer really think about the competition?

[ ] Is the typical warranty for products/services like mine?

[ ] Are the major trade or consumer shows customers go to?

Where

[ ] Is the customer using my product or the competitor's?

[ ] Does the customer gain value from my services?

[ ] Are the major and minor customers located?

[ ] Do customers buy products/services similar to mine?

[ ] Do customers learn how to use or fix my product?

[ ] Do customers go first to buy products/services like mine?

Why

[ ] Does the customer need more than one supplier?

[ ] Do my ads create so few or so many worthless sales leads?

[ ] Does the competition use the distribution channels they do?

[ ] Do customers just look around the store and not buy?

[ ] Do customers buy from my competitors?

When

[ ] Does the customer usually buy products/services like mine?

[ ] Is the normal payment period for invoices?

[ ] Is the typical delivery of the product/service expected?

[ ] Does product/service performance have to pay back the price?

[ ] Is product/service training and maintenance expected?

[ ] Will a replacement technology or service be available?

How

[ ] Does the customer define profit margin?

[ ] Many units does the total market buy?

[ ] Many dollars are spent to buy all the units?

[ ] Many sales calls does it take to get an order?

How (concluded)

[ ] Many units do customers usually buy at one time?

[ ] Many sizes, shapes, and colors should be offered customers?

[ ] Many of the customer's employees help make the purchasing decision?

[ ] Many times do customers expect me to visit them in a month?

[ ] Much margin does the distribution channel expect?

[ ] Much detail is needed in customer price or work proposals?

[ ] Many units are each of my major competitors selling?

[ ] Many revenue and profit dollars are my competitors getting?

When you can answer most of those market questions confidently there will be:

• Fewer new product failures.
• Lower probability of your going out of business.
• Greater profits for your business and shareholders.

VITAL THOUGHTS

• Constantly collect customer and competitor facts and opinions to reshape your business strategy.
• Prioritizing questions about your business as vital, essential, important, and trivial helps identify your key business questions.
• Converting market-based answers into business change actions is the end product of marketing intelligence.

CHAPTER 3

THE BUILDING BLOCKS OF MARKETING INTELLIGENCE

WHAT IS MARKETING INTELLIGENCE?

Before we can develop intelligence about a market we must understand our business and how it fits the needs of the market. Marketing intelligence is a collection of facts about our customers and competition used to form *reasonable* market conclusions. These conclusions are then used to make decisions to change our product, service, and distribution method to satisfy the customers' evolving needs.

Elements of the Marketing Intelligence Process

1. *Intelligence* is the merging of meaningful facts, observations, and opinions.
2. *Market* or *business research* is the process used to select the right questions, to get answers, to organize and evaluate the information, and to form business strategies and tactics.
3. *Market knowledge* is knowing your customer and competitor.
4. Decisions to change a business to meet customer preferences must be based on these facts.
5. Changing your business's strategies and tactics can keep your competitors from satisfying your customers' product or service needs before you do.

Here are some marketing terms, some of which may be new. We'll be using these words throughout the book.

Marketing Intelligence Glossary

Buyer: the person who decides what to buy.

Channel: the links of a supplier chain to the customer.

Competition: my opposition who wants my customer.

Customer: anyone who needs a product or service.

Discount: the selling price below list price.

Distribution: flow of goods from manufacturer and user.

End user: someone who uses my product/service.

List price: what the manufacturer suggests I sell it for.

Market intelligence: knowledge for decision making.

Market or business research: a process to collect information.

Middlemen: the same as resellers.

Perceptions: not facts, but beliefs or feelings.

Performance: how well the product/service does the job.

Preferences: supplier performance wanted by the customer.

Price: what's paid to get the product or service.

Purchaser: the person who commits to buy.

Purchasing: the process of buying.

Resellers: anybody who buys and then sells the products.

Retailer/dealer: the last supplier selling to the customer.

Supplier: anybody who sells the product or service.

Value: the customer's view of performance plus price.

Value-added reseller: a reseller who adds product performance.

Wholesaler: a regional supplier that sells to retailers.

As we go through the day, you'll want to add additional terms.

I've listened to your description of vital questions—now let's add a few more. Here's what I would want to know if I were running each of your businesses.

VITAL QUESTIONS

John: How do I differentiate my business?

Susan: How do I identify new product features?

Bill: How do I expand my business and locate new customers?

Betsey: How do I secure new products and set sales forecasts?

Peter: How do I find new distribution and track competition?

Anne: How do I change the business and build in-store traffic?

Any other additions or changes?

JOHN

> In addition to positioning my business as better than the competition, I'd like to get more consulting assignments from the calls made on potential customers. You know, increase my new-customer-to-sales-call ratio.

You need more than simple selling skills like smiling and being positive. You need to know how to *close* more sales.

SUSAN

> Along with getting ideas for new products, I want to know how high a price the end user, in our case the parents, would pay for our toys. We have been setting our prices based on what it costs us to make the toys. Then we add in the discounts that distribution needs and that becomes the end customer's price. Maybe we could set higher prices if we knew beforehand what value they might place on the toy.

Set the price at what the customer perceives the product is worth. Perfect.

Bill, how about you?

BILL

> You know, I did say we want to expand the business. But I'm not sure how much more of a market for our product line is available. We really don't know what share of the market we now have. So I have to find out what the total market is. Also, I don't know how many customers our competitors have taken from us. If I know answers to these questions, I can plan a sales campaign to either take back lost customers or get new business from a market potential that I didn't know existed.

Exactly. Those are usually the first questions: how much, how many, who, and what. This is a good place to define *total market* and *share of market.*

CALCULATING A TOTAL MARKET

How do we determine market size? To determine a total market requires knowledge of only two of three sales transaction elements. They are

- Total number of units sold.
- Total dollars paid to buy all the units.
- Price of a single unit.

As an example, let's take mops:

- Total units of mops purchased by all customers = 20.
- Price customer paid = $5.
- To figure the total dollar market, the number of units is multiplied by the unit price (20 (units) × $5 (price) = $100).
- If we know the total dollar market and the number of units, to figure an average price, divide the dollars by the units ($100 (dollars)/$5 (price) = 20 mops).
- If we know the price and total dollars, to figure the number of units, divide the dollars by the price ($100 (dollars)/20 (units) = $5).

[*I know this looks like sixth-grade arithmetic, but I have to review to get them used to the three elements that make up a market forecast. I'm trained to use these elements all the time, but most marketing people spend their time trying to figure out the dollar market sizes and don't pay enough attention to the units and price.*]
    Back to the basic questions.

BETSEY

My need is to determine whether we could sell new party food items to other caterers or resellers. Can I build a line of catering business accessory products? I might be changing the direction of my business and that could be distracting.

That's certainly possible. The trick will be to find resellers who are not potential competitors.

ANNE

> It may be minor, but should I have a more accurate book subject profile to satisfy customers that come to my door or shop in the mall? Right now I just take the recommendation of the publishers' salespeople, but they don't know *my* customers. Maybe people who buy books are not all the same. Does that make sense?

You have to offer customers what they want, not what, in this case, the book publishers want to sell you. Marshall Field was one of the finest consumer merchandisers of all time. He created and built a large retail and mail order catalog business on one principle: "Give the lady what she wants." Stock books they'll want to buy. So you need to know what ways you should use to find out the subject preferences of people who come into your store.

PETER

> I'm going to stick with my two points. It will be a big job just answering what new distribution channels are available. Also the who, what, and how much about my competitors.

Let's stop here and list the new questions you've brought up:

John: How to be perceived differently than the competition? How to close more sales?

Susan: How to get new product definitions? How to find the highest price customers will pay?

Bill: How to expand business and find new resellers? How to determine the total market potential?

Betsey: How to define new products and set sales forecasts? How to locate new distribution?

Peter: How to identify new distribution channels? How to track the competition?

Anne: How to change the business? How to build store traffic? How to inventory best-sellers?

Throughout the day we will be discussing a variety of methods and techniques to gain market intelligence. You will recognize the right set of questions and hear about the marketing tools to get answers to those questions that uniquely pertain to your business. [*I can't interrupt the teaching flow to point out when or how each one of their particular business questions can be answered. It's much more constructive if they are constantly trying to apply any and all techniques to their market information needs.*]

Before we start developing the right questions for your businesses, we have to understand how customers decide to buy. To do that, we must:

- Characterize the perceived value that customers consider when they select products or services.
- Locate the places where they go to buy.
- Understand the costs of distribution to deliver products to the place of purchase.

BACK TO MARKETING FUNDAMENTALS

We've worked up the foundation questions of marketing intelligence for all businesses. Many of you either learned the basics in school or during each day you intuitively used marketing concepts and truths in your decision making. But I want you to refresh your memory, so let's explore perceived value, distribution, and reseller costs. Be particularly mindful that your competition wants to replace you as the customer's preferred supplier. Framing the basic questions to understand what competitors are doing to satisfy customer needs is vital to your business survival.

CUSTOMERS—USERS AND PERCEIVED VALUE

What is value?

BILL

> The way the product or service performs. The way it does the job. Performance, coupled with the price, equals value.

The only way a customer will make a value decision is by combining the performance our product or service delivers with the price we charge.

Here's an example. Everyone take your pen and hold it up in the air. Okay, let's see. We have Bics™, lots of black roller tips, there's a Cross pen, and a couple of Monte Blancs. Isn't that interesting? They all make marks on paper, clip onto a pocket, and have black or blue ink. Performance, I would say, is about equal. What about price? The Bics are less than a dollar, roller-tips about $2, Crosses around $20, and well, for the very wealthy, the Monte Blanc is a steal at $125. Now, why do Monte Blanc and the Bic buyers perceive the value of pens differently? What did Monte Blanc discover by market research that led them to confidently set their pen price at $125? What additional features did Cross add to their pen to separate themselves from Bic? Think about that.

Now, everybody take off your watch and hold it up. We have the same situation: there's a Timex™, some Seikos, a few fake Rolexes™, and one antique Hamilton. What's going on here? They all tell time and are reasonably accurate, but there is a price range from under $20 to $3,000. Now think about cars, houses, boats, haircuts, computers, hotels, and shop tools. Similar performance and utility, but definite price differences. Isn't it interesting that the items we buy have almost identical performance but such a wide price difference?

All customers, whether consumer, industrial, or commercial, make value purchases by defining their performance needs and then deciding how much they can pay to have their performance preferences met.

GOOD, BETTER, AND BEST—VALUE WORDS

I like the Sears value models that have been used for more than a century. They satisfy customers with three distinct value strata: good, better, and best. Price and performance buying options are offered to customers from the bottom of good to the very top of best. (See Figure 3–1.) The triangle is divided into three levels—good, better, and best. The ascending arrow on one side represents increasing performance, as well as price.

Each customer has a different minimum performance expectation that must be met before the sale can take place. That's

FIGURE 3–1
Performance + Price = Value

Value strata descriptors are good, better, and best.

easy to see when we look at the best buyer. In all my years of analyzing internal and external buyer patterns, whether consumer or industrial, my conclusions reflect conventional marketing wisdom that of the total range of value, the best buyer represents the smallest percentage of all buyers—typically 5 to 10 percent. These are customers who will pay almost anything to own the perceived highest performance. Note, I said *perceived*. That 5 to 10 percent group includes the Rolls-Royce™ and Porsche™ car buyers, and the Monte Blanc pen buyer, for example. At the very bottom of the good range is someone who just wants transportation and is content with four wheels, no air conditioning, and plain cloth seats. The Bic pen buyer is sitting in the passenger seat. Let's look at Betsey's catering customers. Best buyers must have fresh shrimp, caviar, and aged beef while the good buyer opts for sliced ham and celery or carrot sticks. This is important because everything from the low end to the high end is the total market. Remember to picture in your mind the value triangle: it applies to all goods and services, whether for the consumer, industrial, or commercial buyer.

How about the low end or good performance, as Sears defines it? How many of you have a dryer at home? What happens? We open the door, put in the clothes, close the door, set the temperature and timer, and push "on." Functionally, all dryers are the same: a motor drives a belt; the drum rotates; a fan blows hot air into the drum; and the clothes dry. Why then are there higher prices as we move from good, to better, to the best dryers?

BETSEY

The more expensive the dryer, the more features you get.

Of course—like more temperature and fabric settings, quieter motors, a window to see your clothes drying, and shorter or longer dryer guarantees. Sears knows people will pay higher prices for a higher level of performance. Now make a triangle for cars. Always start defining value from the very bottom of good and then move up. Think about all those features we pay for until we reach the tip of the best value level.

Somewhere in a triangle for your business, your customers will stop wanting more performance and will not pay any more. That's the value level we must satisfy before our competition does.

Consider the car example in Figure 3–2. You write in automobile brand names on the left side of the triangle at the value level where you think they belong. I've put my perceptions of value on the right. Maybe we differ?

Now, let's try one for air travel. What's the good?

JOHN

Coach or cattle.

The best?

BILL

First class.

Better?

SUSAN

That would be business class.

Now you've got it.

FIGURE 3–2

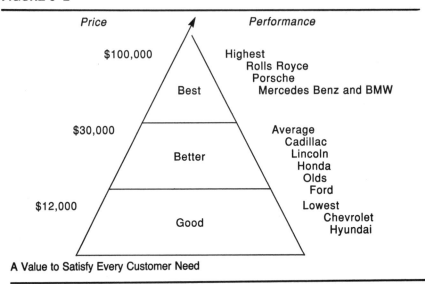

A Value to Satisfy Every Customer Need

Most units of goods and services are purchased in the good category. Most of the dollars are spent in the *better* value category. We generally prefer greater performance than is offered in the *good*. We want dryers that offer more than just hot or cold drying air. Not Rolls-Royces, but not just four tires and a steering wheel. Not the fanciest hotel, and not the flea bag in Center City. Think about restaurant menu choices. Not the *good* baked chicken or the *best* Peking duck, but a mid-priced beef, lamb, or seafood entree in the better value stratum. You get the idea. So, *good* buyers purchase the most units, but (again, this is my experience) *better* buyers create the most dollars.

But what about the airline example? Fact: there are far fewer passengers riding in first or business class than in coach or tourist class. Why don't people fly business class? As consumers, we have difficulty justifying services or products that cost more than $1,000. Business class, like first class, is usually more than $1,000. That's why most airline seats are in coach and are usually priced at half those prices. We will tolerate lower performance for a short flight and choose, if you accept the airline restrictions, to buy a coach ticket at a much lower cost than business or first class. [*I haven't talked about needs versus wants as the driving force for justifying value. This airline exam-*

ple is great. People need *to get from airport A to airport B, and they may* want *the perceived luxury of first class, but they won't buy it.*] Now let's use Peter's weighing scales to demonstrate value levels. How do scales differ in performance? It seems to me that in moving from *good* to *best*, scales would show the weight in more exacting ounces, pounds, or kilograms. Some are more accurate than others. Some are larger or smaller, faster or slower, and so on. Let's put an *X* in the Figure 3–3 triangle where Peter thinks his customers perceive his scale performance.

COMPETITOR'S VALUE

PETER

That's a tough question. Everyone in our engineering department says we're the *best*. The salespeople say we're only equal to the competition. But I'll guess we're between *better* and *best*.

Now put another *X*, with a circle around it, where your price is.

FIGURE 3–3
Peter's Scales

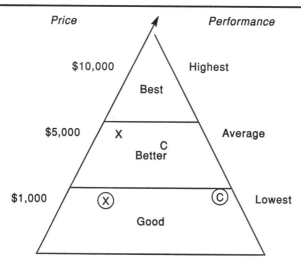

Performance + Price Positions = Value

PETER

> As product manager, I do know we price below the industry average even though we are perceived as the market leader. So I'll put it just below the *good* line.

Alright, tell us where to put a *C* for your competitor's performance and price.

Compared to competitive products, you're giving the customer more performance than you charge. Your price doesn't match performance. The perceived value is not aligned.

PETER

> Doesn't the customer see us as the more valuable supplier? Our lower prices are a great deal.

Sure, but your job is to maximize profits. I'm suggesting there may be an opportunity to raise your price—maybe not all the way to the competition's, but enough to still be perceived as the better value. You would also add sales revenue. We have to constantly ask whether there is an opportunity to raise prices. You said earlier that you were the market leader. Is that in unit sales, dollar sales, or profit?

PETER

> In units sold. That's how we measure our market leadership. Isn't that the right criterion?

It's only one way to define a market leader. Offering greater performance than your competitors at prices below the competition explains why you are the unit volume leader. The trick here is to determine which performance features customers want next, get them to the customer first, and at that time take the opportunity to raise prices. The extra profit is then used to continue the process of adding performance value. The goal is to become the profit leader. That's the sustaining business formula. Maintaining a long-term market perception as the supplier of greater value is the only way to remain the market leader.

Is it worthwhile to gain marketing intelligence to really know how your scales perform? Maybe you need to ask some questions to verify whether you could raise prices. We're going to cover how to ask questions to get objective answers in the next chapter.

THE 80/20 RULE

After performance and price comes the next important marketing element: high volume versus low volume buyers. Let's start with an old and accepted distribution or volume segmentation rule of thumb: 80 percent of the products and services for sale in each value stratum are purchased by approximately 20 percent of the buyers in that value stratum. Here are a few examples:

- 80 percent of all dry cleaning services are bought by 20 percent of all people who dry clean their clothes.
- 80 percent of all gourmet food purchases are made by 20 percent of all gourmet food buyers.
- 80 percent of all golf balls are bought by 20 percent of all golfers.
- 80 percent of all suntan lotion purchases are made by 20 percent of all suntan lotion users.

[*I'd be surprised if someone doesn't challenge this rule. Sure, these examples would have to be researched to validate the percentages and there are always exceptions to every rule, but my hunch is I'd be close.*]

Almost every item, including food, cars, catering, wooden toys, and janitorial supplies will come out this way. I talked earlier about the 13 or 14 million small businesses having less than 50 employees. That's a perfect case where 80 percent of all the firms probably buy only 20 percent of all the goods and services. Figure 3–4 illustrates this rule.

Looking for the volume purchasers, finding where they live and what they really want, and knowing what the competition is doing to satisfy their thirst for units continue to be our challenges.

FIGURE 3–4
The 80/20 Rule of Thumb

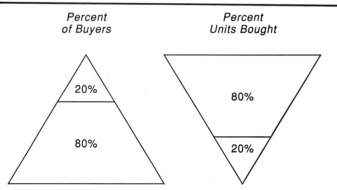

Twenty percent of the customers buy 80 percent of the goods/services.

VITAL THOUGHTS

- Identifying key questions about your business starts the marketing intelligence process.
- Determining the total market requires knowing only two of these three facts: units sold, dollars paid, and total dollars paid for all units.
- Creating customer value is a combination of your performance and your price.
- Finding high volume buyers is done by using the 80/20 rule.

CHAPTER 4

THE DISTRIBUTION PROCESS AND PRICE

Each day, marketing becomes more vital to business success and distribution becomes more essential. Identifying and reaching large volume buyers in the different value strata (good, better, and best) is the job of distribution. Marketing intelligence will detail:

- Where the customers are.
- What advertising is the most effective to pull customers into the reseller outlets.
- What price and performance approach will make our product or service attractive.
- What the competition is doing.
- Why resellers should buy, stock, demonstrate, and sell our goods and services.

Distribution is the pipe or conduit we push our products and services through to reach the customer.

Who are the distribution players? What other methods are available to reach the end customer? How many purchasing decisions are made before our product or service is sold to the end user? Figure 4–1 illustrates the possible participants in the distribution channel.

THE END USERS OR CONSUMERS

To the far right is the end user, which can be any consumer. The end user can be a factory or office worker using Peter's scales, a child who plays with Susan's wooden toys, one of Bill's maintenance customers, one of Anne's coffee drinkers and (hopefully)

FIGURE 4–1
**Distribution Alternatives: Product and Service Channels to the
User/Customer**

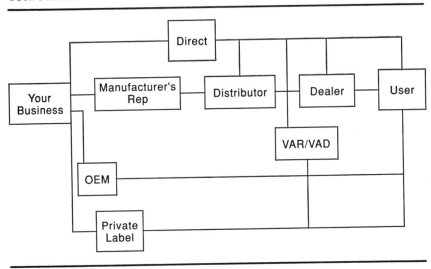

book buyers, John's small business owner struggling to understand his operating numbers, or perhaps Betsey's social or business host or hostess needing catering expertise. Everyone is an
end user of something.

SPECIFIERS, BUYERS, AND PURCHASING AGENTS

Selling to industrial or commercial users requires us to know
about three other influences on the buying decision: specifiers,
buyers, and purchasing agents. What does a specifier do?

BILL

> That's someone who knows what's needed for the application. Spec-
> ifiers compare competitive products and services and decide on ac-
> ceptable performance for their use. Then they describe or write up
> the requirements for purchase from vendors.

You said *vendor.* That's a new word. What does it mean?

BILL

Anybody who has a product or service to deliver to a customer—actually, everybody in this room.

It sounds like the specifier makes the real decisions on what to buy.

BILL

Yes and no. Yes, they determine and define what the user needs. And yes, their recommendations carry a lot of weight in the final choice. But a purchasing agent actually negotiates price, delivery, and terms of the purchase. A purchasing agent is the same thing as a buyer.

So let's review. Users state preferences for a product or service performance. Specifiers describe, either verbally or in writing, the key performance to meet application needs. The buyers or purchasing agents use the performance description to select the lowest-priced supplier. They then order the product or service.

THE IMPORTANCE OF THE SPECIFIER

Let me tell you a story about the key role of the specifier in the purchasing decision process.

In the late 1970s the hierarchy of a major, worldwide religious organization put together a 10-year program called "The Decade of the Family." This project was to furnish training materials, attractive signs, banners, bumper stickers, and other resources to create an awareness that the family was the core of ethics, morals, and human needs. Each local church across the country was to form a committee to encourage participation among its members to improve their immediate and extended families.

The American headquarters created colorful brochures, workbooks, training materials, and a program promotion package to be used at the individual church and at the regional administrative level. (The administrative regional office is like a sales manager with the local churches reporting to it.) My wife and I were asked if we would create the bumper stickers, banners, and little rubber stamps with the logo and program symbol to imprint letters. We were given exclusive use of the "Family Life" design to use on the items they wanted us to supply. We were told that our little company would be promoted in their mailings to all the churches as the place to order these support materials. I asked for and received a letter endorsing our company as the exclusive provider for the 10-year national "Family Life" project. What greater opportunity could a small company want? We agreed to sell the materials at our cost plus a nominal profit to cover administrative expenses.

Practicing what I preach, I did some marketing intelligence work. First, I counted the number of local churches to get banner potential. I made estimates of the number of cars owned by the churchgoers and calculated the bumper sticker potential. I looked up the average number of families per church and made an estimate of the rubber stamp potential. The program was planned to be active for 10 years, so I multiplied my annual estimates by 10 to form a total revenue projection. We spent money to develop, print, and inventory the materials, and awaited the launch of the program at a big meeting in Kansas City.

Let me review the players in the purchasing decision chain. I assumed the individual church families were the users. The national headquarters was the specifier. The local church pastor was the buyer because funds came from each church budget. I concluded that there was no other player in the decision-making process.

The Kansas City program launching event was a success. In attendance were representatives from all the regions, including church pastors and the national trainers who would crisscross the country installing the program in all regions. All we had to do was sit and wait for the orders to roll in. We waited and waited. Nothing happened. I kept calling the headquarters to get progress reports. The answer came back, "these kinds of programs take time."

Meanwhile we had inventory waiting to move. Weeks went by. Months went by. We took a half-page advertisement in a magazine that was promised to arrive on the desk of each pastor.

Still no orders. Only then did I start more intelligence gathering to find out what the problem was. I called regional administrative offices (the sales managers) and was told the program was under review. I talked to pastors who said they had heard of the program but they were waiting for authority to implement the activity. Waiting for authority! What more authority did they need? The national office was launching a positive, noncontroversial program called "Family Life." Who was this authority the pastors were talking about?

Finally, after six months and two trips to the national offices, it became clear that the national administration had no authority to force programs into existence at the regional or local level. It was the regional administrators, not the individual church pastors, who decided on participation in national programs, and the regions were not buying the program.

Well, we sold perhaps ¹⁄₂₀ of our initial inventory. The national offices didn't need or want to buy the balance of our inventory. I assumed the program vanished and we learned a great marketing intelligence lesson. Always find out: who really has the ultimate authority to authorize purchases? who in fact is the specifier? We didn't find that out. We did not validate the assumption that the national administration had the decision power. It did not.

DEALERS/RETAILERS, VALUE–ADDED RESELLERS (VARs), AND DISTRIBUTORS

Let's go back to the distribution diagram. The next distribution channel participant is the retailer or dealer, just to the left of the user. Their function in the chain is to stock, display, and present products to buyers, specifiers, and end users. We're all familiar with dealers. Almost everything we buy is from a dealer. As we move to the left, we run into distributors and VARs. What value do these kinds of businesses add in the movement of goods and services from supplier to user? What is their role? Can anybody tell me?

ANNE

In my bookstore, I rely very heavily on distributors to quickly deliver any book I don't stock. They tell me about new books and set up promotional displays in my store that draw customer attention to the sale books. Best of all, distributors extend credit to me to buy the books.

BILL

I'd like to talk about distributors. Anne's right about all the services she said distributors provide. We give our cleaning supplies customers more by taking back damaged merchandise. We also train dealers to show and sell customers the products. We'll even go with dealers to visit end users and help them close the sale. Another important activity is arranging for factory people to visit the dealers or retailers and end users. This helps the product supplier understand what it's like out in the field. Our function is to warehouse, grant credit, train, and provide end customer support. We are the link between the product manufacturer and the real users.

Betsey, do you deal with distributors?

BETSEY

Yes, they add lots of value in my catering business. Just yesterday, I needed some frozen seafood, but the distributor didn't have any in stock. The distributor contacted the supplier and had it flown in just in time for a party I did last night.

Why couldn't you just call the prime supplier and save a step by not going through the distributor?

BETSEY

Because, as a small user, I have no clout with the manufacturer. The distributor is a big customer and they really get fast service.

Great examples of the distributor's value-added role. Peter, we left out VARs. You're the expert here. Tell us what they do.

PETER

Not expert, but we do use VARs and distributors. The VAR buys off-the-shelf products or services and puts them together with other system pieces to create a better total solution for the end user. VARs usually support end customers with all the other distributor services Bill mentioned. The exception is they don't inventory these systems because everything they sell is customized or tailored to solve an end-user problem.

Some other examples of VARs are swimming pool and landscape sprinkler contractors, and home or office security and telephone system installers. Let's continue on distributors. Susan, how important are distributors in the toy business?

SUSAN

> We get quite a bit of damage from shipping and dealer breakage trying to put toys together for floor samples. The distributor takes the damaged goods back under our product return policy. A "no questions asked" return policy really helps to keep retailers and distributors loyal to us.

THE ORIGINAL EQUIPMENT MANUFACTURER (OEM)

Look back at Figure 4–1. The last goods or service purchaser in the distribution chain, the participant closest to the manufacturer, is the OEM, or original equipment manufacturer. Peter, do you sell scales to OEMs, and if so, what role do they serve?

PETER

> OEMs buy a large volume of scale parts or components. They use these pieces and parts to build a larger weighing instrument that offers their customers greater performance functions than our scales. They are not VARs. The OEMs' products have their brand names and numbers on the label. While an OEM's product is a larger and more complex solution for the customer's needs, it is not a system. The distribution channel used by OEMs will most likely be the same one we use because they serve the same kinds of customers we do.

Well, aren't they competitors?

PETER

> No, our market is for table or benchtop weighing applications. They satisfy more complicated weighing problems. We see the OEMs as an opportunity for extra business. We watch them closely because they may decide to build smaller units. Then they really would become competitors.

Let's keep talking about the OEM. What does an OEM add to distribution?

PETER

The additional advantages are that selling expenses are lower, advertising and promotional expense is minimal, and OEMs are large volume customers.

Again, it sounds like they become competitors.

PETER

Well, they do in a way, but most suppliers to OEMs want the unit volume of parts or subsystems to reduce their manufacturing cost.

The OEM buys in large volume and requires minimal sales or marketing effort and expense for the manufacturer. OEMs demand and usually get a 65 percent discount from the manufacturer's list price. It's great business, but most manufacturers need to be very careful not to let OEMs dominate their revenue stream. I've seen too many small suppliers become slaves to large volume buyers.

PETER

That's part of it. The OEM doesn't want our packaging, the sheet metal cases, or even the electronics. They build their own more complex product. So the parts we sell them cost us much less than what it costs us to build a whole scale product. A discount of 65 percent is a little confusing. We would never take the parts we sell to the OEM and market them separately at a list price. It's like comparing apples and oranges. We are not price comparing the same products for sale.

Let me inject a true story about how the OEM obscures the base manufacturer's brand and is really a competitor. Back in the 1960s I was at 3M Company and had responsibility as a product manager to sell magnetic computer tape to large OEM computer manufacturers like RCA, Univac, and Honeywell. [*Funny how times change. None of these companies are major computer business players now.*] We also sold in bulk to IBM, who packaged the tape in their branded boxes and sold directly to their customers.

New tape competitors were eroding our OEMs' market share at user accounts and forced us to change our marketing strategy. We decided to market the very same computer tape being supplied to OEMs but sell directly to customers under the 3M Scotch™ brand label.

It took about a year to launch our branded product. Pricing was set well below the OEM level, but slightly above the competition. We were sure the perceived value of the Scotch brand would sell and be accepted immediately. The field sales force was brought in for training, advertisements appeared in the right journals, press conferences were held, and direct mail literature was sent to all major data processing managers. It was a perfect product launch, but nothing happened. No phone orders; the salespeople went silent—something was radically wrong.

The phone calls we did get were from our good OEM customers asking why we had suddenly turned into a competitor. My boss said, "Get on a plane and find out what's going on!" I lined up visits with the largest 20 percent of computer tape users at insurance companies, banks, and government agencies. We didn't know the people. We had never made a computer tape sales call. Our OEMs did that. One visit after another produced the same responses:

- 3M? Oh yes, you make the sticky tape.
- Really? I didn't know you made computer tape.
- Sure, I know you make IBM's tape, but now you'll have to qualify just like your competitors.
- How do I know the Scotch brand is exactly the same?

We regrouped. Our conclusion: the market didn't connect 3M with computer tape. My God, 3M practically invented computer tape! We were the largest supplier in the free world . . . through OEMs. We were totally obscure to end users. Data processing managers—the specifiers—had no firsthand knowledge of our quality, reliability, and service, and didn't know a soul in the company. There is a happy ending to the story. We quickly changed our communication messages, delivered test samples, and smothered the major accounts with sales effort. The sales plan slipped about nine months, but in the end we achieved the market-share goal for Scotch brand computer tape sold direct to users. I learned a lot from that experience:

- OEM unit volume business is rewarding, but the risk of being hidden as the prime manufacturer is high.
- Never assume that end users will immediately transfer the OEM product quality perception to an OEM supplier product.
- Customers build loyalties on brand performance and the people behind the brand.
- Look before you leap—do the marketing intelligence work.

Here's another model. The OEM is a volume buyer of parts of another supplier's whole product or services. Peter's whole product is a scale. Part of his scale is a unique balance spring that the company designed and makes in its factory. An OEM needs this kind of spring for a product it is manufacturing and offers to buy large quanitities of springs from Peter. The large unit spring volume, added to Peter's normal business, will reduce his cost to make the spring. There is very little marketing expense for Peter to get this cost-reducing and revenue-increasing business. The OEM can become a competitor, but Peter decides the risk is remote and takes the OEM order.

Let me be clear on the OEM as customer. They are great customers and many companies adopt a business strategy to market product only to an OEM. However, an OEM can become a competitor if its market conditions require lower manufacturing costs and it can make the product more cheaply than you can. The message is, just be careful.

WE'RE ALL OEMs

I want you to realize and remember that we are all OEMs. We put together pieces and parts to form our own products or services. Let's take a look.

John takes crumpled up invoices and bills, cash register receipts, and bank statements. Then, as an OEM, he adds value by manufacturing a more useful product called a financial statement. Susan buys wood, screws, rope, and paint and becomes a toy product OEM. Peter purchases springs, metal cases, and electronic chips and becomes a scale OEM. Bill uses catalogs and in-house customer training and delivers useful products in a timely manner to become a distribution system OEM. Betsey merges food, drinks, napkins, glasses, decorations, creativity, and trained servers to create a food service system. Anne is an intellectual OEM using books, coffee, and a conversational setting as the parts for her product.

Get the idea?

To do business we all create a product. Sooner or later we become original equipment or service manufacturers. A manufacturer is an OEM of products. Someone who links people and products to solve customer problems is an OEM of services. As a teacher, I am an OEM. I create a product and service solution for learning by combining slides, relevant student handouts, teaching skills, knowledge, experience, and speaking style to provide training performance for you, the customer.

PRIVATE LABELING

Another market condition, like selling to the OEM, is private labeling or branding. Particularly in consumer markets, like a wooden toy manufacturer or Betsey's catering business, suppliers will allow a large reseller to buy products with the reseller's brand name on the product or service. An example of a service private label is Sears. Roof repair, painting, drapery making are all done by outside contractors, not Sears's employees. These contractors allow Sears to market their services under the Sears brand.

Because the private label volume is usually very large, suppliers are willing to sell the private brand at very low prices.

In Figure 4–2 (on p. 56) you will see that the private brand price is sold at a deep discount from the $1 list price. A smart supplier balances OEM or private label sales opportunities with its own product brand business. The strategy is not to let OEM or private label become too dominant a part of its business or capture too much market share as a competitor. [*OEM and private label accounts can kill a company. I've emphasized the point as much as I could. I hope the message sticks.*]

FIGURE 4–2
Rule of Thumb—Value-Added Chain Costs

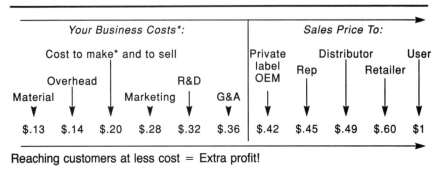

Reaching customers at less cost = Extra profit!

*Costs are accumulated. Example shows: total cost to make is $.20; to market & operate business is $.16 more; your price to OEM is $.42, or a $.06 pre-tax profit; selling to a retailer at $.60 = $.24 profit.

Susan, do large consumer merchandisers, like Sears or Toys "R" Us, request private label of your wooden toys?

SUSAN

Sure, they ask for private label all the time. But we have decided not to do that. Being the highest quality line, at the top of the triangle, we don't want another competitive brand name in our niche market. We don't care how large the orders are.

That's a good strategy, but you must monitor the competition closely to detect when customers and distributors perceive that competitive quality is equal to yours. At that point, a competitor's strategy may be to try to build unit volume by private labeling for these large merchandisers. Your company should consider a policy change when you learn that your competitors are about to get a private brand order from your customers who now just resell your brand. Then make your tactical move to sell to the large retailers and block competition from making a significant market entry. Now, let's move to the left in the distribution diagram, Figure 4–1, to manufacturers' representatives.

MANUFACTURERS' REPS

So far we've learned about several ways to communicate with customers using reseller intermediaries who take possession of products and then move the product to the user. Now, there are only two ways a prime supplier can meet and ask for a reseller or customer order. The *first* way is to talk directly to distribution and end customers. This is done through travel, the telephone, or written communication from our place of business to the customer. The *second* alternative is to employ independent sales representatives, known as reps, who specialize in selling certain types of products or services to industries, usually within a specific geographic area. The reps' role is to make sales calls, in person, on distribution targets and end users. They earn commissions, usually 5 to 7 percent of the sales revenue they generate, for doing this work. The company only pays this commission after it receives the money from the reseller, so one advantage of a rep, versus a direct sales employee, is the improvement of cash flow. Hiring regional independent representatives to make sales calls costs far less than paying the salaries of a direct sales force.

JOHN

> This whole discussion on distribution is of absolutely no help to me. I'm a local bookkeeper. Why do I have to know about independent reps, resellers, or VARs?

Let me make the connection. You are a solo business person. There are just so many hours in the day for you to do accounting work for clients, complete all the administrative demands of running a small business, and do the life-sustaining job of getting new customers. Distribution is an extension of your marketing efforts to new customers. Who might your resellers be, John? How about insurance agents, local bankers, newspaper advertising salespeople, personal financial planners, and other suppliers to your potential customers? We call these *third-party referrals*. Could you employ them to tell your story? Yes! Could you pay them a commission or small fee for a referral? Yes! The message here is clear. Consider any person or organization that is credible in the mind of your potential customer as a candidate to distribute the story of your services. See the connection?

JOHN

> I've never heard of an accountant paying a commission.

So what? It takes creativity and bold action these days to reach customers and displace your competition!

WHAT THE VALUE–ADDED CHAIN COSTS—FROM SUPPLIER TO END USER

Let's examine the value-added chain. Each step, from manufacturer or service vendor to the end user, adds value by selling, warehousing, demonstrating, creating systems, and servicing your customers. The prime supplier spends profit to buy distribution. Look back at Figure 4–2, the Value-Added Chain, which illustrates the cost of distribution.

It costs money to achieve distribution. In Figure 4–2, I assume the end users pay $1 to purchase the performance they need. Moving from right to left, we see that retailers purchase that product or service for $.60 and they receive $.40 compensation for reselling. Distributor receives $.11 and so on. Typically, the prime supplier, using all the levels of distribution, should expect revenue of $.06 to $.24 for every item that is sold to end users for $1. Now move all the way to the left of the diagram and let's look at what it costs the supplier to get that revenue. Materials or contract labor will typically cost about $.20. Marketing, engineering or product/service development, and administrative expenses will consume another $.16, for total costs of $.36. The difference between what the company sells for $.42 and the cost of $.36 is a 14 percent profit of $.06.

Cut out or make a copy of Figure 4–2. It's a great reminder of the available distribution options and ways to increase profit. [*As suppliers, we get set in our ways to distribute to users. I want them to realize it's okay to consider by-passing traditional channels and to pick up extra profit. It's hard to change old habits.*]

THE SELLING PROFIT MARGIN—A MARKUP OR A DISCOUNT?

Businesspeople define *profit margin* in several ways. We must make sure that a person talking about margin has the same meaning we do. Let's look at a few examples.

Here's the first one. We did market research and determined a consumer product had a $100 value when bought in a retail store. We'll say Susan has new wooden reading tables and bookcases. Her marketing strategy is to sell these through bookstores, like Anne's. Look at the $1 at the far right of Figure 4–2, and make that $100 for this example. Anne added value by telling people how strong the table was. She described how the bookcase could be used to teach children about putting toys away. She moved the customer to buy the furniture because the set was available right off the floor. She deserves to earn profit for this distribution service. Anne gets $100 from the customer, the suggested list price set by Susan't toy company. But she only paid $60 to the distributor who delivered and probably set up the table and bookcase as a floor sample. Anne has a profit of $40 on the sale, or a markup margin of 66 percent on her cost of $60. Look at it another way: she bought a $100 library set for $60, or at a 40 percent discount from list price.

SUSAN

> I don't fully understand the difference between markup and discount. Isn't the list price of $100 and the $60 paid the same, either way?

Good question. [*It's rare that people get a clear idea of the difference until they go through the numbers once or twice, or view these margin concepts from two perspectives.*] The dollars are the same. It's just the way you look at profit margin. A markup is looking up from what you paid, $60, to a $100 selling price. When Anne sells at $100, her $60 cost is returned, right? She gets an additional $40, or 66 percent more than she paid. When she looks down from $100 to what she paid, $60, that is a 40 percent discount.

The following table illustrates markup and discount.

| | Selling Margin | |
	Markup	Discount
List price	$100	$100
Cost	60	60
Dollar margin	40	40
Percentage margin	66 percent	40 percent

Consumer distribution resellers describe the difference between what they buy and sell products for as markup margin. Industrial and commercial resellers call what they pay for a product a discount from selling price. There is no difference in the numbers, just in the language. The reseller is either looking up from cost, or down from selling price.

Whenever you hear the word *margin* from anyone who sells anything, ask the question, "Do you mean a markup from your cost, or a discount from list price?" This is extremely important. Let me show you why. The chart I put on the board had a markup of 66 percent and a discount of 40 percent. The price of $100, cost of $60, and $40 profit margin were identical. The percentage margins were different. Now we'll keep the price and profit margin of 40 percent the same and see if the cost or dollar margin changes. Look at what happens.

	Selling Margin	
	Markup	Discount
List price	$100	$100
Cost	71	60
Dollar margin	29	40
Percentage margin	40 percent	40 percent

On a markup of 40 percent, the cost increased from $60 to $71, and the dollar margin decreased from $40 to $29. Do you see how we can get misled if we only hear, "I get 40 percent on your competitor's product"? We must know whether that's a markup or a discount. I've seen many companies set prices either too high or too low because they were not clear on how distribution was defining margin.

Take Peter's scales as the second example. They typically sell to the user through an industrial or commercial dealer. The unit price, say, is $1,000. Unlike consumer retailers, these kinds of dealers usually pay $750 from a manufacturer or distributor. What's the discount? To get the answer, just subtract $750 from

$1,000 to $250, then divide the $250 by $1,000. The discount is 25 percent.

SUSAN

> Why do the retailers selling to consumers get a 40 percent margin, and industrial dealers only get a 25 percent margin? Don't they both provide similar value in reselling the product or service?

Yes, a major reason for the margin difference is that the consumer reseller unit price is normally less. Your wooden library set sells for $100, and Peter's scale has a price of $1,000. Because the prices are lower for your type of products, the dollar margin is less, too: $40 for yours versus $250 for his. The consumer dealer needs a higher price-to-cost percentage margin to run the business. However, the industrial dealer is willing to operate at a lower percentage discount because it earns more dollars from each unit sale. The industrial and commercial dealers also have lower expenses to make a unit sale than consumer resellers have.

SUSAN

> Yes, but it's unfair for equal value-added work.

Each distribution channel has traditional business methods. Understanding how our potential markets and distribution do business is of real strategic importance in developing marketing plans.

What would happen if we sold our products or service directly to the consumer? What if we reached the end user through direct mail or our own selling activity? What would we quote for the wooden library set and scales? John, what do you think?

JOHN

> If you mean what price, I would say $100 for the library set and $1,000 for the scale. Is that right?

Right, because we asked the potential users what they would pay for product or service performance, and they said $100 and $1,000. We don't need to sell for anything less than the customers' perceived value.

Let's take another look at VARs. VARs sell directly to the end customer, but add value by creating systems or service solutions. They add more value than most resellers and deserve a greater profit margin. Most VARs serve the industrial or commercial business. We'll use the selling price of $2,000 for a system, and typically their cost is $1,400. The VAR discount of 30 percent is between the dealer's 40 percent and the distributor's 25 percent.

THE IMPORTANCE OF DEFINING YOUR BUSINESS

This is a good place to revisit the notion of defining your business. Having a clear idea of what we want our business to be leads us to the questions that, when answered, will guide the setting of our strategies. Continuously creating and seeking answers to our business questions is vital.

Internal company information as well as past, lost, current, and potential customers have our answers. We need company business facts or customers to tell us:

- What business we appear to be in, or they think we are in.
- Their needs, or what they have bought.
- About our competition.
- Where we fit in the performance triangle.
- What our niche value is in solving their problems.
- The price they have paid or would pay for performance.
- Where we've sold or they would buy our performance.

Customer and competitor information is the cornerstone to defining and building business strategy, looking for signals of change, and taking corrective action.

John, having heard all this, do you have any changes in how you describe your business?

JOHN

I now think I am describing what I do too narrowly, or for that matter, what I want to do. Seems I should broaden my financial services.

Maybe you should be looking for a narrower financial niche definition as a competitive advantage. John's business is a good example to use. As a financial services provider, are you a banker, a bookkeeper, a stockbroker, a bill collector? Tell me the niche you're really in.

JOHN

> I'm actually a bookkeeper, but I also show my clients how to better manage their cash flow.

That helps us to focus on what you really do. Your vital cash management service is at the heart of the small business solution. Detailed records, positive cash flow, and satisfied customers keep the business doors open.

What I want to know is, what do your clients think you do best—keep books or counsel on cash? Remember when we discussed product performance? A supplier always emphasizes its strongest performance, whether that's a product or a service. So which one do you perform best, and which one gives you more professional satisfaction?

JOHN

> Thinking about it like that, my customers say I'm really good at helping them increase cash coming in the door and slowing down money going out. I guess I enjoy the cash management.

Sounds to me like your primary financial consulting specialty is really cash management. Your secondary expertise is bookkeeping, which gets you in the door to use your cash flow skills. That's more understandable to me and I'm sure it will be to your clients. By the way, sole proprietors who really enjoy what they do are more successful than those that just want to make money. So, when your potential new clients say, what do you do, John? You say, I am a cash management consultant! Much better.

BILL

> I'm starting to think distributors should or can have greater impact on customer profits by offering new solutions. Having the right cleaning products and training and knowing when and how customers want them is really decided by our management. *We*

insist on the minimum number of units they can buy. We deliver when *we* want to deliver. We train when it fits *our* schedule.

I want to think about how to improve our perceived value in the customer's mind. That value may include a greater partnership with the customer. Maybe new quantity pricing and training policies can reduce customer purchase costs and improve their workers' efficiency. I think it's too early to clearly define my primary and secondary business.

My sense is that it is too early for all of you. Do you know why? Because you don't have enough marketing intelligence to form strategies that leverage your performance strengths. Your perspectives on customers and competition are only from your experience and your point of view. Therefore, your views are biased. What you think the customer wants is only a reflection of your current customer policies and business strategies. What market intelligence forces us to do is stand in the shoes of the customers and competitors and look objectively at our businesses. The view is interesting and sometimes frightening. Constantly ask yourself, what business am I really in?

COMPETITORS—A DEFINITION

What is a competitor? The dictionary tells us that a competitor is a rival. Pretty good word. A rival is a person or organization competing with us for the same goal. That goal is the customer's business. A rival tries to equal or surpass our perceived product or service quality in the mind of the customer. Very simple. A competitor, or group of competitors, wants your customer's business. They will use any combination of perceived value and distribution to replace you as the customer's supplier.

Consider some competitors that can impact your business.

1. *New technology* is a competitor that will replace the product or service solution we now sell to meet customer performance demands.
2. *Time* is a competitor that insists we quickly meet customer performance criteria or rival activity with new products and services.

3. *Distance* is a competitor that physically separates us from knowing what end users want.
4. *Money* is a competitor that permits rivals to invest and create performance, price, and distribution that our customers want.
5. *Distribution* is a competitor that strives to offer greater value to our customers.
6. *Innovation*, whether in performance or distribution, is a competitor when developed by rivals.
7. *Resistance* to change is a competitor that delays our adoption of new policies and business methods to meet competition.

We're all so close to our day-to-day struggles that we fail to see competition in these terms.

Competition also is

* The store down the street.
* The invading distributor from the next county.
* Far Eastern and European suppliers moving into our markets.
* Catalogs mailed directly to our customers offering lower prices.

These rivals are all real and can significantly impact our business. But the broader competitive threats of new technology, time, distance, money, distribution, innovation, and resistance to change, if not constantly monitored, will threaten our survival. It is critical that business management take time to consider how to manage these competitive forces. Without this knowledge, it can not retain or advance its market position.

Remember the who, what, where, when . . . in Chapter 2? Well, I extracted competitor questions to be answered by marketing research. Consider the following:

Who

Is the nearest reseller to the customer?
Is the current competition?

Is the potential competition?
Are the competitors' major customers?

What

Product/service can replace what the customer now uses?
Is the competitive technology or service that could replace me?
Is the current distribution channel for products/services?
Are the real and perceived good and bad points of the competition?
Does the customer really think about my competitors?

Where

Is the customer using my product or the competitor's?
Are the major and minor customers located?

Why

Does the customer need more than one supplier?
Does the competition use the distribution channels they do?
Do customers buy from my competitors?

When

Is the typical delivery of product/service expected?
Will a replacement technology or service be available?

How

Much of a price discount does the distribution channel expect?
Many units are each of my major competitors selling?
Many revenue and profit dollars are my competitors getting?

PETER

There isn't a question about getting to market on time to meet customer needs and beat competition. Put this on the list: how long is the development timetable to introduce advanced performance?

Good addition. But isn't that the same as, when will a replacement technology or service be available?

PETER

Not quite. I understand that question to mean a whole new way of doing something. My statement asks about the time to develop additions to the current technology. Is that reasonable?

You have made your point. Let's add your comment. Any more?

BETSEY

How about asking distribution to collect market information to overcome the problem of distance in reaching and understanding customer concerns.

That's valid. How would you ask that as a question?

BETSEY

How much information can distribution collect from customers to define new products or services? and, how can this be accomplished?

Fine, but let's put a *what* in the question. Here then are your and Peter's additions:

What

Are the methods or incentives that will motivate distribution to collect customer information?

How

Long is the development timetable to introduce advanced performance?

In the appendix you will find the complete list of who, what, and so on, questions brought up in our discussions.

LAST WORDS ON *VALUE*

The customer perceives value as a combination of the product or service performance coupled with a price. Performance solves a customer problem better and at a reduced cost. Performance is grouped into three levels—low, average, or high performance (or good, better, and best). Price has similar divisions of low, medium, and high.

LAST WORDS ON *DISTRIBUTION*

Please review the distribution channel diagram. Distribution is involved with telling customers the value story and delivering products and services. The distribution channel participants are users, specifiers, buyers, resellers, distributors, VARs, OEMs, private label accounts, and independent sales representatives. Each distribution participant adds value for the prime supplier and receives profit for doing its distribution work.

We must know:

- Where and from whom customers want to hear our selling proposition.
- How quickly customers want product or service delivery.
- What after-sale service and training customers expect.
- How much distribution will cost to reach customers.
- What distribution the competition will use.

Only then can we strategically and tactically adjust our business to prevent the competition from satisfying our customer.

MORE WORDS ON *COMPETITION*

Competition consists of time, distance, money, distribution, innovation, and our resistance to change. In addition, there are the specific who, what, where, when, and how questions about the competition to address. While we sleep, the competition is trying to get more business from our customers. They work to offer better performance and price to change the customers' perception of value in order to replace the existing supplier. They are creating new, different, and effective distribution channels to reach our customers. They will not rest!

VITAL THOUGHTS

- Constantly consider these core business tasks:
  Find and attract new customers.
  Define products and services customers will buy.
  Set prices at what customers will pay.
  Select the best distribution to reach customers.
  Know the market potential.
  Know and track the competition.
  Identify media to get sales leads or customer traffic.
  Determine after-sale service and customer needs.
  Specify continuing intelligence to be gathered.
  Monitor replacement technologies or services.
  Find import or export sales opportunities.
- Extend your marketing effort to old and new customers through new distribution.
- Know the difference between markup and discount—it's vital for setting distribution pricing.
- Set your price at the *customer's* perception of your value.
- Build business strategy with past and current internal company information, customers, and competitors in mind.

CHAPTER 5

FRAMING VALUE QUESTIONS

Now, what's most important about all the questions I've asked so far today? The answers tell us where we are. They form a strong strategic foundation. Look, we certainly know something about competitive pricing. We understand the quality our existing customers demand. The competition sells to those people we don't. We must know what their quality of performance is and how much their customers are willing to pay to get it. So let's dig even deeper into price, quality, and our competitors' customers.

A COMPETITIVE STORY

Here's a short story about price, quality, and competition. The message to listen for is that even if you have the best product, a fair price, and good service, you may not get the business.

I started my career selling fresh meat products in the Midwest for Armour & Company. My job was as a route salesman calling on grocery stores, butcher shops, and restaurants. The fresh meat business buys on price. Each day I received brand-new price sheets reflecting whether our cattle buyers in Chicago had bought higher or lower than competitive buyers for the same quality meat. Now, I had been trying for some time to replace the competition in Michael's Meat Market in Goshen, Indiana. No matter how many times I called on them, or what promotions we had, I could not get them to order. All the other markets would either buy from me or my competition depending on what the prices were. But not Michael's.

So one day, our pricing came through very low and I knew I could really beat my competitor at Michael's. The prices I had in my hand would surely get the business. Michael was in and we sat down to talk about an order. No, no, no—that's all Michael would say as I went through my price book. Finally, I said, "Why won't you buy from us? Armour quality is tops. My prices are right, and we have the best delivery of all our competition." The perfect market equation—price, quality, and service. He replied that I was absolutely right. If all things were equal, he said, he would buy. I asked, "Well, what's not equal?" Michael finally gave me the answer: "Do you know Frank, the competitor's salesman? He's my brother-in-law."

If I had just asked the other butchers in Michael's shop and Michael's competitors, "Hey, how come Frank, my competitor, gets all of Michael's business?" I would have found out he was family, and that I would never get the business. This story is about how price, quality, and service sometimes lose to the competitor's unfair advantage. I sure wasted a lot of time because I didn't gather enough marketing intelligence.

PERCEIVED VALUE

We saw in the value strata charts that all buyers or customers have certain performance price ranges they will pay to get what they need or want. It's called the *value price point*. We have to know the questions or market conditions that give us enough information to allow changes in our pricing strategy. We have to know the elements customers use to establish a value. Knowing this perceived value really tells us what they will pay. The elements, again, are product or service performance, the quality (whether real or perceived) and delivery of the product or service, and what price they will pay. [*Again, if I say these words enough times, they will make it part of their thinking.*]

Have you ever been in a restaurant that the newspaper reviewed as an "outstanding dining experience"? You go there and at the door you are greeted and shown to a pleasant corner table. You open a crisp, well-printed menu and notice the prices are high. A professional server gives glowing suggestions about the menu items. Your order is confirmed as the best choice. The candles give off just the right light over a clean tablecloth, while soft music plays as you wait to be served. The order arrives on sparkling white, warmed plates. But the food is terrible. Is it your taste buds? It couldn't be the chef.

After paying the bill, your dining companion asks, "Well, what did you think about our dinner?" "All in all," you say, "it was worth it." That's perceived value. The total product performance included soft music, candles, hot plates, bad food, good service, and high prices. Would you go back? The food was not what you expected, but overall you enjoyed the restaurant. What's going on here? You went in there for dinner—to eat. But you were satisfied with the whole performance of the dining experience, the attitudes and professionalism of the service, the table location and candles, the overall dining environment. The bad food was just one part of the product and service experience.

Now think about the time you ate in a fast food restaurant. Let's say you ordered a grilled sirloin pattie in the fancier restaurant and paid $10 just for the meat entree. In the fast food restaurant, that's called a hamburger. You would never pay more than $3. Why not? Because we are not willing to spend more money for essentially the same products or services if they are presented in a manner that we perceive demands a lower price. Maybe the soft music is everything. See the difference? Comparable product quality but unequal service or delivery. The perceived total performance of the fast food restaurant resulted in a lower perceived value. But what about the performance advantage of speed offered by a fast food meal?

I'll let you think about different performances and values. Does anyone have another situation where similar products or services delivered in different ways create different perceived values?

SUSAN

> We do that now with our wooden toys. We and our competitors use only oak to make our toys. But we advertise our oak as coming from 100-year-old trees. Instead of just oak, we say it's white oak and specially treated to give extra long life. Then we say that each large oak slab must pass a careful inspection for knots and cracks before it is used to make toys. We describe the noncorrosive screws and bolts to firmly hold toys together. We talk about the wood sealers as being nontoxic for child protection, and about how mar- and scratch-resistant the toys are.

Do you actually provide this kind of product quality? What about competitive products?

SUSAN

> Sure, we provide the quality, but as to inspecting the wood, that's all done by machines. The customer assumes that real people look at every slab to make sure there are no knots. All manufacturers must use nontoxic sealers—it's the law. We all get wood from 100-year-old trees . . . but *we* advertise the fact. For some reason, they don't.

Does this perceived performance enhancement bring you higher prices? Also, how did you find out that customers would pay more for this perceived higher product performance?

SUSAN

> It does get us higher prices because it allows us to claim we have higher costs to offer these product advantages. How did we find out about them? Many of our employees have small children and they have concerns about toxicity when their kids chew on the toys. They told us how much the toys get abused and that we should make sure we put finishes on the wood so the toys did not get all marred and gouged. We didn't do a formal study of our employees. It was just a collection of comments and suggestions.

Your performance was defined from inside the company, versus sitting down with a wide cross-section of potential customers.

SUSAN

> Yes, these perceived value-building statements about our products surfaced over a period of time from inside our company. We added one selling feature and then another.

Don't you think you could have raised your price earlier in the life of the product if you knew about all these features at one time? You could have set up a pricing strategy to block the competition before they got to your customers. Susan, consider doing outside research before you price your next new products.

BETSEY

> I try to enhance perceived value all the time. In catering, you've got to merchandise the main food dishes. I put the roast beef on a

shiny silver platter. I have the servers in white aprons, wearing huge chef's hats. They wield large sharp knives while standing beside a steaming tray of au jus. But the customer sees our performance as the server-chefs, the steam, and the beef. Same thing with shrimp. I serve the shrimp, not too many, arranged on a big mound of ice, with lemon slices all around, and add sprigs of parsley for color. We charge a lot more for each shrimp than you can buy it for in the fish markets. Is that merchandising, or am I really adding performance value?

I say merchandising *is* adding value. It creates a perception, not deceit. Customers want to believe whatever they buy or think about buying has the right performance for them. As suppliers, you and Susan are telling about or showing us additional, nonessential elements that justify paying more for your product or service, even though I know I can pay less someplace else. Your decorations, knives, and chef's hats have increased or added value in the customer's mind.

Now, how did you decide to use those strategies to create more perceived value? Do your competitors merchandise in the same way? It costs more money to add these values. Did you ever really ask a customer how they wanted the food served or what additional performance they would enjoy?

BETSEY

Well, now that you ask it that way, I don't remember asking. For that matter, I have never asked anyone—the customers, the guests, or even experts in the field. I don't know why. I guess I just trusted my own judgment that I knew what the customer wanted. Maybe if I did ask, I would find a higher price point for the dishes we serve.

Although you guessed what customers wanted, you're probably more right than wrong. But I'm going to tell you, like I did Susan, customers know more about what they want than you do.

Here's an approach that works almost every time to explore customer preferences. We're all constrained in asking for what we really want. We've built barriers and defined norms in our mind about what products or services now cost, what our societal position requires us to use, drive, or wear, and what technology or our circumstances permit us to have. For example, fifteen years ago I said that what I'd really like is a portable typewriter that would correct my spelling, be able to move paragraphs all around the page, and allow me to erase every word I wanted without messing up the paper. A dream then. Today that performance, the personal computer, is sitting on my desk or in my briefcase.

You can open the respondent's mind to imagine the perfect product. You can do that by mentally taking away the constraining thought barriers. Here's how to set the stage. Say something like this to anybody: "If money were no object," and then continue on about a circumstance involving a product or service, or ask, "If, right now, I could solve the most troublesome problem in getting your work done"; or, "I'd like you to imagine the perfect product." Then ask, "What is that? Describe it to me. How big is it? How much does it weigh? Where would you put it? How fast would it go?"

The respondents will need encouragement during this dialog because they're relaying thoughts far beyond the perimeters of what they know is normal. Use and reuse the barrier-breaking phrases, "money is not an issue," "believe that you can have it now," and "any feature or performance is possible." These idea streams always suggest opportunities for new product or service features to design for and execute now. Try it on any of your customers. You'll be surprised at how responsive they'll be in telling you what they really want if they could only get it.

Let's try to summarize what questions to ask. You need structure. By now, you should have a feel for the content of questions. Who, what, why, where, when, how much, and how many: just keep repeating these words and adding the vital specific information you need to form strategies to change your company's direction.

TEN BUSINESS QUESTIONS

We've covered, where are we? When you fill in the answers on Figure 5–1 you should have an even better feel for where you are. But what about the other two strategic questions: where are we going? and how are we going to get there? We can't say where

FIGURE 5–1

Vital Questions

	Users/Customers	Resellers	Competitors
Where am I?	_____	_____	_____
Who?	_____	_____	_____
What?	_____	_____	_____
Where?	_____	_____	_____
Why?	_____	_____	_____
When?	_____	_____	_____
How many?	_____	_____	_____
How much?	_____	_____	_____

Copy this chart to a larger paper or write real small. Now put one of your vital questions in each box. Make two charts and ask someone who also knows your business to fill it out. Then compare questions.

---

we're going because we need to collect some marketing intelligence before we decide our objectives. Turn back to Figure 2–2. Compare how you would either change the questions, add new ones, or rank them differently.

HOW TO ASK UNBIASED QUESTIONS

By now we know the questions. But how do we know we're getting straight answers from people? Why are they going to tell us how they really feel about products or services, or about the competition? Does anybody have ideas about getting objective answers?

PETER

> I remember hearing in school that you have to ask unbiased questions to get real answers.

Correct. Usually, people constructing or asking questions in an ad-lib manner unconsciously bias their questions to get the answers they want to hear. It's not intentional, but that's what happens. Let's demonstrate the point.

We've been at this workshop for a while and I need some feedback, or marketing intelligence. Here is my question:

I like to teach, I really enjoy it, and I've been doing it a long time. Marketing intelligence is an interesting subject and I hope the handouts and my board diagrams have been helpful. I'm very pleased you seem to understand what I'm saying. We've had a few laughs and you appear to be enjoying the back-and-forth conversation. Please tell me, *honestly*, don't you think I'm a pretty good teacher?

What kind of answer do you think I'm going to get from you? Because I prejudiced your response—told you my bias and preferences of how I want you to view my teaching skill—it is unlikely that you'll give me an honest response. It's the same with any question.

We solicit biased responses from our employees. "Max, the company is really depending on you to get these orders shipped on time. You don't mind working overtime, do you?" "Eileen, how do you feel about flying to the coast on Sunday to get the biggest order the company has ever received? You won't mind doing that, will you?" And Max and Eileen say, "Sure, boss, why not?"

In each of these examples the person asking the question knew the answer he or she wanted to hear. We usually don't realize we are adding our bias in phrasing questions. It is just a habit we have built over the years as we dealt with children, parents, employees, friends, neighbors, and spouses. The person we bias most is ourselves. We want to hear what we want to hear. In gathering marketing intelligence, we must be very careful to really think about the way we phrase questions and to not prejudice the person we're talking to or surveying.

Consider the following examples, first biased, then unbiased.

Biased

I want to show you how two cleaning solutions take grease off this pan. The product on the left is my competitor's cleaner. This one is our new, improved formula. Notice the new easy-to-hold pistol grip on my sprayer, compared to my competitor's old plunger-type sprayer. Now watch when I spray on both cleaners. Look, my competitor's cleaner is just rolling over the grease. But mine is foaming. Tell me, do you think mine works better?

Unbiased

I want to show you how two cleaning solutions take grease off this pan. I have purposely put tape around the labels so you can't see which one is our cleaner. Now watch when I spray the pan with both cleaners. Which cleaner do you think is doing the better job?

Notice, I left out the advertising words "improved formula," "easy-to-hold pistol," "competitor's old plunger," and the comment that the competitor's is just "rolling over the grease." In the biased question, I described mine as "foaming," which was my message that it was doing a better cleaning job. Maybe foaming has nothing to do with cleaning; I don't know. Then I asked which one was doing a "better job." I planted the answer. I prejudiced the response. In the unbiased question, I only asked which one the respondent thought did the better job. Subtle differences in asking, but the unbiased will get the most honest and objective opinion. The next set of examples involve Betsey talking to one of her catering customers.

Biased

I'm thinking of expanding my business by offering new products to my satisfied catering customers. I'd like you to help me by answering a simple question. I see you contracted with a local printer for announcements for the party we're catering for you. Suppose I could offer you announcements as part of my catering service. Do you think that's something you would buy from me?

Unbiased

I'm considering expanding my catering services by offering customers additional products or services. I would like your opinion on a simple question. Please tell me a service or product you have bought for this party that could also be supplied by a caterer.

See the difference? In the first question you said you were thinking about expanding your business. You were telling the person (or, in marketing intelligence terms, the respondent) that you were not really committed to expansion. You signaled that a less thoughtful answer was alright. I changed "thinking about" to "considering," which is more businesslike.

You then prejudiced how they would perceive your new product by saying "my satisfied customers." The word *satisfied* told the respondent that others had tried your products, and the quality was good, so he or she shouldn't worry about shifting business from a specialized supplier, like the print shop, to you. You implied that your announcements would be of the same performance as your catering. That's advertising. So I took all that out of the unbiased question.

Last, I had you preferentially ask the respondent, "Do you think that's something you would buy?" Now what's going on? The respondent is either satisfied with your past catering work or you have come with good recommendations. You said you are only thinking about expanding and now you ask the respondent if he or she thinks the printing could be supplied by you. Nine out of 10 times the respondent would say yes. Why? Because you did not ask for a decision. Everybody will think about something. That doesn't mean they are going to do it. More companies have misspent more millions of dollars on unsuccessful new products or services from bad market information. The person answering the question was not asked to take a position on whether he or she would actually buy—just whether he or she would think about buying. The open-ended "tell me a service or product" question allows the respondents to give more input than whether or not they would buy announcements.

We shy away from asking a direct question because we may hear a negative response. Then we go on to believe that when we heard "yes, I'd think about giving you business," and, "yes, it looks like your cleaner does a better job," it really meant, "I'll buy yours."

ANNE

> How do I ask the coffer drinkers whether they came here to drink coffee or buy a book? Also, how do I find out why they don't drink more cups while they're here and whether they would like something else to eat with the coffee. I may not want to learn that they'd like to eat something too. . . . I'll have to be in the restaurant business!

Here's the way I would phrase both types of questions:

Biased

Excuse me, I am the store manager and I'm asking customers a few questions. First, this is a bookstore, but we've provided what I think is a nice area for you and your friends to have some coffee. What I would like to know is, did you come here to drink coffee, or did you come in to look for a book and then decide to have some coffee? Also, if you don't mind my asking, do you think you will just be having that one cup of coffee, or will you be ordering another cup? By the way, are there any other food items you think would go good with coffee? Something like rolls or donuts, for example.

Now, if the customer didn't jump up and leave because of my directness, I'd ask the same questions like this:

Unbaised

Excuse me, we are doing a customer survey. Do you have a minute to give me your opinion on a few topics? What was the reason you decided to come into the store? (Pause for answer.) About how many cups of coffee do you normally drink when you are with friends in a setting like this? (Pause for answer.) How about when you are sitting alone, do you have one or several cups? (Pause.) Last, we are considering adding some food items to go along with coffee. What are your preferences?

In the biased question what were the prejudices?

ANNE

Well, it sounded like I was trying to sell them more coffee or I was annoyed because they didn't buy a book.

It did sound angry and authoritarian. The words *store manager* conveyed authority. Also, you were emphatic that this is a bookstore. You also transmitted that you are not happy it's a coffee shop—at least, it may have sounded that way. They should either drink a lot of coffee or buy a book; that was your bias. Then by saying, "Will you just be having one cup," you sounded like you wanted them to order another. How about the food items question? Didn't you sound indecisive, a little like Betsey, by using the words "think would go good"? That bias did not permit a choice of desserts or whatever; you really forced your preferences when you gave examples of foods.

Now think about the unbiased question. I took out "store manager" and said, "We are." That got rid of the authority. Next, we asked the question about why they came into the store in a slightly different manner. The biased question assumed they either came to drink coffee or look for a book. However, it may have been for some entirely different reason: just passing by, saw a friend through the window, to come in out of the rain, or to use the telephone or lavatory. Who knows? Well, the respondent knows and you have to ask. To find out, we say, "What single reason brought you into the store?" Let the respondent tell you. It may very well be it was for coffee or to buy a book, but don't prejudice the answer.

What about the number of cups of coffee and the food? By adding the word *normally*, you allow the respondent to visualize his or her coffee-drinking routine. It creates a picture in the respondent's mind about different coffeetime environments. Anne, your goal, as I hear it, is to either increase the cups of coffee bought per customer or validate the value of coffee as a traffic builder. So we want to understand *what's* in the coffee drinker's mind. Again, the word *normally* transports the person answering the question to be ready to describe that setting to you. From the answer, you may get strategy information to change your bookstore environment and increase coffee purchases. Last, on the food question, the unbiased question asked for the respondent's bias with "what are your preferences." We didn't suggest donuts, rolls, etc.—we left the respondent wide open to express his or her likes and dislikes. This line of questioning provides lots of data.

GATHERING COMPETITIVE INFORMATION

PETER

How can I frame questions to get information about the competition? How can I objectively find out what users think about competitive product performance and price?

Remember that we talked about the people involved in the buying decision?

PETER

> There is the user, the individual who actually uses the product or service in a specific application. The specifier translates the performance requirements into a specification or requirements statement. The buyer actually goes out to vendors for prices, negotiates the terms of purchase, and sees to it that the product or service gets delivered. That function is also called a purchasing agent.

And there is one other decision maker or activity as part of the sale.

PETER

> The financial or budget approval.

Correct. These four activities all have some say in why customers buy from one supplier versus another.

Additional competitive information can be generalized as follows:

- How and how well the product performs.
- What price competitors are willing to accept for their products.
- How many sales representatives they have calling on distribution.
- What incentives they offer resellers to demonstrate, warehouse, and deliver.
- How they can offer prices lower than ours.
- What their costs are to make the product.
- Who their suppliers are.

We'll add these to the list of questions we talked about earlier.

Here are basic questions for the user, specifier, buyer or purchasing agent, and the financial approval authority. These questions work for any industry, as well as the individual consumer, and apply to large and small companies.

The User

How are you using the product or service in the application?
What performance feature allows you to do your job better?
What are the good and bad features of different products you have tried?
How many or how often do you use the product in your workday?
What happens if the product or service fails while you are using it?
What single feature would you change to make the product or service better?

The Specifier

What criteria do you use to select the right tools for an application?
How much detail do you need to define the product or service?
What product or service characteristics go into the purchasing document?
How helpful are product brochures in your work? How would you like them improved?
How do suppliers help you with product selection?
What are company policies about buying from only one supplier?
How often do you make changes in the purchase specifications and why?

The Buyer/Purchasing Agent

What supplier performance criteria do you use to select a supplier?
Who determines what kinds of products or services to buy?
What is the most important purchase criterion: price, quality, or service?
How often do suppliers ask for your business?

What help do you get from suppliers to make your job easier?

Who makes the final decision to buy from one supplier or another?

What policies do you have about single suppliers, low bid, and quality issues?

What are your invoicing and payment policies?

Which suppliers of products or services like mine are the most valuable?

Why do you buy from our company or our competitor?

The Financial Approval

What documentation and justification do you need to approve purchases?

When are the various budgets approved for products or services like mine?

What policies cover single suppliers, low bid, and quality issues?

What role in the purchasing process do users, specifiers, and buyers play?

Again, competition is working while you are sleeping. They are trying to replace you as the preferred supplier to your customers. Simple, true, and frightening. That's why we must ask the right questions to all the purchasing decision makers to get a clear picture of the competitor's market strategy and tactics.

Peter, here are some biased questions for the user: Someone said you're using our product to measure ball bearings. I'd like to ask you a question or two about how our scales are performing for you. Although our product is not perfect and we are always trying to improve it, have you been offered a competitor's scale to test? And can you tell me what you found wrong or deficient about our competitor's product?

What's biased in those questions and how would you fix it?

PETER

Let's see. I said I was the current product supplier. That would probably bring me an answer that the person thought I wanted to hear. The user won't want to hurt my feelings. Because I was not specific about changes we might make, the respondent would have nothing to gain or lose by telling me what he or she really thought we should change in the product. This is how I would reword it. "I see you are using a Global Scale. Your supervisor said it would be okay to ask you a few questions about the different scales you use or have tried."

Good, but the user doesn't know who you are. Are you going to get open and unguarded answers?

PETER

I think so because I referred to his supervisor saying it was alright to ask some questions. The supervisor is really giving me credibility and legitimacy to be talking to the person.

In the question I posed, there was "someone" who told me the respondent was using the product. As you suggested, saying "supervisor" does convey that it is okay for the user to answer the questions. You have detected the subtle difference in phrasing a question to put the respondent at ease. Any other biases?

PETER

There are two more big biases. Your question stated, "Our product is not perfect and we are always trying to improve it." I told the user he might expect improvements in anything he was finding wrong with our scales. Next I planted in his mind that the competitor's products had problems with their performance. That came across when I said, "tell me what you found wrong or deficient." Let me try to make those two points unbiased. I would leave out "our product is not perfect," and "trying to improve it." I would just say, "You have several choices of scales to do your job. Which ones have you tried?" Then I would ask, "I know each manufacturer claims to be the best, but are there some good and bad performance features about the different makes of scales you have tested?"

Great. Let's go to the specifier and ask some questions. Your supervisor said it would be okay to ask you a few questions. As I understand it, your responsibility is to decide which tools and instruments workers should use to do the job. Then you write up the purchasing documentation to get them here on the factory floor. We make our brochures very clear so you can understand our scales. What additional information can we add to our technical manuals? Are there any specifications that would be of help to you?

What do you think about that question?

PETER

It sounds fine to me. I don't see any bias.

There are no biases and I didn't try to plant an answer, but I used a tone that would probably get a biased answer. Did anybody detect the tone?

PETER

You made the specifier look dumb when you said, "We make our brochures very clear so you can understand them."

Right, I was talking down to the specifier. The answer I would get back would be, "yes (I'm no dummy), everything in your literature is perfectly clear. You couldn't add a thing to make it easier for me." Get the idea? So let's change that part of the question to, "We want to make our brochures more complete. Do you have any suggestions about how or what we could do to improve them?"

We haven't covered the buyer or financial decision maker. The unbiased questions we would ask them are variations on what we have already covered.

VITAL THOUGHTS

- A good business strategy moves us to a more competitive position.
- Examining your current business patterns provides new information.
- Customers know what they want—just ask them.
- Unbiased questions result in objective answers.
- Competitive information sources are the user, the specifier, the buyer/purchasing agent, the financial approval authority, and the distributor.

CHAPTER 6

FINDING AND COLLECTING
SECONDARY INFORMATION

We're drowning in information. Bombarded by television, newspapers, thousands of magazines, journals of all descriptions, and now with the availability of electronic data bases, we're awash in data. It's true. Every time I go to the library I feel intimidated because I know that all the answers to whatever questions I might have are there somewhere. If I only had the time to absorb all this information, how smart I'd be!

I know the direct pathways to the information I really need. This understanding has increased my business efficiency. Your business and mine are fundamentally the same, so what we're going to talk about will help you, too. Let's spend a few minutes understanding the sources of data and information that make collecting marketing intelligence efficient.

The world has been sorted into neat information piles about people, geography, economic structure, habits, likes and dislikes, governments, and prophesies about the future. Professionals work at synthesizing information into manageable units of knowledge. Their efforts are aimed at identifying current and future trends, signals of change, shifts in buying preferences, and attitudes of customers about what they want. Because satisfying customers is now a global effort, customer information is more abundant and accessible. Knowing what to look for, where to find it, and how to apply it is marketing intelligence in a nutshell.

Right now, the information you need is lying somewhere on a shelf, idling in a computer memory, or tucked in the mind of an expert. So how do we make our way through the information maze?

The first level of information is customer and market demographics. I often refer to demographics as "age, rank, and horsepower"—the basic data. For example, let's take everyone who lives in a community of 1 million people. They are tall and short, young and old, wealthy and poor, black and white, male and female, married and single, educated and uneducated, employed and unemployed. The community includes businesses that are profitable and unprofitable, big and small, young and old, and so on. Each of these categories is a demographic unit. Each has been counted and put into groupings. We can put this information to work and get answers to our questions. Let's look at Figure 6–1. It depicts an example of how demographics are organized.

What's interesting is that these demographers cannot only dissect a city, they can also give similar data for specific city sections broken down by census tracts and grouped ZIP codes. They cluster cities and suburbs into a regional or metropolitan composite. The regions are added together to get state or provincial totals in all these categories, and finally the states are added to form a national picture. It doesn't stop there. Because

FIGURE 6–1
Population Data Tree

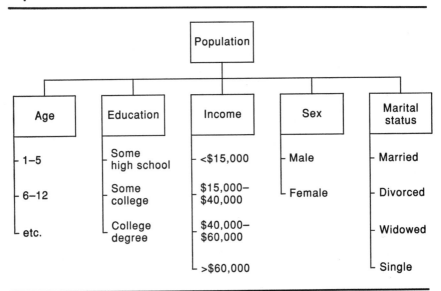

we are a global society, our country is merged with all other nations to form a worldwide set of demographics by each of these characteristics. Here's a sampling of the ways we can get geopolitical data:

- City blocks.
- Groups of blocks.
- Census tracts.
- Places (such as cities, villages, and towns).
- Counties.
- ZIP codes.
- Congressional districts.
- Metropolitan areas.
- States.
- Clusters of states.
- Regions (Southeast, Northeast, etc.).
- Total United States.
- Continents.
- Hemispheres.
- World regions.

Figure 6–2 displays the geography of where we live and work. A key point to remember is that most industrialized nations have data on their population in approximately the same level of detail as the United States. With such a deep information base, market planners and researchers can forecast unit demands and identify locations where your goods or services would seem to be needed.

Consumers, industries, and businesses are general classifications to keep in mind. Let's identify the industries you are in.

JOHN

I'm in the accounting and financial industry.

PETER

The weighing industry.

No, I would say you are in the instrumentation, instruments, or measuring industry.

FIGURE 6–2
Partial World Data Tree

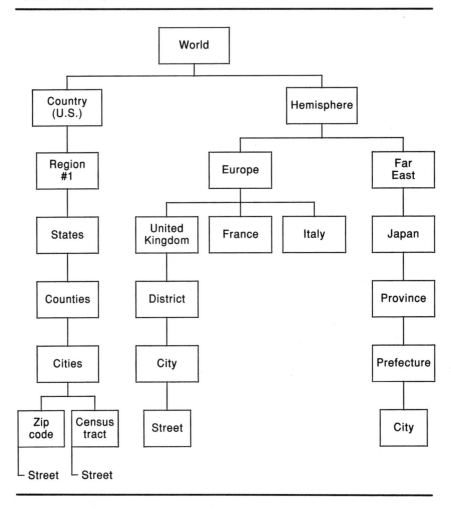

ANNE

I'm not sure. It could be the publishing or retail industry.

Let's talk about that. Yes, you retail published books, but I think you are a specialty retailer, or bookseller, and that's the industry classification you should look to for information about your business.

JOHN

Well, doesn't that mean I am a specialty service company in accounting?

I guess we have to clear up what we are. We're talking about defining our business into industries so that we can go look for information in targeted information pockets. Finding the right pocket will depend on how we've defined what we're looking for.

John, if you were trying to see what the trends are for the accounting or bookkeeping business, you would look into service business data sources that also collect facts about accounting or bookkeeping, which are specialty service businesses.

That would hold true for Anne if she were trying to find out whether book sales were up or down. She would look at the facts about the publishing industry. To see how well she was managing a specialty retail business, she would look for information about book retailing. In other words, a business can fall under two or three classifications, depending upon what function of the business we are interested in, such as sales and marketing, finance, or costs of the goods we are making.

SUSAN

That means I am a manufacturer of a certain size as measured by employees or sales or whatever. I'm also in the specialty toy industry, and have some connection to the children's toy retailing industry. Right?

Perfect. You're all three. Looking for data in those three areas should produce a composite of your business. What we have to do is step back, look at our business activity and our customers, and then define ourselves in several ways. Doing it this way, we have more opportunities for insights into industry trends, customer behavior, and relevant comparisons about how our business performance matches that of our competitors.

Now, let's understand how demographers classify industries and businesses for easy use. Most countries have adopted a system for standardizing classification of all economic or business activity. The system in the United States is known as the *Standard Industrial Classification Code*, or the *SIC code*. The SIC code is a series of number groupings from two to seven digits, depend-

FIGURE 6–3

Excerpt, Standard Industrial Classification Manual

Each business activity has its own identification number.

34	FABRICATED METAL PRODUCTS	59	MISCELLANEOUS RETAIL
341	Metal Cans and Shipping Containers	591	Drug Stores and Proprietary Stores
3411	Metal cans	5912	Drug stores and proprietary stores
3412	Metal barrels, drums, and pails	592	Liquor Stores
342	Cutlery, Handtools, and Hardware	5921	Liquor stores
3421	Cutlery	593	Used Merchandise Stores
3423	Hand and edge tools, nec	5932	Used merchandise stores
3425	Saw blades and handsaws	594	Miscellaneous Shopping Goods Stores
3429	Hardware, nec	5941	Sporting goods and bicycle shops
343	Plumbing and Heating, Except Electric	(5942)	Book stores
3431	Metal sanitary ware	5943	Stationery stores
3432	Plumbing fixture fittings and trim	5944	Jewelry stores
3433	Heating equipment, except electric	(5945)	Hobby, toy, and game shops
344	Fabricated Structural Metal Products	5946	Camera & photographic supply stores
3441	Fabricated structural metal	5947	Gift, novelty, and souvenir shops
3442	Metal doors, sash, and trim	5948	Luggage and leather goods stores
3443	Fabricated plate work (boiler shops)	5949	Sewing, needlework, and piece goods
3444	Sheet metal work	596	Nonstore Retailers
3446	Architectural metal work	5961	Catalog and mail-order houses
3448	Prefabricated metal buildings	5962	Merchandising machine operators
3449	Miscellaneous metal work		
345	Screw Machine Products, Bolts, Etc.		
3451	Screw machine products		
3452	Bolts, nuts, rivets, and washers		*Susan's customers-resellers*
346	Metal Forgings and Stampings		
3462	Iron and steel forgings		
3463	Nonferrous forgings		
3465	Automotive stampings		*Anne's bookstore*
3466	Crowns and closures		
3469	Metal stampings, nec		
347	Metal Services, NEC		
3471	Plating and polishing		
3479	Metal coating and allied services		

Source: U.S. Dept. of Commerce, *Standard Industrial Classification Manual* (Washington, D.C.: Government Printing Office, 1987).

ing on the level of activity detail. Look at Figure 6–3 for an example of some government data. You'll get the idea. In the first column is the SIC designation for the product area, and then to the right is the type of business or industry.

Now we'll look for your businesses in multiple classifications and at several SIC activity levels:

	Group	SIC Code	Description
John	Major	87	Engineering and accounting services
	Sub	872	Accounting, auditing, and bookkeeping
	Minor	8721	Bookkeeping services
Betsey	Major	58	Eating and drinking places
	Sub	581	Eating places
	Minor	5812	Caterers
Susan	Major	39	Miscellaneous manufacturing
	Sub	394	Dolls, toys, and games
	Minor	3944	Wagons, children's
Bill	Major	50	Wholesale trade—Nonfood
	Sub	508	Machinery, equipment, and supplies
	Minor	5087	Janitorial supplies
Peter	Major	35	Industrial/machinery
	Sub	359	Miscellaneous Industrial/commercial machinery
	Minor	3596	Scales & balances
Anne	Major	59	Miscellaneous retail stores
	Sub	594	Miscellaneous shopping goods store
	Minor	5942	Book stores, or
		5812	Coffee shops

We can also find information about all the demographics—productivity, profitability, number of employees, sales, imports, and exports—about these specific classifications. The data is available at the census tract, ZIP code, city, regional, national, and global levels. SIC codes are very powerful tools. Use them to find calibrating market information.

KINDS OF MARKET INFORMATION

I said that marketing knowledge is available from two sources—primary and secondary. The following are my definitions of these sources and the differences between them:

1. Primary Data.
   a. This is data collected for the market research project at hand (i.e., asking customers what they like or dislike about the product, service, or company). We get answers directly from others outside or inside our business.

2. Secondary Data.
   a. If it's been published as market or sales history or forecasts, future trends, study results of customer attitudes, etc., we can classify it as secondary market information. There are two kinds of secondary data—internal company data and external facts and opinions.
   (1) Internal data is a company's own information about its business. It includes records of sales, shipping reports, incoming telephone calls per day, repeat orders, and customers added or lost. A great source of internal market information is managerial experience and wisdom. [*They'll always want to give you their opinions. However, my experience is that managers' views are the least reliable source because managers usually are not objective about customers and competitors.*] We'll talk later about specific internal data elements and how to get new insights into our business by arranging the information differently.
   (2) External secondary information comes from outside the organization and is found in magazine articles, journals, technical papers, studies, newspapers, and books.

Let's look at secondary information sources more closely.

SECONDARY DATA—DEMOGRAPHIC DATA SOURCES

Market area and potential customer demographics are the cornerstones of secondary data. Remember the Family Life church program story I told about making buying decisions and finding out who is responsible? Well, Figure 6–4 illustrates where I got part of the data for my market potential of churches and church member customers.

Look at how easy it was to estimate potential customers from the "membership" column, and the number of resellers from the "churches reported" column. One small chart saved me hours of hunting through many different religious directories.

FIGURE 6-4
The Basis for the Family Life Forecast

Use this and average family size from Figure 6-8. Here's what I did:

$$\frac{membership}{3.17} = Family$$

Religious Bodies—Religious Congregations

No. 77. RELIGIOUS BODIES—SELECTED DATA—Continued

[See headnote, p. 56]

RELIGIOUS BODY	Year	Churches reported	Member-ship (1,000)	Pastors serving parishes	Sunday school enrollment[1] (1,000)
Bodies with membership of 50,000 or more—Con.					
Polish National Catholic Church of America..	1960	162	282	141	(NA)
Presbyterian Church in America	1987	924	191	1,062	91
Presbyterian Church (U.S.A.)	1987	11,513	2,968	11,365	1,096
Primitive Baptists	1960	1,000	72	(NA)	(NA)
Progressive National Baptist Convention, Inc	1967	655	522	(NA)	(NA)
Reformed Church in America	1987	925	338	837	100
Reorganized Church of Jesus Christ of Latter-day Saints	1987	1,097	192	16,929	(NA)
Roman Catholic Church, The	1987	23,552	53,497	34,791	7,147
Romanian Orthodox Episcopate of America	1987	34	60	28	2
Russian Orthodox Church Outside of Russia, The	1955	81	55	92	(NA)
Salvation Army, The	1987	1,097	434	2,582	111
Serbian Eastern Orthodox Church in the U.S.A. and Canada	1986	68	67	60	(NA)
Seventh-day Adventist Church	1987	4,096	676	2,241	512
Southern Baptist Convention	1987	37,238	14,723	37,150	7,937
Triumph the Church and Kingdom of God in Christ (International)	1972	475	54	860	(NA)
Ukrainian Orthodox Church in the U.S.A	1966	107	88	107	(NA)
Unitarian Universalist Association	1986	956	173	(NA)	(NA)
United Church of Christ	1987	6,395	1,663	5,116	436
United Methodist Church, The	1986	37,750	9,125	21,201	(NA)
United Pentecostal Church, International	1988	3,410	500	(NA)	(NA)
Wesleyan Church, The	1987	3,217	186	2,656	(NA)
Wisconsin Evangelical Lutheran Synod	1987	1,187	419	1,404	49
Bodies with membership of less than 50,000	(X)	15,461	1,557	13,872	295

- Represents zero. NA Not available. X Not applicable. [1] Includes pupils, officers, and teachers. [2] Estimate of size of Jewish community provided by American Jewish Yearbook. Estimates of the number of Jews holding membership in synagogues or temples of the four branches of Judaism amount to 3,750,000.

Source: National Council of the Churches of Christ in the United States of America, New York, NY, *Yearbook of American and Canadian Churches*, annual. (Copyright)

Used this data to cast units

Once I had the national data, I then went to another source to get the breakdown of the churches by city, region, and state. I developed a mailing list from a more comprehensive directory that had each pastor's name, address, and telephone number. This level of data would be invaluable if I wanted to conduct some "primary" market research in a mail or telephone survey.

Remember that all industries collect and publish data about the activities of businesses in that industry, usually to the finite levels of the five-digit SIC code. Data is available from many sources: government documents, industry trade associations, industry trade publications, and the general business press.

Bill Communications, Inc., issues two reports each year which serve as my standard bases of data:

1. In the *Survey of Buying Power*, each region, state, city, and town are analyzed, and total and specific household expenditures are estimated. The report also calculates the "effective buying index" (EBI) of that locality by taking census data on personal income. An index for the whole country is then created. The EBI for the United States is 1.00. The report then analyzes San Diego, for example, to find the average income. The results indicate that San Diego has a higher average income than the country's average. The EBI for San Diego, according to the 1990 Edition of the *Survey of Buying Power*, is 1.108, or 10.8% higher than the country average. The market researcher is able to determine which sections of the country, region, state, or town have higher buying potentials. It's a very effective tool, particularly for manufacturers, retailers, and wholesalers of consumer products.

2. In the *Survey of Industrial Buying Power*, each region is segmented to the same level as in the consumer buying power report, but the data focuses on specific manufacturing activities detailed by SIC-coded industries and products. The report lists the number of factory sites, the number of employees at each site, and the value of shipments from those sites, and calculates the number of manufacturers that produce the majority of product shipments.

PETER

Is this *Survey of Industrial Buying Power*, or any other annual forecasts done by trade publications, reliable? Should I use the data?

The answer to your question is yes, you should use it, but here's my philosophy on all market and product data published annually by reputable firms like Bill Publishing, McGraw-Hill, Dow Jones, etc.: I use their published data, but I do so under several assumptions:

- Numbers cannot be 100 percent accurate.
- The methods to derive the data, year after year, are consistent.
- The publisher is diligent to accurately collect primary and secondary data from reliable sources.
- The publisher corrects and reports significant data errors in subsequent forecasts.

So, Peter, my rule of thumb when using these published forecasts is: I know the data has a margin of error, but I trust that it is reliably put together. I use the information year after year to spot trends, to get approximations of market sizes in units and dollars, and to build a marketing intelligence base on these forecasts. All market truths are built on **reasonable** assumptions.

PETER

Should I use these sources for determining my market share or looking for new product opportunities?

Yes, these forecasts are a great source, but just remember my assumptions when using them. The key here is that we are dealing with secondary information put together by somebody else for some other purpose not identical to ours. The best way to feel more comfortable with market data collected by others is to validate the findings by calling the publisher and finding out how they got their data. What rationale did they use to group markets, customers, and locations? Also, collect your own primary data. I can tell you most managers will not accept other people's work, particularly if the data doesn't tell the "right" story. To feel confident about market conclusions, you must make the effort to validate this outside data.

WHERE IS ALL THIS INFORMATION?

Collecting secondary market information is the easiest way to build marketing intelligence. Most of the needed information is right in your own business files, in the public or university library, accessible through electronic data bases, or available from government files and reports.

Internal Secondary Data—It's in Our Own Files

Now let's talk about one of the most overlooked sources of marketing intelligence: the wealth of records and documents kept to conduct our day-to-day business. Internal company data is easy to find. There is no need to ask permission to get it. It is an incredibly relevant source in supporting market intelligence conclusions.

Here are some ideas of what you can learn from company files:

Customer Order Files

- The 80/20 Rule applies—or doesn't apply.
- The percent of customers who are local, regional, or national.
- Average order sizes in units and dollars.
- Sales coverage—too many or too few customers per salesperson

Invoices Sent to Customers and Backorder Reports

- Average price of goods sold to big and small customers.
- Shipping times from customer order to delivery.
- Peak and low ordering times during a month, quarter, or year.
- Percent of orders shipped 100 percent complete.

Bill Sent to You by Vendors

- Average discounts from large and small vendors.
- Inventory histories of out-of-stock and partial shipments.

Returned Merchandise Forms and Repair Records

- Percent returned by large and small customers.
- Frequency and number of complaints by specific problems.

- Length of time to resolve customer complaints or repair merchandise.

Warranty Cards Sent Back by Customers

- Profiles of customer demographics.
- Distribution channel sell-through time.
- Reseller identification and effectiveness.

Cash Register Receipts

- Peak selling periods.
- Clerical accuracy—customer under- or overcharging.
- Customer checkout lane preferences.
- Checkout lane speed.

Parking Lot Validation Stickers or Records

- Average time spent in shopping area.
- Peak and low traffic periods.
- Average additional cost of sales support parking.

Incoming Sales Department or Service Phone Call Logs

- Ordering periods for large and small orders.
- Average time to take orders and answer sales questions.
- Average time to handle service calls.
- Determine where local reseller support is needed.

Trade Show Inquiries

- Peak and low booth attendance periods—hours and days.
- Show attendee demographics.
- Booth attractiveness to large or small potential customers.

Telephone Bills

- Length of call times to large and small customers.
- Effectiveness or value of incoming "800" number lines.
- Value analysis of outgoing "800" lines.

Outside Sales Call Reports

• Efficiency of sales call patterns.
• Frequency of calling patterns to different customer types and sizes.
• Number of sales calls per order.
• Proportion of sales calls to large and small customers.
• Competitor's image according to customers of different types and sizes.
• Competitor's image by price, quality, or service.
• Market share of each competitor by type of customer.

Accounts Receivable Histories

• Average time customers pay by size and type of customer.
• Payment patterns by sales coverage, partial shipments, etc.
• Terms and conditions violations by customer size and type.
• Payment histories by large and smaller customers.

Literature Requests from Advertisements

• Effectiveness of each advertising medium.
• Effectiveness of different styles of advertisements.
• Effectiveness of different advertisement insertion times.
• Demographics of advertisement respondents.
• Average time from inquiry receipt to sending of literature.

Company Personnel

• The switchboard operator and receptionist are sensitive to customer moods and attitudes.
• Employees, in general, have attitudes and observations about the product or service offered by the business.
• Sales representatives (or anybody who calls on customers) have firsthand knowledge about shifting buyer preferences.

In short, any captured transaction record related to the business premises, the field or selling effort, on the customers is a valuable resource tool. I am not going to detail how to collect this information or detail the analysis techniques because it really only involves:

- Identifying the question that needs to be answered.
- Locating internal documents that hold the answer.
- Collecting the information in a structured and organized manner.
- Constructing arithmetic expressions of the answer.
- Developing conclusions.

An analysis of this internal data usually doesn't take long to sort out. Once arrayed, it presents a clearer picture of the business. The key is that we must have questions that the data can answer. [*These examples are obvious, but I just want to open their minds to the information possibilities that are all around them in company records.*]

Libraries

Let's take a moment to refresh our knowledge about how most libraries work and the most efficient ways to use them in collecting market data. All libraries are organized in about the same way, and for our purposes we need not consider geographic sections or book and periodical collections that don't relate to business activity.

Most business-related information is in the following library sections:

- Business and industry.
- Social sciences.
- Government documents.
- Science and engineering.
- Reference.

The information is contained in the following formats:

- Books.

- Magazines, journals, and pamphlets.
- Government reports.
- Newspapers and newsletters.
- Directories.
- Microfiche and microfilm.
- Maps and charts.
- Computer data bases.

These business publications are in most libraries:

- *The New York Times* (newspaper).
- *The Wall Street Journal* (newspaper).
- *Barron's* (newspaper).
- The local or regional newspaper.
- Dun & Bradstreet's *Million Dollar Directory* (directory).
- Moody's *Manuals* (directory).
- Standard & Poor's (directory).
- *Statistical Abstract of the United States* (report).
- *U.S. Industrial Outlook* (report).
- Annual Reports of Fortune 100.
- *The Thomas Register of American Manufactures* (directory).
- Local chamber of commerce membership directory.
- *Encyclopedia of Associations* (directory).
- Directory of elected officials (local, regional, national).
- *The United States Government Manual* (directory).
- White and Yellow telephone pages (local, regional, and national).
- Import-export and foreign trade directories.
- *Business Week, Fortune, Forbes, Inc.* (magazines).

If the library is a government depository (there are some 1,300 in the United States), you will also find:

- Census data—local, regional, and national (reports and pamphlets).

- Special government reports, such as:
  Commerce Department reports.
  Federal Drug Administration reports.
  Environmental Protection Agency reports.
  Department of Defense reports.
  Federal Trade Commission reports.
  Patent abstracts.
  Transcripts of hearings before the state and federal legislatures.

Business school and university libraries will usually have these additional materials:

- *The Wall Street Transcript* (newspaper).
- Master's theses on a variety of subjects (pamphlets).
- Wide selections of trade and industry periodicals (magazines).
- Foreign government and trade directories.
- International business publications (newspapers, magazines).
- U.S. Securities and Exchange Commission publications, such as:
  Annual industry reports and composites by SIC.
  Public company annual reports (pamphlets).
  10K reports (more extensive annual data).
  8K reports (more extensive quarterly data).
- *Sales Management* Survey of Buying Power—*Sales Management Magazine* (report).

Science-based university libraries will usually have these additional materials:

- Multidiscipline technical papers (journals).
- Annual buyer's guides (directories).
- Scientific industry publications (magazines).

Getting to the specific documents is now easier. Most large city and university libraries have put books, periodicals, journals, and reference collections into computer indexes. The traditional published indexes are still an excellent first source to locate information. Each index is arranged by subject and is accessed through the use of keywords. Peter, what are your keywords?

PETER

> *Scales, balances, instruments,* and maybe *export* or *foreign distribution.*

Good, but export alone may be too broad. I would modify it by connecting the keywords with *and* to get *instruments and export.*

Anne, what keywords would you use for the bookselling business?

ANNE

> *Bookstore, bookstore and coffeehouse, bookstore and retail, publishing,* and *trends.* Can I use words like *and, or,* and *not* when I use these indexes?

Yes, the software or programming used for data bases is usually standardized around what are called Boolean search methods and it allows tying several words together. The computer can then search for your specific requirement faster and more precisely. The library reference person will help you get started and the computer terminals there have easy-to-follow instructions.

The traditional card catalogs, *Reader's Guide to Periodic Literature,* and microfiche indexes are also available to find keyword references. Let's discuss electronic data bases not found in the library. These data sources allow the scanning of mountains of information, and finding just the right references takes only a few seconds.

Electronic Data Bases

Computers are now essential for all business people. [*I can't imagine running a business, managing a product line, being in sales, or servicing customers, and not being able to use a computer.*] Soon all computers will come equipped with a modem to communicate through any telephone to the outside world. I know all of you don't have this capability yet, but you will, so I must describe the electronic data base information sources that are really helpful in finding market information leads.

What is an electronic data base? Well, the simplest way to think about one is that someone, somewhere, found all the printed information about a subject, like wooden toys, scales and balances, business accounting, or cooking for each country. Then they sorted these articles, reports, and technical papers from a wide variety of sources and created an index by subject, author, and publication date. These specialty information boutiques manufacture an information product, but they need distribution to get to the information users. They use the telephone lines or satellites to transmit instructions between your computer and theirs, as well as to send the information for browsing or saving. Almost all new computers are equipped with modems. They are also inexpensive to use with your older computer and well worth the investment.

Many specialized data bases are available, but the ones I now find most useful are Dialog, the less expensive Knowledge Index (a division of Dialog), Compuserve, Prodigy, and Data Star for foreign coverage. Appendix 4 includes the telephone numbers and addresses of these companies, should you wish to secure more information. It takes a little practice to enter and search these data bases. The fees to use the service may at first appear to be high, but the cost to find information electronically is far lower than the value of your time spent in physically going to libraries. Data base searching does not solve market problems, but it does quickly generate a bibliography of articles, locate experts and gurus, and illuminate pathways to information before you go to the library.

Let's take a quick look at how to use these data bases. Finding information is very straightforward. Each data base company furnishes you with a catalog of specific information collections. Figure 6–5 is an extract from the Knowledge Index catalog.

Once your modem signs you on to the data base, you are asked which collection or data base you want. After typing the collection code name from the catalog, you are ready to search. For example, by typing "find scales or balances," you will produce a count of how many citations of those keywords are in the data base. The actual search result is shown in Figure 6–6.

The information about the citation is available for viewing at three levels. They include everything you need to locate the

FIGURE 6–5
Examples, Electronic Data Base Subject Categories

Business Information –

✱ BUSI1	ABI/INFORM⁸
BUSI2	TRADE & INDUSTRY INDEX™
BUSI3	HARVARD BUSINESS REVIEW
BUSI4	CHEMICAL BUSINESS NEWSBASE
COMP4	COMPUTER DATABASE™
✱ CORP1.4	STANDARD & POOR'S NEWS
CORP2	ICC BRITISH COMPANY DIRECTORY
CORP3	STANDARD & POOR'S CORPORATE DESCRIPTIONS
CORP5	STANDARD & POOR'S REGISTER – BIOGRAPHICAL
CORP6	STANDARD & POOR'S REGISTER – CORPORATE
ECON1	ECONOMIC LITERATURE INDEX
MAGA2	CANADIAN BUSINESS & CURRENT AFFAIRS
✱ NEWS1	NEWSEARCH™
NEWS3.4	UPI NEWS
NEWS5	FACTS ON FILE⁸
REFR6	CONSUMER REPORTS

Directories & Reference –

✱BUSI2	TRADE & INDUSTRY INDEX™
BUSI3	HARVARD BUSINESS REVIEW
CORP5	STANDARD & POOR'S REGISTER – BIOGRAPHICAL
CORP6	STANDARD & POOR'S REGISTER – CORPORATE
EDUC2	PETERSON'S COLLEGE DATABASE
EDUC3	GRADLINE
EDUC6	THE EDUCATIONAL DIRECTORY
MAGA1	MAGAZINE INDEX™
MAGA2	CANADIAN BUSINESS & CURRENT AFFAIRS
NEWS1	NEWSEARCH™
NEWS2	NATIONAL NEWSPAPER INDEX™
REFR1	QUOTATIONS DATABASE
REFR2	MARQUIS WHO'S WHO
REFR3	EVENTLINE™
REFR4	MAGILL'S SURVEY OF CINEMA
REFR5	DISSERTATION ABSTRACTS
✱REFR6	CONSUMER REPORTS
REFR7	EVERYMAN'S ENCYCLOPAEDIA
REFR8	PUBLIC OPINION ONLINE (POLL)

✱ Ones I use a lot.   *Data base name.*

FIGURE 6–6
Finding Technical Articles for Peter (in and out of the data base in less than 2 minutes!)

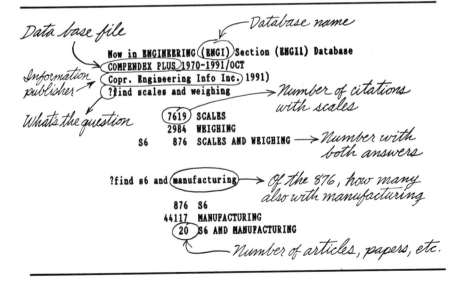

actual article or book at the library. Figure 6–7 depicts level 1, 2, and 3 searches. Here's how it works. I look at the level 1 information in the citation to make sure it matches what I want. Then I choose the citations of interest, and proceed to levels 2 and 3. Level 1 is the title of the article or paper. Level 2 provides the author's name, publication data, the name of the journal, magazine, or book in which it was published, and some notations on the library call numbers. Level 3 is a detailed summary of the article. Many collections within the data base offer the convenience of the complete text of the article.

Even if you don't have a modem on the computer you're using, find a friend or neighbor who has one and try out a search on a subject interesting to you.

BETSEY

Isn't using electronic data bases too sophisticated for most business people like me? I'm really trying to think of what the benefit would be.

Let me give you a few examples of what I would look for if I were running your catering business.

Specialty Collection	Topics	Keyword Example
Newspapers, magazines	Recipes	Southwestern
	Business trends	Customer entertaining
	Franchising	Franchisee
	Employees	Food servers
Books	Management	Hiring and firing
	Franchising	Marketing
	Recipes	Ethnic food
Reports	Market potentials	Eating out, entertaining
	Customers	Entertaining expense
	Competition	Income and profitability

That's not a complete list, but you get the idea. The real benefit is that it saves time, and your time is valuable. Just think about trying to hunt down those topics by rooting through newspapers, magazines, books, and reports. It would take weeks. My guess is you could find the references to whatever you need from my list within one hour. I sound like I am selling electronic

FIGURE 6–7
More Details and What They Mean?

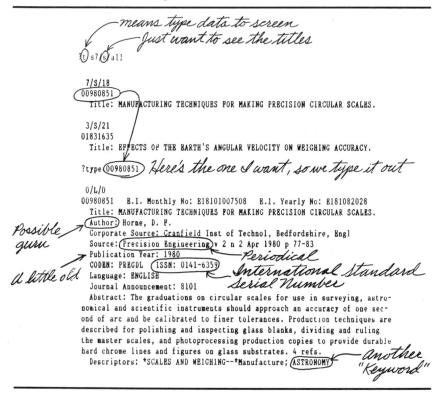

data base services, but as a small businessperson myself, I know saving time is important.

PETER

How would you track competition?

That's easy in a data base. Leading business publications like *Business Week, Fortune, Harvard Business Review, The Wall Street Journal, Barron's,* and major newspapers like the *New York Times, Washington Post, Los Angeles Times, London's Financial Times, Chicago Tribune,* etc., are all available in the electronic data bases. All that's necessary is for you to go into any or all of these specialty collections and use the competitor's name as your keyword. The search will bring back citations of any article where your competitor was mentioned. Likewise, you could ask for *scales or balances* and the competitor's name as keywords to get even more specific competitive activity information.

Data bases scan every article written within the last several years in a matter of seconds. These data base service firms allow you to transfer what's on the screen, including the full text of the articles, to a diskette and printer. That's one way to keep up with your competition.

Let me summarize the external sources of secondary information:

- Information collected by governments, institutions, universities, and trade associations, usually referred to as census or trade data.
- Directories of business or special interest areas.
- Published articles, papers, and reports.
- Local, regional, or national libraries.
- Electronic data bases accessed via your own computer.

VITAL THOUGHTS

- Secondary information is published, while primary information has not yet been collected.
- Published information validates or refutes your experience and business intuition; primary and newly gathered data provides market opportunities.
- Internal company data is your best, first information source about the markets you serve.
- Governments and institutions have analyzed world populations; the information is yours to use.
- SIC codes standardize historical business activity to aid in analyzing commerce.
- Libraries probably have what you need; start marketing intelligence work there.
- Computers, telephone lines, and electronic databases are an efficient means to locate secondary source materials, gurus, and information leads.

CHAPTER 7

COLLECTING PRIMARY DATA

PRIMARY DATA COLLECTION

After you've exhausted the secondary data sources in search of market knowledge, you're ready to collect real-world primary information. There are five key sources or methods to access primary market data. Reflecting on marketing intelligence methods I've used, here's a list in descending order of effectiveness:

1. Personal interviews—face-to-face meetings.
2. Telephone interviews and surveys—one-on-one.
3. Mail surveys—questionnaires sent to targeted respondents.
4. Focus panels—group interviews of targeted respondents.
5. Observational study—just watching subject behavior.

At this point let me summarize the characteristics of the most used primary market research methods:

	Interview Methods				
Factors	Personal Interviews	Telephone Interviews	Mail Surveys	Focus Groups	Observational Study
Advantage	Quality information	Medium cost	Low cost	Opportunity for interaction	Unbiased
Disadvantage	Access	Too quick	Low reply	Time	No subject communication
Ease of performance	Difficult	Not hard	Easy	Difficult	Easy
Subject cooperation	Limited	Good	Good	Very good	Very good
Time to complete	Days	Hours	Weeks	Weeks	Hours
Amount of data	Low	Medium	High	Very high	Medium
Cost to collect	High	Medium	Low	Medium	Low

The question is, why do we use different methods to extract essentially the same information? Personal, telephone, mail, and group interviews are communication devices designed to ask people questions. All we're looking for are facts and opinions. Most people are open or closed to answering questions. They will be open if they trust the person who is asking the questions. They won't be open if they feel embarrassed about answering a question. They may not be open if they are concerned about giving the right or wrong answer.

Choosing an interviewing method comes down to:

- the desired comfort level of the respondent.
- the costs involved.
- the time element involved.
- whether we want more or less comprehensive answers.

SAMPLE SIZE—RULE OF THUMB

How many people do we have to talk with to get the truth? We're not going to spend much time on sample sizes because there are many books devoted to the development of appropriate statistical modeling, sample size selection and cross-demographic respondent requirements. You'll find these at most public libraries in the business or economics sections.

The world is divided into essentially two market piles. They are consumers, like you and me, and industrial/commercial users. Here's the general rule about the number of people who must be asked a question before we can be comfortable with the answer.

How Many Consumers?

For consumers, statistical laws indicate that to assure nearly 100 percent accuracy, we must collect about 300 responses for each demographic characteristic. For example, we should get 300 answers from people 25 to 30 years of age, and then 300 from the 30 to 35 age group, and so on. Another 300 from males and 300 more from females; 300 from high school graduates and 300 from those that completed college; and 300 from the east, west, north, and south of the country. Just be aware that when you need information from groups of people who are very different from one another, you may get inaccurate information unless an adequate number of opinions are gathered from each group. You get the idea.

[*We just can't get into the complexity of sample sizing. What's more, only a tiny fraction of the business community needs to be concerned with that level of sampling detail. But I had to signal that there is a great deal more depth to statistical accuracy of picking market research respondents.*]

National opinion polls are conducted by major newspapers, magazines, or polling organizations. They usually interview 2,000 to 3,500 people. The blend of respondents in the sample size yields sufficient accuracy and the validity of the data can be trusted. The large consumer products companies can afford the cost of this large sample base, but most businesses can't.

What do market researchers do to find out what individual consumers want? They must ask *enough* people and get *enough* answers to feel sure about what the customer really wants.

BETSEY

> Enough! That definition of a sample size doesn't seem to be very professional. I want to conduct the right number of interviews. It's my money I'm going to invest to expand my business based on market research.

Alright, let's remember the function of direct interviews. They are used to validate other secondary, experiential, or assumed information about the subject. Suppose you gained quite a bit of market knowledge through your trip to the library. You uncovered a report on a large survey conducted by others, a poll of trade association members, or a trade or consumer magazine reader survey about the catering business or consumer attitudes about caterers. Let's say the information was not exactly on the point you're interested in, but the data was there. All you need is validation of the facts produced by the large secondary report. That's when additional *primary* information is needed. You get this through interviews.

The point is, you don't need the large sample base to get the accuracy, because others have reported on that work. What you need, as I said before, is *enough* additional information. How much? For consumer markets I would say:

- Personal interviews: 25 to 50.
- Telephone interviews: 50 to 75.
- Mail surveys: 100 to 150.

This is a consumer sample rule of thumb. *Enough* people must be polled for you to feel comfortable.

How Many Industrial/Commercial Market Respondents?

The primary data collecting process in industrial/commercial markets is similar to the process in consumer markets. Do your secondary research first. Users, specifiers, and buyers in the commercial markets are far less demographically diverse. Their preferences or subject interests are very narrow. They only need products and services to do their job and their attitudes have a single focus—product or service performance. For that reason, getting enough market information from industrial/commercial markets is faster, takes fewer interviews to validate assumptions, and costs much less than polling individual consumers.

What we're looking for in conducting primary interviews is the repetition of attitudes, opinions, and facts. You keep asking different respondents the same questions, in the same way, until you start hearing the same answers. That's it. How many interviews? Here's another rule of thumb for the typical number of interviews needed to reach a consensus opinion in industrial/commercial markets:

- Personal interviews: 5 to 10.
- Telephone interviews: 10 to 15.
- Mail surveys: 25 to 50.

The reason this low sample rate works is that the questions are narrowly focused on performance, competitors, trends, price, delivery, and so forth. There is less invasion of the respondent's ego, biases, or privacy than when polling individual consumers. These are business questions directed to businesspeople. We don't ask the respondent to mix business answers with their personal biases. This detachment permits more open opinions.

Let's talk about interviewing methods.

THE PERSONAL INTERVIEW

Why Will People Talk to You?

The word *personal* means *private* and *one-on-one*. When I conduct a personal interview with consumers, CEOs, presidents, or
business owners, I am usually in their office. The door is closed.
Nobody else is in the room. I tell the person that whatever we
talk about and the information we exchange will be held in strict-
est confidence. In my final marketing intelligence report I probably will directly quote what that person said, but I will not
identify who said it. I go on to say that in the report I will identify all the people I talked with, but the quotations will not be
linked to individuals.

Now, how can the respondents feel sure that I will hold their
comments confidential? How will they get at ease so they can
openly discuss the matters I am investigating? Let's think about
that. We all get comfortable with other individuals we don't
know by looking into their eyes, noticing their dress and groom-
ing, and observing their level of professionalism. Those are factors we use to make a decision to trust another's word that a
conversation will be kept private. The personal interview is the
only medium of exchange in the market research world that provides that forum of confidence.

Getting the Respondent Comfortable

Why do these people grant a personal interview with a perfect
stranger, take time out of their business day, and risk their egos
by opening up on business issues, buying preferences, and attitudes about competition? It's quite simple—here's how it works.
For example, I'm in Joe Smith's office because:

- I told him I was engaged by a client to understand potential buyers' needs, concerns, and preferences.
- I probably told him that, if the market conditions were
  appropriate, my client's goods or services would be introduced for sale and those products or services would be

cheaper, better, more easily available, or easier to use in his business.

- I tell him that my purpose in meeting with him is only to validate existing, industry-specific knowledge.
- I would also say that I had chosen him as someone to interview because:

  He is an expert in the field.

  His company is a potentially large user of my client's offering.

  Others in the industry, neighborhood, or community said, "If Joe thinks it's a good idea, we'll buy it."

What's going on in Joe's mind? He's been told or sees:

- He is an expert or tough customer whose opinions are valued by others.
- That my client may bring out a product or service that could benefit his business or home life.
- That I'm trustworthy and his comments will be held confidential.
- That he is in control because we are in his office.
- That nobody else is around to hear the exchange.
- That my credentials and manner are professional.

Weighing all these factors, he will usually decide that the potential rewards of providing information are greater than the risk of denying the interview. We'll then talk for 30 to 60 minutes, covering my marketing intelligence gathering agenda.

No other interviewing environment, including telephone interviews, mail surveys, or focus panels, provides the opportunity to collect the quality of information better than the personal interview.

JOHN

Are you talking about big business again? What about owners of little companies? Some don't even have an office with a door on it.

That doesn't matter since they perceive their role as owner in just the same way as the CEO of General Motors perceives his role. They have the same kinds of apprehension about divulging their opinions and attitudes to a stranger. The key here is that, as interviewers, we have to set people at ease, gain their trust about talking confidentially, and persuade them that new benefits may be available to them as a reward for their information. Interviewing is just selling a product or service, and Joe is the customer. He doesn't owe me an interview. I must convince him that it is in his best interest to openly and objectively give me information. I must give him what he wants—privacy, interviewing professionalism, and the potential of a future benefit.

Here's how the personal interviewing process works.

The Interviewing Process

There are five elements to executing the personal interview:

1. Locating interview candidates
2. Making the appointment
3. Preparing the interview agenda
4. Conducting the interview
5. Reporting the results

I will cover some of these elements in more detail.

Locating Interview Candidates

We're validating the information we've read, informally heard, or observed about the market. The individuals we will interview may be recognized authorities on the subjects we want to understand, or they may be typical users in the market environment of our interest.

How do we get the names of people or firms that hold this information about the market? The best source is from our secondary research. Every magazine, newspaper, or journal article will cite industry experts, concerned citizens, association or organization officials, and managers of involved firms; this is where we get the names of possible interviewees. Think about how many times you have read articles that state:

"According to _____, vice president of XYZ firm. . . ."

"_____, a noted expert in the field, commented. . . ."

"_____, CEO of XYZ, said. . . ."

"The XYZ firm, the market leader. . . ."

"A study just completed by _____, an NYU professor. . . ."

"The homeowners in ABC neighborhood have demonstrated for. . . ."

All we have to do is carefully read the secondary data and extract the names of individuals the writer identifies as leaders, experts, and authorities to validate the facts and opinions expressed in the article.

Other secondary sources, like directories, membership rosters, and book and report bibliographies, are also places to gather the names of potential personal interview candidates. Don't forget to include journal article authors themselves as candidates.

Another way to find the right person is to ask a company, agency, or organization. It's worked for me almost every time. I'll use Bill's products (janitorial supplies) as an example.

1. Select a target firm where your potential interview candidate should be working.

2. Telephone into the switchboard and simply say, "I'm not sure who I should speak with, but the person I am looking for is probably responsible for all the maintenance for your offices and factory."

3. The keywords heard by the operator are *all* and *maintenance*. To the operator, the word *all* probably means overall, executive, decisions, supervisor. The word *maintenance* probably means plant engineering, janitorial, operations, plant management. Then the operator will say, "I'll put you through to Jo Stokes in Plant Engineering." At that point ask how to spell Jo's last name. If you weren't given the last name, ask for it. In this instance, you're keeping the operator engaged in helping you get to the right person. Interestingly, most operators will continue to help as long as you are patient and show appreciation in both your words and voice. Before you get transferred, ask one last question about the level of Jo's authority by asking if she is responsible for *all* of the maintenance in the company. The typical response is either, "Yes, she is the vice president of plant engineering" (now you have a title), or, "No, that would be Bob," followed by a title. If the operator is still uncertain where you should be directed, you will hear, "I think you should speak to

the CEO's secretary, who can direct you to the right person."
Repeat the keywords of *all* and *maintenance* to the secretary.
Here are some keywords to avoid with an operator:

- "I'm a *customer* interested in . . ."—you'll be directed to the sales department.
- "I'm a *shareholder* trying to find . . ."—you'll be directed to finance or shareholder relations.
- "I'm looking for some *technical* information . . ."—you'll be switched to engineering, field service, or sales.
- "I'm interested in your *purchasing* or *buying* plans . . ."—you'll be directed to the purchasing department.
- "I'm interested in discussing *product liability* . . ."—you'll be directed to the legal department.

By saying, "I don't really know, but . . ." you prevent the operator from jumping to a departmental conclusion. The danger of getting into the wrong department is that you may become trapped by an expert in the company who doesn't know what he or she is talking about. You may not be able to get referred on to the right person. When I'm trapped in this situation, I just hang up after we've finished talking, redial the company and start over. It works.

Making the Appointment

We've all made appointments. You make a phone call, compare calendars for the day, set the time and place, then meet the appointment on time. However, most of our appointments are to buy or sell, meet a friend, or discuss a mutual problem. Getting appointments with total strangers, to probe into their minds and get them to tell you things they may not have even thought about, takes an artful approach.

Getting appointments with consumers is really no trouble. You stand on the street, in a mall, or anywhere you think the best interview candidates may be. If you're dressed appropriately and your demeanor is pleasant, the majority of people will accommodate your interview request.

The industrial and commercial candidates are different. They are apprehensive and you must diffuse their hesitation.

The key element in getting the appointment is clearly stating to the candidates or their intermediaries:

- Who you are.
- Why you want to see them.
- What you want to talk about.
- How long you think it will take.
- Where the answers are going.

Important people (such as your interview candidates) respond to appointment requests from other *important* people or people from important companies. That's reality. Seeking and gaining an interview appointment if you are in the important category should not present a major problem. Important would mean anybody with a respectable title from a Fortune 500 company, an elected official, the head of a major association or nonprofit agency—or an IRS auditor.

Barriers to Appointments

But what if you are not perceived as *important* by the interview candidates or their intermediaries? Let me say a word about intermediaries, such as secretaries, administrative assistants, and associates. Their job is to erect barriers that keep *un*important people away from Mr. (or Ms.) Right. So, what do you say or do to get the appointment? This is where some selling comes in. Always remember, we must give the customers what they want. Mr. Right wants to spend time only on important matters, so our request for an appointment must satisfy his needs. Getting answers to your questions is important but how can you make it important to him or the intermediary?

These are some techniques I use to get cooperation from intermediaries:

1. I give my name and where I'm calling from.
2. I say that Mr. Right has been referred to me as someone who:
   - understands,
   - has responsibility for,
   - has written about,

- has made a speech I heard or read about,
- is an official of an organization related to the subjects I am investigating.

3. Next I say that I would like a few minutes of his time to discuss his opinions on a few topics. I do not say I would like to have him answer questions. The word *answer* sounds like an interrogation and puts them on the defensive, and they want to protect Mr. Right from some sort of quiz. Never say, "I'd like to meet with Mr. Right because I think he could help me." Mr. Right doesn't know you, so why should he agree to help you?

4. Then I'm asked what company I am with. This is the difficult part because my company is only important to me and my clients, and none of us are important to Mr. Right. Straightforwardness is the only way to meet this question. "You have never heard of my company or my client, but we believe if we could get a deeper understanding of the subject I want to cover with Mr. Right, your company could benefit in the future from new or additional goods or services we may be able to offer. Mr. Right's opinions would be very valuable to us now, and perhaps to your company in the future."

5. Then the intermediary will agree to check with Mr. Right or convey the request. If Mr. Right is available, he will usually get on the phone to hear first-hand your reasoning as to why he should agree to the interview. He will also weigh the risk of granting the interview against the possibility of a future reward, should his information be translated into a benefit for himself or his firm.

I've had occasions where the intermediary will say, "he wouldn't be interested in talking to you." My response, depending on the attitude of the voice on the other end of line, is, "How do you know Mr. Right wouldn't be interested? Is it your responsibility to make Mr. Right's decisions about the future value my company or client could bring to Mr. Right?" This is tricky, so tact and a controlled but somewhat forceful voice is very important. This usually pierces through even the most ada-

mant intermediary. (Obviously you can't be this aggressive with Mr. Right, because he will just hang up.)
6. We've got the appointment. You should always confirm the personal interview in writing, stating the time, place, topics, and anticipated length of the interview, and include some credibility material such as a business card or brochure on your company.

Identifying the Interview Sample

Let's keep in mind that we have to discover what the customer wants and also find out what the competition is planning to do to satisfy their needs. Finding people to interview, whether in person, over the phone, or by mail, requires making every effort to get just the right set of people to interview.

I make no real distinction between individual consumers and commercial or industrial users. Methods to find product or service interview candidates are identical and locating national or international candidates uses a similar process.

What Are Gurus and Where Are They?

Webster defines a guru as "an influential teacher; a revered mentor." In marketing intelligence circles the guru is anyone who has the most information on a particular technology, customer base, or market niche. Many proclaim themselves gurus, but few are. In every facet of our society or business world there are these unique individuals who can instantly answer your core questions. They are the invaluable resource used by marketing intelligence researchers. They are by far the best source to consult on any market element, whether price, cost, or distribution. They usually are willing to discuss their expertise, have egos large enough to not feel threatened by questions, and will refer you to other gurus if they fail your quiz.

Clients often challenge that I can't find the right niche market guru within two hours. I usually win the bet. Here are the steps I take:

1. Clearly understand the market niche definition: what product area, geographical area, distribution channel, or technical question.
2. Sort through all the trivial information and get to the *vital* questions.
3. Sit back and visualize: the type of customer who will use the product or service, where that customer is located, and how he or she will use the product.
4. Think about and define who, other than the customer, should know most about and have unbiased opinions about the application environment, problems, or needs of that customer, and competitive methods to solve the problem. Likely candidates are suppliers of complementary equipment or service support, doctors, lawyers, academics or other researchers, trade or consumer magazine editors, the list goes on. Don't be afraid to imagine very strange and different people or occupations that may be associated with the customer.
5. Identify where that guru is right now. Maybe he or she is at work somewhere in government, employed in or as a consultant to that industry, or selling insurance around the corner. **The guru you need to talk to is out there and near a telephone.**
6. Consult your secondary resources for name leads. Look for a technical article author, the key researcher in government or a university, or a speaker at a niche market conference.
7. Validate your selections by calling the staff editor or columnist of two niche trade publications. This is very simple. Get a copy of the magazine, find the masthead, usually in the front of the publication, and look up the editor's name. Make the call and just ask the editor for two or three recommendations of experts for the information you need.
8. Call the most referenced or cited guru!

BILL

I can't believe that works. Who would imagine there's a guru in the maintenance supplies business?

Bill, I'd call you if I had a marketing intelligence assignment from one of your competitors. Let's turn that around; you could call your competitor's sales manager either here in your territory or in another state. Maintenance is maintenance wherever it takes place. Someone else I might call is the *Factory Maintenance Engineer* magazine, if there is such a publication, and talk to one of the editors.

Take a minute and think about how you would find the guru for your business questions.

The Sample Collecting Process

Let's go step by step in collecting the interview sample base for personal, telephone, mail, and focus group questioning targets:

1. Assemble interview candidate resources.
2. Select geographic interviewing boundaries.
3. Estimate how many completed interviews will be *enough*.
4. Select respondent demographics.
5. Choose specific sample names.
6. Enter names into a computer data base or build a list.

Purchased mailing lists, directories, white and Yellow Pages, backward telephone books, and culled names from speeches or trade articles produce a sufficient interview candidate base.

Geographic Interviewing Boundaries

The world is available for all forms of interviews; it's just a matter of cost. We can confine our sampling to a ZIP code, a town or city, state or nation, global regions, or the entire world. The key here is to stop and think about whether the opinions of individual customers in one location are representative of those in all locations.

For example, Susan's wooden toys are purchased by parents for small children. We probably could assume that small children will react to a wooden wagon the same in Los Angeles as in Chicago or Dublin, Ireland. A question: is it necessary to interview parents in all those cities to feel comfortable that we have representative opinions from parents? We need only select one or two cities or towns.

How about Anne's bookstore patrons? Those interviews must be confined to the ZIP code areas she serves. Peter's distribution questions are global and he would select interview candidates from those countries that proportionately represent the most business. Bill's customer base is regional and that's where to draw the sample. John's interests are represented by small businesses whose needs are the same everywhere. He could draw his sample from any location, provided the business owner demographics are a match to his target customer profile.

Try to minimize interview costs by confining the location of potential interviewees to as few locations as possible.

How Many Candidates Are Enough?

Recall that each interview technique demands a minimum number of completed interviews to accumulate enough market information to feel comfortable to build a market strategy or plan. We covered these numbers earlier, but here they are again. For consumer markets:

- Personal interviews—25 to 50.
- Telephone interviews—50 to 75.
- Mail surveys—100 to 150.

For commercial and industrial markets:

- Personal interviews—5 to 10.
- Telephone interviews—10 to 15.
- Mail surveys—25 to 50.

These are my rules of thumb. The selection of sample sizes is now a rather exacting science, particularly in the field of consumer market intelligence. I urge you, if you are uncomfortable with my practical sample sizing, to go to the library and consult the many excellent market research books that will guide you through an exacting process of sample selection techniques. [*I hope they remember to sample more than my rule of thumb if the kinds of people are very different from one another.*]

How Many Will Answer?

We decided on how many completed interviews are needed to feel comfortable, but not everyone who is called or mailed a questionnaire will agree to be interviewed or send back the questionnaire. My rules of thumb on response rates is shown below:

Market	Completions Needed	Estimated Percent Return	Total Sample Size
Consumer	Personal—50	40	125
	Phone—75	30	250
	Mail—150	20	750
Commercial/Industrial	Personal—10	70	15
	Phone—15	50	30
	Mail—50	25	200

Use this chart when it comes time to pull names for interviewing. Assemble enough candidates to achieve the required number of completed interviews.

Selecting a Demographic Mix

We'll build a few examples to demonstrate how selecting the demographic mix works. I have said we need a *representative* sample. What does that mean?

BETSEY

The number of people you talk to with various traits is equal to the ratio of people with those traits in the population as a whole.

That's right! The secondary census or industry survey data of consumers, commercial or trade customers, and industrial users usually provides the basis to determine the right ratios. Here are where and how I would find the ratio information. I'll assume Susan's interview population need only come from two sources: (1) families with children under six years of age; and (2) grandparents, represented by householders over 55 years old. I'm also going to assume other demographics, like income or education of the parents, are not relevant. Figure 7–1 displays the census data on families.

Let's extract what we need. *First*, the families with children. The 1988 data shows the total number of families is 65 million. There are only about 14 million families in the United States that have children under the age of six. These are the target candidates. Here's the ratio: approximately 1 in 5 fami-

FIGURE 7–1
Household Data for Susan's Sample

Of no use except that 1 in 2.5 households called will say, "no children."

Important in family life, for me!

Families With Children

NO. 66. FAMILIES, BY NUMBER OF OWN CHILDREN UNDER 18 YEARS OLD: 1970 TO 1988

[Except as noted, as of **March** and based on Current Population Survey; see headnote, table 65. See also *Historical Statistics, Colonial Times to 1970*, series A 353–358]

RACE, HISPANIC ORIGIN, AND YEAR	NUMBER OF FAMILIES (1,000)					PERCENT DISTRIBUTION					Average size of family
	Total	No children	One child	Two children	Three or more children	Total	No children	One child	Two children	Three or more children	
ALL FAMILIES [1]											
1970	51,586	22,774	9,398	8,969	10,445	100.0	44.1	18.2	17.4	20.2	3.58
1980	59,550	28,528	12,443	11,470	7,109	100.0	47.9	20.9	19.3	11.9	3.29
1985	62,706	31,594	13,108	11,645	6,359	100.0	50.4	20.9	18.6	10.1	3.23
1988	65,133	33,213	13,578	11,911	6,431	100.0	51.0	20.8	18.3	9.9	3.17
Married couple	51,809	27,209	9,904	9,576	5,120	100.0	52.5	19.1	18.5	9.9	3.24
Male householder [2]	2,715	1,669	657	296	94	100.0	61.5	24.2	10.9	3.5	2.69
Female householder [2]	10,608	4,335	3,017	2,039	1,217	100.0	40.9	28.4	19.2	11.5	2.98
WHITE FAMILIES											
1970	46,261	20,719	8,437	8,174	8,931	100.0	44.8	18.2	17.7	19.3	3.52
1980	52,243	25,769	10,727	9,977	5,769	100.0	49.3	20.5	19.1	11.0	3.23
1985	54,400	28,169	11,174	9,937	5,120	100.0	51.8	20.5	18.3	9.4	3.16
1988	56,044	29,426	11,299	10,217	5,102	100.0	52.5	20.2	18.2	9.1	3.12
BLACK FAMILIES											
1970	4,887	1,903	858	726	1,401	100.0	38.9	17.6	14.8	28.7	4.13
1980	6,184	2,364	1,449	1,235	1,136	100.0	38.2	23.4	20.0	18.4	3.67
1985	6,778	2,887	1,579	1,330	982	100.0	42.6	23.3	19.6	14.5	3.60
1988	7,177	2,982	1,803	1,338	1,054	100.0	41.5	25.1	18.6	14.7	3.49
HISPANIC FAMILIES [3]											
1970	2,004	597	390	388	629	100.0	29.8	19.5	19.4	31.4	4.28
1980	3,029	946	680	698	706	100.0	31.2	22.4	23.0	23.3	3.90
1985	3,939	1,357	904	865	833	100.0	33.9	22.9	22.0	21.1	3.88
1988	4,588	1,597	1,047	1,080	864	100.0	34.8	22.8	23.5	18.8	3.79

[1] Includes other races, not shown separately.   [2] No spouse present.   [3] Hispanic persons may be of any race. 1970 Hispanic data as of April and based on Census of Population.

Source: U.S. Bureau of the Census, *U.S. Census of Population, 1970* (PC-2-4A), and *Current Population Reports*, series P-20, No. 437 and earlier reports.

What to expect in different ethnic areas

more data found here

Source: U.S. Dept. of Commerce, Bureau of the Census, *Statistical Abstract of the United States* (Washington, D.C.: Government Printing Office, 1990), p. 51.

lies, or 20 percent, will be good interview candidates. Susan may have to make five interview attempts in order to find a respondent that meets her criteria.

Second, the grandparents. We'll assume they would buy a wooden wagon as a gift. The 1988 census data in Figure 7–2 shows some 91 million households. The difference between the 65 million families we talked about earlier and this figure is the 26 million families without children. [*I always carefully read the legends of government documents to make sure I am "comparing apples and apples."*] Of the 91 million total, there are about 32 million householders aged 55 or older. That means the grandparent potential is 35 percent of all the households.

FIGURE 7–2
More Data for Susan's Sample

Total households

NO. **58.** HOUSEHOLDS BY CHARACTERISTIC OF HOUSEHOLDER AND SIZE OF HOUSEHOLD:
1970 TO 1988

[As of **March.** Based on Current Population Survey; see headnote, table 55. See also *Historical Statistics, Colonial Times to 1970,* series A 335–349]

CHARACTERISTIC OF HOUSEHOLDER AND SIZE OF HOUSEHOLD	NUMBER (mil.)							PERCENT DISTRIBUTION				
	1970	1975	1980	1985	1986	1987	1988	1970	1975	1980	1985	1988
Total [1]	63.4	71.1	80.8	86.8	88.5	89.5	91.1	100.0	100.0	100.0	100.0	100.0
Age of householder:												
15–24 years old [2]	4.4	5.8	6.6	5.4	5.5	5.2	5.2	6.8	8.2	8.1	6.3	5.7
25–29 years old	6.1	7.8	9.3	9.6	9.8	9.7	9.6	9.6	11.0	11.5	11.1	10.6
30–34 years old	5.6	7.1	9.3	10.4	10.6	10.9	11.0	8.8	10.0	11.5	12.0	12.0
35–44 years old	11.8	11.9	14.0	17.5	18.0	18.7	19.3	18.6	16.7	17.3	20.1	21.2
45–54 years old	12.2	12.9	12.7	12.6	13.1	13.2	13.6	19.5	18.2	15.7	14.6	15.0
55–64 years old	10.8	11.3	12.5	13.1	12.9	12.9	12.8	17.1	15.9	15.5	15.1	14.1
65–74 years old	7.7	8.9	10.1	10.9	11.2	11.3	11.4	12.1	12.5	12.5	12.6	12.5
75 years old and over	4.8	5.4	6.4	7.3	7.4	7.7	8.0	7.6	7.6	7.9	8.4	8.8
Male	50.0	54.3	58.0	60.0	61.0	61.7	62.8	78.9	76.4	71.8	69.2	68.9
Female	13.4	16.8	22.8	26.8	27.4	27.7	28.3	21.1	23.6	28.2	30.8	31.1
White	56.6	62.9	70.8	75.3	76.6	77.3	78.5	89.5	88.5	87.6	86.8	86.2
Black	6.2	7.3	8.6	9.5	9.8	9.9	10.2	9.8	10.2	10.6	10.9	11.2
Hispanic [3]	(NA)	(NA)	3.7	4.9	5.2	5.4	5.7	(NA)	(NA)	4.6	5.6	6.3
1 person	10.9	13.9	18.3	20.6	21.2	21.1	21.9	17.1	19.6	22.7	23.7	24.0
Male	3.5	4.9	7.0	7.9	8.3	8.2	8.8	5.5	6.9	8.7	9.1	9.7
Female	7.3	9.0	11.3	12.7	12.9	12.9	13.1	11.5	12.7	14.0	14.6	14.4
2 persons	18.3	21.8	25.3	27.4	27.7	28.6	29.3	28.9	30.6	31.4	31.6	32.2
3 persons	10.9	12.4	14.1	15.5	16.1	16.2	16.2	17.3	17.4	17.5	17.8	17.7
4 persons	10.0	11.1	12.7	13.6	13.8	14.0	14.1	15.8	15.6	15.7	15.7	15.5
5 persons	6.5	6.4	6.1	6.1	6.3	6.2	6.1	10.3	9.0	7.5	7.0	6.7
6 persons	3.5	3.1	2.5	2.3	2.1	2.2	2.2	5.6	4.3	3.1	2.6	2.4
7 persons or more	3.2	2.5	1.8	1.3	1.3	1.3	1.3	5.0	3.5	2.2	1.5	1.4

NA Not available.   [1] Includes other races, not shown separately.   [2] 1970 and 1975, persons 14 to 24 years old.
[3] Hispanic persons may be of any race.

Source: U.S. Bureau of the Census, *Current Population Reports,* series P-20, No. 437 and earlier reports; and unpublished data.

32 million potential grandparents

Source: U.S. Dept. of Commerce, Bureau of the Census, *Statistical Abstract of the United States* (Washington, D.C.: Government Printing Office, 1990), p. 46.

Okay, let's further assume that the potential purchase of a wagon for the child is equally weighted between parents and grandparents. The demographic mix model is constructed of the two potential buyers added together to create a new combined potential total market. The percentage each buyer represents of the total is then calculated. We've determined that not everyone will respond. We must draw a total sample of 125 names for the personal interview, 250 for the telephone interview, and 750 to complete the mail survey. The necessary sample base is multiplied by the percentage each buyer represents to determine the mix for the interview method. The following illustrates the sample demographic mix:

	Number of Households	Percent of Total	Personal Interviews (125 Minimum)	Telephone Interviews (250 Minimum)	Mail Survey (750 Minimum)
Under 6	65 million	67	84	167	500
Over 55	32 million	33	41	83	250
Total	97 million	100%	125	250	750

Does that make sense to you, Susan?

SUSAN

> Yes, our warranty card analysis from a card packaged with the toy indicates that grandparents and parents are equal purchasers of the toys. How did you know they would be equal potentials?

I didn't, but that's what I mean about sitting back and asking who has the answers. I'm a grandparent and we buy toys. Marketing intelligence is about the real world. Using our common sense to consider what and who to ask is far more useful than most scientific approaches. Of course, that's my opinion.

Okay, let's try to figure out John's ratio of candidates. His base data can be taken from the small business population chart (see Figure 1–1). Here's how I would create John's candidate mix. I'll rule out certain firms as not potential customers. I'll assume firms with less than five or more than 99 employees are not potential customers. Figure 1–1 shows that the firms with five to 99 employees number approximately 8,745,000. We'll use the same calculation methodology as we did to create Susan's mix. John's potentials are commercial customers, so we'll use the total sample needed of 15 personal, 30 telephone, and 200 mail survey candidates. I'll round off the Figure 1–1 numbers. Here's the mix:

Number of Employees	Number of Firms	Percent of Total	Personal Interviews (15 Minimum)	Telephone Interviews (30 Minimum)	Mail Survey (200 Minimum)
5–9	4,400,000	50.3%	8	15	100
10–19	2,345,000	26.8	4	8	55
20–49	1,500,000	17.2	2	5	34
50–99	500,000	5.7	1	2	11
Total	8,745,000	100.0%	15	30	200

Is that clear, John?

JOHN

Sure, but I don't know where I will find the specific firms of those sizes.

You have rosters, directories, and lists of companies in your city. They're at the library, the chamber of commerce, and even the newspaper office. All you have to do is go through these data sources, look for the number of employees, and copy the business names down for sampling.

Let's use Betsey's catering business as another example to give you a feel for creating a sample mix. The assumption is that her household customer base has discretionary income to afford catering and is earning more than $50,000 per year. I'll further assume her commercial business is from larger firms with over 50 employees. What do you think about that, Betsey?

BETSEY

I'll agree with those assumptions. I've never sorted my customers that way, but it seems right.

If you haven't looked at your business from a demographic standpoint, you'll find it extremely interesting. Figure 7–3, from the *Abstract*, shows the 1986 demographic profiles of

FIGURE 7-3
How Much Do They Have to Spend?
Discretionary income buys toys, catering, and books

How many
How much

Income, Expenditures, and Wealth

No. 723. Households with Discretionary Income—Selected Income Measures: 1986

[Households as of **March 1987** and income figures are for the preceding year, expressed in 1986 dollars. Discretionary income is the amount of money which would permit a household to maintain a living standard comfortably higher (30% or more) than the average for similar households. For methodology, see source]

CHARACTERISTIC	ALL HOUSEHOLDS		HOUSEHOLDS WITH DISCRETIONARY INCOME						
			Households		Average income		Spendable discretionary income		
	Num-ber (1,000)	Aggre-gate income after taxes (bil. dol.)	Num-ber (1,000)	Per-cent of all house-holds	Before taxes (dol.)	After taxes (dol.)	Aggre-gate income (bil. dol.)	Aver-age in-come (dol.)
Total	89,479	2,165.1	25,869	28.9	56,605	41,940	319.0	12,332
Age of householder:								
15–24 years old	5,197	78.0	972	18.7	38,241	30,124	7.6	7,790
25–29 years old	9,652	205.9	2,646	27.4	48,547	36,618	24.2	9,130
30–34 years old	10,850	264.3	3,419	31.5	54,243	40,067	37.3	10,919
35–39 years old	10,155	280.2	3,349	33.0	60,049	43,585	41.5	12,405
40–44 years old	8,549	259.1	2,605	30.5	66,133	47,891	36.5	13,999
45–49 years old	6,888	218.3	2,299	33.4	69,412	49,968	33.2	14,448
50–54 years old	6,323	193.0	2,008	31.8	68,181	49,079	27.2	13,550
55–59 years old	6,443	178.5	2,252	35.0	61,480	44,906	32.8	14,584
60–64 years old	6,424	157.8	1,848	28.8	61,001	44,262	26.5	14,356
65–69 years old	6,086	125.3	1,523	25.0	50,447	38,968	19.7	12,921
70 years old and over	12,912	204.6	2,946	22.8	39,117	32,344	32.5	11,015
All other households	47,376	800.7	10,376	21.9	42,768	32,817	104.1	10,030
Occupation:								
Managerial and professional specialty	17,826	653.9	9,512	53.4	67,743	48,138	151.8	15,961
Technical sales and administrative support	15,767	425.4	5,210	33.0	57,570	41,963	62.6	12,021
Precision production, craft, repair, operators, fabricators, and laborers	21,553	533.6	5,551	25.8	49,874	38,029	47.3	8,519
Service, farming, forestry, and fishing	9,158	171.3	1,433	15.6	50,371	38,510	13.8	9,633
Nonworker or in the Armed Forces	25,175	380.9	4,163	16.5	41,066	34,146	43.5	10,444
Household income:								
Under $15,000	26,984	205.8	197	.7	13,855	13,213	.2	1,014
$15,000–$19,000	9,303	142.5	694	7.5	17,570	16,108	1.6	2,304
$20,000–$24,999	8,617	164.5	1,011	11.7	22,558	19,303	3.5	3,438
$25,000–$29,999	7,733	175.6	1,662	21.5	27,460	22,733	6.2	3,737
$30,000–$34,999	7,078	186.4	2,248	31.8	32,327	26,323	10.6	4,700
$35,000–$39,999	6,089	182.0	2,278	37.4	37,453	29,990	13.3	5,841
$40,000–$49,999	8,667	302.6	4,807	55.5	44,767	35,190	32.4	6,746
$50,000–$74,999	10,085	455.6	8,146	80.8	60,163	45,618	93.6	11,493
$75,000–$99,999	2,938	180.5	2,885	100.0	84,785	61,466	65.8	22,818
$100,000 and over	1,984	169.6	1,940	100.0	140,759	86,745	91.8	47,320

[1] Hispanic persons may be of any race.

Source: U.S. Bureau of the Census and the Conference Board, *A Marketer's Guide to Discretionary Income, 1989*

Potential grandparents

much more detailed info

Source: U.S. Dept. of Commerce, Bureau of the Census, *Statistical Abstract of the United States* (Washington, D.C.: Government Printing Office, 1990), p. 448.

households having discretionary income. I have purposely included all the census data so that you can get to know the household customer.

Look at all the data. We have their ages, race, where they live, size of family, education, the number of earners and what they do to earn money. Their average income amounts are listed in the far right column of Figure 7–3. Of the 89.4 million households, the total number with incomes over $50,000 is 15 million or approximately 17 percent of all households (add the number of households with income from $50,000 through "$100,000 and over"). So if you randomly called households, only one family in six would have an income over $50,000.

I said Betsey's customers probably had discretionary income for catering. Look at the *Households with Discretionary Income* columns in the table. The total number equals about 26 million, and households with over $50,000 total about 13 million, or 45 percent. Quite a difference. We want to narrow the interview candidate search so the trick now is to find where families with discretionary income live.

I would look for residential areas with homes having values approximately three times the target candidates' incomes. This should lead us to neighborhoods where houses sell for about $150,000. Local realtors or the Sunday classified section should specifically identify the discretionary income residential areas. The backward phone directory provides the names to call. A second way to locate where these families live is to study the U.S. census reports such as the *Census of Income* and *Census of Housing* data to get families with incomes over $50,000 by ZIP code. To get the right commercial market mix, we'll again use Figure 1–1 to determine the sample size needed to complete interviews of companies with more than 50 employees.

Number of Employees	Number of Firms	Percent of Total	Personal Interviews (15 Minimum)	Telephone Interviews (30 Minimum)	Mail Survey (200 Minimum)
50–96	500,000	53.7%	8	16	107
100–500	358,000	38.5	6	12	77
500–999	36,000	3.8	1	1	8
1,000–4,999	29,000	3.2	1	1	7
5,000–9,999	4,000	.4	1	1	1
10,000+	4,000	.4	1	1	1
Total	931,000	100.0%	18	32	201

Selecting the Names to Interview

This process is not complex. To create an unbiased sample, I recommend choosing names from telephone directories or neighborhood lists on a random basis. Just decide to take every fourth name, or every 10th name. In marketing intelligence jargon, that's called selecting every *n*th name. The "*n*th" method removes the bias of picking names you like, or streets that sound good to you. Your secondary work has led to the appropriate data sources—the best ZIP code or street area—to meet your demographic criteria. The random or every *n*th name method is the best selection method.

Specific personal judgments should be used to select commercial or industrial interview candidates. Vary the business type when you are constructing a sample using business *size* as the major demographic criteria. Pick some retail, some service, some manufacturing, and some professional firms. This will give you a good cross-section within the size category. If you are only interested in a certain *type* of business, like retail, then vary the number of employees to get diversity.

Entering and Assembling the Sample

Computers are wonderful. You can use word processing, data base, or spreadsheet software to create the sampling information. Here's the format I prefer:

Interview candidate first name—Jo.

Interview candidate last name—Stokes.

Title—vice president of plant engineering.

Company name—Nominal Widgets, Inc.

Street address, apartment or suite number—8 E. Elm Street.

City—Nartow.

State, ZIP or mail code—Browmenter.

Country—United States.

Telephone and fax number—(777) 555-2222, fax—(777) 555-2221.

Data base and spreadsheet software allow you to arrange the lists by any one of several data fields. A *data field* is any discreet information from the file. For example, the first and last name of the candidate are *fields*. So are the address and telephone number. Let's say you wanted to sort your candidates by ZIP code. The computer will do this almost instantly by designating ZIP code as the priority or primary sort criterion. Just a suggestion: if you don't have a computer or don't want to take the time, there are many service companies listed in the Yellow Pages under *computer services* that will do this job for you. They will take your marked-up directories and lists and convert them into data base files, and create a telephone list or mailing labels of candidates sorted to the priority or field preference you want. The cost per candidate is nominal.

Interviewing Consumers

For personal consumer interviews, the sample selection procedure is very simple. Go to where the consumers are likely to be, such as a bookstore, a shopping center, a car wash, a neighborhood park, or a ballgame. You're trying to match where and who to personally interview with what kind of information is needed.

Anne should ask questions of people who are leaving a competitor's bookstore across town, people visiting the public library, or people sitting in the park or on the beach reading a book.

John should approach people who have just picked up IRS tax forms at a federal building, business owners coming out of a bank, or different small business owners at their locations.

The Interview Agenda

We've combed the secondary information, talked to our gurus about the interview subject matter, and created questions that should provide answers. Let's review the environment of a commercial or industrial personal interview.

The interviewee is an authority, a decision maker, an expert, and a busy person who has granted you "a few minutes." In deference to the interviewee's time, your interview will take place in his or her office. In my view, it's not the best environment. I prefer an off-site or neutral setting, but the interviewee will usually feel more at ease in his or her office. Chances are that the person has not asked that telephone calls be held so that the interview would not be interrupted. Interruptions are terrible during an interview because they break concentration and information flow, as well as provide a reason to terminate the interview. I address this problem with a direct request: "I'm not going to take very much of your time, and it will help if we aren't interrupted. Would mind having your calls held?"

By granting the appointment, they've agreed to help you, but they don't want to spend time on chitchat, except to establish confidence in your credibility, trustworthiness, and professionalism. They want to get on with the important issues you came to talk about.

To satisfy our customer, the respondent, arrange the questions in a sequence so that if interruptions do occur, or the respondent does end the interview earlier than expected, you have found out what you came to learn. The simple sequencing of questions from *vital* to *urgent* to *important* assures good interview data. *Trivial* questions have no place in a personal interview.

Key Interview Steps

Here are the personal interview steps:

1. Thank the person for taking the time to meet and be interviewed.
2. Present your business card and tell the interviewee who you are, your affiliation, what your business does, and who your client is if you have one and have permission to divulge their identity.
3. Describe why he or she was selected and how you got his or her name.
4. Summarize what kinds of questions you would like to cover.
5. Ask for and respond to any questions the person may have.

6. Cover topics in the ranked order of vital, urgent, etc.
7. Ask for comments on topics the interviewee feels are important to the subjects covered.
8. Request referrals to others inside or outside the company who you could talk with.
9. Close by thanking the interviewee again for his or her time, insight, and information.
10. Thank the interviewee's secretary or assistant for his or her help in arranging the appointment, and leave your business card with that person for future reference.

Key Interviewing Techniques

Interviewing takes practice and is more art than science. Here's the way I do it:

- Sit down and review my interview agenda.
- Re-review the sequence of questions.
- Begin the interview.
- Maintain constant eye contact.
- Concentrate on what this person is saying.
- Watch their body language signals.
- Take the opportunity to dig deeper.

Here are some key interviewing techniques that will maximize the time you have with the interviewee and the information you can get as a result.

First, begin with a few simple questions:

- "How long have you been an expert in this field?"
- "What near-term trends are affecting your _____?"
- "Why are other firms in your industry or market operating like _____?"

These open-ended queries get the person comfortable and open to discussing your *vital* questions.

Second, don't ask biased questions. We discussed earlier the way to phrase a question so we don't get back only what we want to hear. Incidentally, most interviewees will quickly detect if you are just asking them to confirm a decision you've already made.

Third, keep the "yes/no" answers to a minimum. When people perceive they should respond by saying yes/no, up/down, sooner/later, or more/less, they get bored. It feels like a test. The personal interview is a way to get in-depth information and opinions. I try to ask open-ended questions that will address my vital issues, such as:

- "Considering the trends, what alternatives do you see to increase _____?"
- "I am familiar with what others think, but what do you believe are the underlying reasons that _____?"
- "We all can make them cheaper, smaller, and faster, but if you could have the perfect _____, describe that to me."

Fourth, get them into your problem-solving framework. Let them talk. Don't interrupt. Nod your head, take notes, lean forward, and listen intently. Convey genuine interest in their opinions.

Fifth, occasionally question their point of view. This opens them up even further. Information they may have been guarding tends to come out.

Taking Notes

You can't be a court reporter and capture every word your respondent says. When you are taking notes, you won't be keeping eye contact to instill trust, conveying interest in their responses, and appearing professional. You also must concentrate on what they are saying so you can quickly follow leads for new information on some comment they make. In most interviews there are always key bits of very important information. Note these for future reference. The note-taking here conveys to the interviewee that what he or she is saying has real value. Remember, you've prepared for the interview from a ranked set of questions. Your antenna is tuned for information about those questions, so don't miss it.

When the interview is over and I have shaken hands and left the office, I keep my mind clear until I can write down all that I heard. Don't make a phone call, talk to anyone for any length of time, or dig out a timetable to make the next appointment. Sit in your car, the waiting room, on a park bench—anyplace it's quiet—and write down everything you can remember. Use the interview guide to help refresh your memory. I guarantee you'll be able to reconstruct almost the whole interview.

Taping the Interview

SUSAN

Is it okay to tape the interview so you don't have to make all those notes or go through the memory test?

Well, that's a really sensitive subject. Here's what you risk with a tape recorder humming along: the person will not become as trustful of your confidentiality; answers will be much more thought-out and less open, and you probably will get less real information from the interview.

Your interviewing skills will get better with practice. As I said, it's not a science; it's an art. You will be very surprised at how much information people are willing to part with when the interview setting and question flow are right—even in your first attempt.

Reporting the Interview Results

1. Make a list of those interviewed, citing name, company affiliation, and title.
2. At the top of separate pages, or in the word processor, put the key questions from the interview guide.
3. Focus on one key question at a time. Go through each set of interview notes, extract the comments, and write them in a list of bulleted statements.
4. When you're through compiling the comments, sit back and read them thoroughly. Now formulate a consensus observation of what all the interviewees said about the question.
5. Repeat this process for each question on the interview agenda.
6. Go back and read all the observations and begin constructing your conclusions as they relate to your business.

The interview report becomes part of your marketing intelligence.

THE TELEPHONE INTERVIEW

Let's look at getting information over the telephone. Today the telephone is truly our access to the outside world, and unfortunately at times, the world also has very easy access to our privacy. There isn't a night, from 7:00 P.M. to 9:00 P.M., that the phone doesn't ring with someone taking a poll, asking for donations, or selling gutters and storm windows. This penetration of our privacy has hardened consumers to unsolicited phone calls and reduced the effectiveness of using the telephone for market intelligence gathering. But it is still the most cost efficient method to ask one-on-one questions and get answers. [*Seems like I'm spending a lot of time on interviewing. But I can't just say, "Go do it." I've got to walk them through step by step or they won't feel comfortable executing an interview.*] Here's how to do it.

Consumer Surveys

The Interview Candidates—Drawing The Sample
People don't want to be interviewed. We usually have to make at least three contacts to get one person to agree to be interviewed. The subject you're going to explore does make a difference in getting a positive response, but my suggestion is to plan on making three calls. We've determined that 50 to 75 completed interviews are required for us to become comfortable about the information, so we must draw a sample of 150 to 225 names and telephone numbers. Here's how we select the interview candidates and where to get their names and phone numbers.

The demographics of our candidates define the caller base of the survey. Let's use Susan's toy company as an example. The census data details ZIP code locations where families with more than one child live. Further digging will specify the streets where they live. Obtaining the telephone numbers and names can come from backward telephone directories that are available for sale or study at the telephone company office. Also, data base service companies sell or rent name, address, and phone data. They supply computer diskettes that can sort information by name, street address, ZIP code, or the first three digits of the phone number. These data base service companies are listed in the Yellow Pages.

Pull the sample of 150 to 225 names and numbers and get ready to start telephoning.

Telephone Sample Selection

Earlier we said that a representative sample of 50 to 75 consumers was sufficient to derive a consensus and that 10 to 15 were needed for commercial/industrial markets. I believe that for the vast number of business decisions, objective information from these seemingly low sample sizes is adequate to yield enough market opinion confidence. Validation using personal and mail surveys will strengthen data accuracy.

SUSAN

> Ar you saying that we must use *all* the interviewing techniques to feel comfortable enough to make marketing or product decisions?

Yes, in my experience, a combination of telephone, personal, and mail surveys reduces overall market intelligence gathering costs and builds a large enough sample base of responses to draw reasonable conclusions. The market data collector—you or me—has to make the judgment call whether there is enough information. Here is where I think a feel for the data becomes the deciding factor on whether or not more information is needed. Remember, marketing intelligence must satisfy several customers:

- You have to feel comfortable enough to recommend further market or product action based on the data.
- Your superior or peers must believe there is enough outside opinion supporting your findings to accept and champion your recommendations.
- Your ultimate customer or user must be satisfied that your marketing intelligence program developed a deep enough composite of customer attitudes, wants, and needs to reflect that user's preferences.

PETER

How do you ever know that for sure?

We get close, but we never get perfect accuracy. If we did, new product or service success would merely require interviewing a large sample base, drawing the project specifications, and offering it through distribution to accomplish 100 percent market niche penetration. Nobody has done that yet, and probably won't. So we have to strive to get closer, but do not expect perfection in understanding the customer.

The Interview Guide or Agenda—Getting Ready to Talk on the Phone

We've drawn the sample from the secondary data of lists, trade directories, telephone books, and industry contacts that appear as experts in our subject. Let's move on to conducting the telephone interview.

As I mentioned, questioning of people over the phone is more structured than when we personally interview people. The interview agenda for personal and telephone interviews is similar, but phone information gathering requires following a strict questioning sequence. Here's what I do:

Questionaire Development

- List all the questions I want to be answered.
- Arrange them from easy to answer, to harder, and then some easier ones again.
- List the introductory remarks, including:
  Who I am.
  Where I'm calling from.
  How I got their name.
  Why I want to talk with them.
  What I am going to do with the information.
  That their answers will be held confidential.
  That no salesperson will call.
  That the interview should only take a few minutes.

- Add some open-ended questions for telephone interviews with commercial or industrial respondents, to cover responses to questions about competition.
- Determine the demographic information for sorting responses into categories (i.e., age, education, income, title, job responsibilities).
- Create a draft questionnaire.
- Test the questionnaire on people at work or home or on close friends to identify questions they don't immediately understand or seem to struggle with.
- Modify the questionnaire and test it again with people who *don't* know you.
- Rework the questionnaire again one more time.
- Start the phone interviews.

Let's try a consumer interview. I'll use Susan's toys as the example. Listen for some of the interview elements and techniques we've discussed:

CONSUMER INTERVIEW

Hello, my name is Jack Savidge and I know I may be interrupting your evening. [*You must be careful here. While you're trying to acknowledge that they may feel invaded, this gives the person an opportunity to say, "Yes, you are," and hang up.*] I've been asked by a manufacturer of children's wooden toys to talk with families with children about new toys that you feel would be good for your youngster. We are also calling other families in your neighborhood and asking just a few questions. Everybody's answers are going to be put together to form a consensus. Will you take just a few minutes?

Fine. Let's start.

1. Do you have small children between the ages of 6 and 10?

Yes _____   No _____

(If Yes, go to question 3; if No, go to question 2.)

2. Do you have children younger than 6 or older than 10?

(*continued*)

Yes _____ No _____

(If No, thank them for their time and hang up.)
(If Yes, go to question 3.)
3. I am going to name some types of toys. Please tell me which ones you have purchased for your child in the last year or so.
- Puzzles _____
- Kites _____
- Push toys _____
- Wagons _____
- Other _____

4. Thank you. Have you found that your children prefer one kind of toy more than another? I'll go over the list again and you tell me which ones they like best.
- Puzzles _____
- Kites _____
- Push toys _____
- Wagons _____
- Other _____

5. Where do you normally buy toys for your children?
- Toy store _____
- Discount toy store _____
- Drug Store _____
- Department store _____
- Catalog _____

6. Let me ask you about toy packaging. Do you find the box size, assembly instructions, or inside packaging materials to be any problem?

Yes _____ No _____

7. You just said yes. Which packaging element do you find most troublesome?
- Box size _____
- Assembly instructions _____
- Inside packaging _____

Now you can go on with all the *vital* and *essential* questions, but just prior to ending the interview, you must get some specific demographics of who you interviewed. This will be important in compiling the data. Asking people for personal information is very sensitive, so the questions must be phrased just right. To this point, you have spent probably 5 to 10 minutes with the respondent and have built their trust in you. They should be open to offering their personal information. Here's a guide to asking personal questions:

CONSUMER INTERVIEW (*concluded*)

You have been very helpful and we do appreciate your time. Just so we can group your opinions with those of other people in your situation, I'd like to ask:

A. What are the ages of your children? _____
B. How many are boys? _____ girls? _____
C. May I ask you how old you are?
   20 to 25 _____, 26 to 30 _____,
   31 to 35 _____, over 40? _____
D. We find education important. Did you complete:
   High school, Yes _____ No _____,
   College, Yes _____ No _____,
   Some College, Yes _____ No _____.
E. One last question and I'll let you go. About what is your family income:
   $15,000 to 20,000 _____, $20,001 to 25,000 _____,
   $25,001 to 50,000 _____, Over $50,000 _____

Thank you.

The Industrial/Competitive Interview

To get a feel for how an industrial telephone interview is conducted, we'll listen to a tape of a mock interview a friend and I recorded. Let's assume a client had asked me to find out what new product features their competitor was planning to introduce. The product area was microscopes used for biological research. The client was not sure what new features the competitor was about to introduce. He had heard that the competitor would claim its microscopes would increase research productivity and that they could be connected to a computer.

Here's how I used the library to find an interview candidate. My preference would be someone working for my client's competitor. I first scanned the electronic data bases using the keywords *microscopes, productivity,* and *computers.* The cited articles yielded a few industry names, but no individuals at my client's competitor. I next looked up microscope-related trade associations, and found several. After a few phone calls to the executive directors of these associations, I learned that a recent trade show in the biological research field featured several technical sessions dealing with microscopes. The librarian directed me to a copy of the proceedings (or technical papers) from the industrial biology show that was in the library's technical collection. A review of this publication narrowed the search to a Bob Smith, the product manager for industrial microscopes from the *right* competitor. He chaired a session on the use of microscopes to improve research productivity. I scanned the high points of the papers presented during Bob's session to get familiar with the language of microscopy and the conclusions offered by the people on Bob's panel. [*Microscopy is certainly different than catering and wooden toys, but it will highlight the points I'm trying to get across.*]

I had the name, I knew where the competitor was, and I had the phone number—all that was needed. I'll start the tape. Listen to the dialog and the comments that emphasize the key interviewing steps and techniques. There are three characters in the process: Jack, that's me; the assistant, who doesn't want me to talk to Bob; and Bob, my friend, playing the competitor's product manager who has the answers. Here's how it went:

JACK

Yes, I'd like to speak with Bob Smith please.

ASSISTANT

May I tell him who is calling? (The assistant is doing a good job to protect Bob from stray calls.)

JACK

Surely, my name is Jack Savidge, but Bob doesn't know me. Let me tell you why I am calling. I'd like to talk with him about a technical matter concerning microscopes. (I gave my full name, acknowledged that Bob never heard of me, and stated the reason for calling him.)

ASSISTANT

A technical matter? Maybe you should speak with someone in our customer service department. (Oh no, I used one of those trigger words that prompts a switch to another department)

JACK

No, this has to do with the technical session Bob chaired at the recent industrial biology trade association meeting. (Okay, back on track. I explained that Bob was the only one I could talk to and also where I came up with Bob's name. Now, the assistant has all the information needed to convey to Bob who is on the phone, and what I want to talk about. The screening job has been satisfied.)

ASSISTANT

Oh yes, just a minute. I'll see if I can put you through.

BOB

Hello, Jack Savidge. I don't think I know you.

JACK

No, Bob, you don't. I'm an independent marketing intelligence consultant working on a project in your industry. I was reviewing the session you chaired at the industrial biology trade conference this year. I have just a few questions; can you take a minute? (Notice a I said a "few" questions so Bob doesn't feel that too much of his important time will be taken.)

(continued)

BOB

Sure, what kind of a project are you involved in? What do you do and where are you located?

JACK

Well, I'm an independent located in San Diego and I'm trying to understand why microscope technology hasn't advanced further to increase microbiology research quality and productivity. As the session chairperson, I thought you might have a few opinions about this subject. Incidentally, as we talk I am going to take notes, so please don't mention anything that you don't think is public or common industry knowledge.

(Three items: (1) I characterized myself as an independent which I'd said before. I purposely avoided his question about what kind of project I was working on. If he doesn't ask for more clarification about my client, I won't volunteer information. (2) I wanted to set Bob apart from his job as a product manager, so I put him back in the position of chairperson. This usually allows people to speak about subjects from another perspective and they become less guarded about their company confidential material. (3) I told him not to tell me anything that was confidential. Therefore, anything he says I will feel free to use.)

BOB

If you read the papers you know there are some advances that are connecting microscopes to computers and it appears system approaches will advance productivity. (Bob is trying to put me off indicating that whatever I need to know is in the papers. At the same time, he sounds more like a chairperson, just what I wanted. I'll get him back into being a product manager, but first I have to establish the rapport and get him comfortable.)

JACK

Yes, I picked that up in the papers. What intrigued me was a comment in your remarks that better microscope lighting might be a productivity improvement tool. I have gone over every microscope manufacturer's product literature and can't find anything new in illumination.

(I have to be careful here not to get too invasive. I purposely used the word *intrigued* so he could hear I thought he was innovative, and that I had a real interest in what he said at the conference. I hope this will open him up. I also gave him some information, which he probably knew, that his competitors' literature doesn't mention his idea about illumination.)

BOB

It's interesting that you would pick up the point on illumination. Have you talked to other manufacturers about that point? (He's biting on my "intriguing" bait and wants to know whether I found anybody else thinking about this idea. Look what's happened. In a very short time he and I are becoming partners. I'm looking for information from him and he wants to know what I know about his competition. I think the rapport has been set and he trusts me. I need to move him back into the product manager position.)

JACK

No. Because you chaired the session, you are the first industry leader I've called. Tell me, why do you think improved lighting on the glass slide will work better? (One more ego boost to open him up, I use the word *leader*. Now, let's get on with specifics about what they are doing to microscopes.)

BOB

Well, we've done a little work and found that if you can vary the angle and intensity of the light that hits the sample, your eye sees new and different information about what the researcher is looking at. (Right, acknowledgement they are doing something new and, more importantly, what the new product enhancements might be.)

JACK

Okay, instead of shining the light straight up through the sample, you let the light strike it from the sides at different angles. That seems very clever, yet practical. What do people see that's different, and how does that improve the number of samples they can process in, let's say, an hour? (Do you hear my position? He's the expert and teacher and I'm the student. That's the relationship you want as an interviewer. Now, Bob, I want to know what you perceive is the performance benefit to customers?)

BOB

Jack, have you ever taken a lamp or flashlight and looked at

(*continued*)

something on a table by moving the flashlight around the object? I'll bet you have. Now, recall whether you saw things about that object that appeared as you moved the light. As far as improving the number of samples they can process, well, if they can move the light to an angle that best illuminates what they are looking for, they can process more per hour, or whatever.

JACK

Yes, come to think of it, you're right. But how can you do that with a microscope? People don't use flashlights in labs. My understanding of microscopes would lead me to think that there is no room to fit something on the scope. (I've got the concept, how is he going to make that into a product?)

BOB

We've been working on how that can done, not using a flashlight, but a device that fits on the scope that allows the microscope operator to vary the intensity of light and the way it strikes the sample. We think it can be an interchangeable accessory designed to fit in where the existing light bulb is. (That's it. I now know what they are going to offer in microscope hardware.)

JACK

That sounds exciting. Was that your idea? (I sense he feels that information is confidential, which it is. To distract him from thinking about the indiscretion, I moved him into an inventor role.)

BOB

As matter of fact, it was my idea, but our engineering group figured out how to make it at a slightly lower cost. Another idea that I had was to connect the illumination device to the computer with simple electronics. You would press a new button on the microscope when the exact light angle was achieved and the illumination information is fed to the computer for the specific sample. (Well, that last question of it being his idea worked. Now I know how they are going to tie the light to the computer.)

JACK

That really sounds like a way to improve the productivity. You said the cost for these new lighting devices and the tie-in with the computer would not be too high. What is that? Maybe a 50 percent increase in price to the customer? (We know about the hardware; now let's find out about how much they believe the customer will pay for these new performance benefits.)

BOB

I really can't say exactly what the price will be, but I will tell you that it is less than a 50 percent increase—more like 25 to 30 percent.

JACK

Really? I can see where this will make a real impact on the market. As it sounds like a complicated addition to the microscope, I would imagine it will be some time before it would be available. (More, Bob. I have to know when you're going to introduce the product.)

BOB

Well, we've been working on this for quite a while and we've already demonstrated it to a few customers. I guess this is industry common knowledge by now. We will introduce this product at the Fall Miniature Parts Show. (He's again concerned about telling me too much. By saying this is common knowledge, he feels better. It may not be common knowledge, but when any manufacturer demonstrates new products to potential customers, the manufacturer should assume it will quickly become common knowledge.)

JACK

This has been very interesting and helpful. You are doing exciting work. As I said before, I have been taking notes. Do you mind being identified as someone I talked with? (I want his permission to tell anyone, such as my client, about our discussion.)

BOB

Sure, you can mention that we talked. We'll probably be on the market with our new products before you've finished with your work.

JACK

Well, Bob, I can't thank you enough for your time and the education. Your company should do well from your ideas. They are very innovative. I also appreciate your permission to use the information. Thanks again.

(continued)

> *BOB*
>
> Great. Nice talking with you. Call me anytime if you have other questions. Goodbye.

SUSAN

What would you have said if he had kept pressing to know about the project you were working on?

Well, I would have stated, "Although I cannot reveal who my client is, it is a manufacturer of laboratory analysis equipment, and my project is to understand a wide range of laboratory productivity opportunities." Bob has three options at this point: (1) terminate the conversation, (2) assume I am working for a competitor, but continue and hope to gain information from me, or (3) continue and assume that my client is not a direct competitor. Remember, I told him not to divulge anything that wasn't industry knowledge. I have responsibility to warn him I may use what he says; he has the burden of not telling me what he doesn't want me to know. He may hang up, and sometimes this happens. But then I go on to call the next industry expert, a user or knowledgeable microscope distribution executive.

[*Here's the reality if you want to get competitive information: once they're warned, there are no indiscrete questions, only indiscrete answers.*]

PETER

I can't believe someone in Bob's position would give a stranger all that information. Do interviews always go that way?

Usually, the key is that the telephone is an anonymous device. Once you have established rapport with your target, they forget or become less guarded about confidential information. Now, it may take two or three interviews to get all the pieces of information you're looking for, but you will get them by following the pattern of questioning you just heard.

ANNE

What about interviewing regular consumers? What we heard was for a commercial or industrial product. How do individuals react? I know that I don't answer questions over the phone when they call me at home.

Good point. Interviewing consumers over the phone requires more structure, but the basics are the same. Let's review the key elements:

1. Who you are.
2. Why it is necessary to call them at home.
3. What information you are trying to get.
4. Why you have selected them.
5. How much of their valued time the few questions will take.
6. Where, how, and by whom the information will be used.

Follow the interview guide exactly.

ANNE

What if they hang up?

Call the next number on your list. I've found the major reason people hang up is that their names are not pronounced correctly. So practicing a difficult name several times before placing the call is important. Another trigger for a hangup is being too friendly—you know, "Did you have a nice day? How's everything at your house?" Look, you're disturbing them for a business matter, not trying to become their friend. Some interviewers try to get too close, and that sets up resistance, which leads to simply hanging up.

That concludes the telephone survey methods and interviewing techniques. Let's move on to collecting information by using mail surveys.

MAIL SURVEYS

At one time or another, we've all participated in a mail survey. It's simple and inexpensive compared to personal or telephone interviewing. Just get a list, write a cover letter, fold up the questionnaire, put it in the mail, and stand by the door waiting for the post office to deliver bags full of market intelligence.

Not so fast. Simple and cheap responses to mail surveys have their problems. Consider the purpose and value of the mail survey:

- It is used to determine trends and general likes and dislikes.
- It is easy to conduct, but has a longer response time than other methods.
- It is less accurate than other methods.
- It is biased and of lesser value than other methods.
- It is nonthreatening to the respondent.
- It is the least expensive way to collect information.

SUSAN

How can it be biased if we construct questions in an unbiased way?

When we don't get back 100 percent of the questionnaires we send out, we don't know the opinions of the people who don't send the questionnaire back. Let's see if this example demonstrates the point.

I'm going to poll all of you. How many like chocolate? Everyone but John and Betsey. Who likes to shop? Everyone but John, Bill, and Anne. Here's the tally:

	Chocolate and Shopping Tally	
	Likes Chocolate	*Likes Shopping*
John	No	No
Betsey	No	Yes
Susan	Yes	Yes
Bill	Yes	No
Peter	Yes	Yes
Anne	Yes	No

I've mailed a questionnaire to your house. I introduced myself and described that the purpose of the survey is to assist a company looking for ideas about a candy store interior for a shop in a nearby mall. The cover letter also states that we want to find out what type of chocolate holiday gifts you might like us to stock.

As an incentive to answer my questionnaire I have enclosed a certificate for a free chocolate sampler that you can redeem at the store.

Some of you will answer the questions. Some of you will immediately throw the questionnaire and gift certificate away. Who do you think will throw the questionnaire away?

JOHN

I will for sure.

John, why can't you take a few minutes to help someone doing market intelligence gathering? You could give the certificate to your wife or a friend. Tell me why not.

JOHN

Because I have no interest in either topic. I wouldn't take the time because any answers I give won't benefit me in the future.

BETSEY

Well, I'm torn. I'm thinking I might answer the questions about the candy shop interior. So, I would probably only fill out half of the questionnaire.

Half the information is better than none.

BILL

I'd fill it out, but I'd ask my wife about the shopping questions.

ANNE

Sure, I'll send it back. My answers on the chocolate would be accurate but I will probably make up anything about the shopping because I assume they want all the questions answered.

I know Susan and Peter will send their answers back and they will be very helpful. Look what's going on here:

John—no data return.

Betsey—data on chocolate only.

Bill—his chocolate data, his wife's on shopping.

Anne—good chocolate data, bad data on shopping.

Susan and Peter—good data on both.

Mail survey data can be biased and an unreliable reflection of the sample base because: (1) we don't know the opinions of people who do not respond, like John; (2) partial answers have marginal value, like Betsey's; and (3) there is no way to know if the answers represent the sole opinions of the selected sample. Bill's answers on shopping are not all his. His wife helped. However, Bill's answers will be analyzed as if they were only his and grouped within Bill's demographics. Anne's shopping answers will be analyzed as accurate, but they are not—she just filled in the blanks. Mail survey bias is not knowing what those who didn't answer think and whether the respondent did all the thinking about the answers. Maybe we shouldn't use mail surveys!

PETER

> Is there a problem if the data is not perfect? We do get information that helps with fundamental issues that can be validated using personal or telephone interviews.

Absolutely. That's the precise attitude to have about mail surveys, whether we're trying to get information from individuals, or commercial and industrial customers. The message is to be careful about mail surveys. They are easy and inexpensive to conduct, but remember the biases. And always wonder about the opinions of the people who did not respond.

Building the Trust of Mail Survey Respondents

We all have biases about products and services, so many of the questionnaires arriving in the mailbox will immediately go in the wastepaper basket. Respondent unwillingness to fill out surveys exists because we feel unsolicited surveys invade our privacy. So on principle, many reject the notion of filling out a survey. Market researchers often try to mitigate this attitude by making some compelling offer to the potential respondent. These incentives to complete the questionnaire include free products, purchase discounts, maps, reports, pictures, plates, clocks, whatever. Incentives can raise the response rate.

We've all received mail surveys. What do we do first?

JOHN

Throw it away.

But do you look at the letter that comes with the questionnaire before you toss it?

JOHN

Most of the time I do. I see who it's from and why they want me to fill it out. Then I throw it away.

You were not sufficiently impressed with the credibility of the organization that sent it to you. You didn't think the use of the answers would benefit you in any way or that the free offer was not attractive enough. So our letter must be engaging enough to get people into the questionnaire, much like the introductory remarks of the telephone interviewer.

Writing introductory letters requires practice and is a highly developed skill. Large consumer market survey organizations struggle to increase the return rate of questionnaires sent out because any fractional improvement in responses reduces their survey costs. But we're not going for completed responses from thousands of people. Our completed sample base should not exceed 150, and we discussed earlier.

My approach to building trust and establishing rapport in a cover letter is to:

- State that they don't know who I am, but the reason I'm asking their opinion is important.
- Refer to something they will perceive as a future benefit; for instance, a product that cleans carpets better or a booklet showing how to pack for a trip.
- State that answers will be merged with all other answers, that no salesperson will call, and that completing the survey won't take more than a few minutes.

I haven't measured the increased response rates against some norms but these trust and rapport elements seem to work.

Setting the Survey Pace

Asking hard questions at the outset causes people to reject going on to the next question. So start with the easy ones—"Do you live in a house, a condo, or an apartment? Have you taken a trip in the last 12 months? Do you wear a uniform to work?" Individuals must become relaxed before they will answer the more penetrating questions.

Commercial and industrial respondents, after becoming trustful, provide answers in a more workmanlike manner. Key to these respondents is their perception that they are not divulging anything they consider proprietary information.

There is a critical pace-breaking element at the end of the survey where basic respondent demographics should be collected. This part is always touchy. The objective is to have the respondent answer the who, what, where, and how much questions. The message to convey is that their private information (no name or address) is important to send back and that we're not invading their privacy. In short, we don't want to cause them to hesitate and stop and throw the survey in the wastepaper basket.

Pretesting the Mail Survey

The comparative cost of mail surveys is low. Including the cost of questionnaire printing, folding, inserting, envelopes, and postage, it is less than other polling methods. Increasing the percentage of the returned questionnaires is of significant importance and merits taking the time to try out the survey. Pretesting the rapport, clarity, and pacing before making the mailing will increase the rate of return.

Here's how to pretest the questionnaire:

- Edit for structure and simplify the wording.
- Delete your biases to make questions objective.
- Read the entire questionnaire aloud and make changes where it sounds awkward.
- Give the edited questionnaire to three neighbors, peers, or friends, asking them to tear it apart; tell them you really want to know what they don't understand; ask them to

underline phrases that make them defensive or offended; and finally, ask them to answer the questions.

* Now ask three acquaintances who represent the target respondent group to fill out the revised questionnaire.
* Personally collect each questionnaire and discuss their criticisms.
* Make the final revisions.

Pretesting questionnaires applies to consumer, industrial, and commercial markets. It is *vital* to collecting valuable information and well worth the extra effort and time.

Assembling a Mail Survey Package

The essential survey package elements are:

* The cover letter: includes who you are, why they were selected, and all the rapport-setting statements discussed before.
* The questionnaire: using, at a minimum, 10-pitch type and printed on white paper.
* The return envelope: pre-addressed and stamped.
* The mailing envelope: letter-quality typed, no mailing labels, addressed to an individual, not to "occupant" or "job title."
* The incentive: this is not mandatory, but if used should increase the return rate.

Knowing Who Returned the Questionnaire

The respondents have been told their answers will be merged with all survey answers to form a consensus. The last sequence of questions covers the respondent's demographics, but we don't ask for their names, companies, etc. However, there are occasions when knowing who has or has not sent back a questionnaire is valuable. I find this is mostly useful in commercial or industrial markets. Here are a few practical ways to identify the respondents. Sequentially number or alphabetize each name on the master mailing list. Then do one of the following:

- On the questionnaire, at the very bottom left-hand corner of the last page print on the original questionnaire "To be analyzed by _____," and hand print the sequential number.
- Hand print the number on the far right side, inside the return envelope.
- On the front side of the return envelope, in the lower left corner, print "Forward to Analyst _____," and hand print the number.
- Ask the printer to sequentially print numbers after "Project Number _____," either on the return envelope or the questionnaire.

You get the idea. The respondents may see these numbers, but they do not get too concerned because they have not divulged their names or addresses.

ANNE

Let me understand. You said the answers would be merged with all other answers. Doesn't that imply anonymity?

Maybe, and my veracity has been questioned on this point. I need to know who didn't answer so I can determine the demographics of bias not to answer. Yes, a small fraction of the polled individuals, upon discovering the hidden code, will abort the survey. But the rewards of knowing who didn't return the questionnaire far outweigh the loss of a few completed returns.

Now this is a matter of style and your own feelings about not being completely forthright. I can tell you this methodology is industry practice, and the reality is that surveyors don't use the private information other than to determine the demographics of who did not answer the questions. Your concern is valid and you must make the choice. I'm not recommending any approach, only describing what others and I have done.

The Mail Survey Form

Let's use what we have just discussed and adapt Susan's telephone survey to a mail survey.

MAIL SURVEY

Letterhead of the Market Research Company or Yours

Address: To an individual, with full name

Salutation: Dear Mr. or Ms._____:

We've also written your neighbors to ask for their help to better understand parent's attitudes about children's toys. Our company has been asked by a manufacturer of children's wooden toys to talk with families to better define new toys. We're also interested in your views about toy performance, where you shop, and how toys are selected. This should take just a few minutes. We've provided a self-addressed envelope for returning the survey.

1. Do you have small children between the ages of 6 and 10?

   Yes _____   No _____

   (If yes, go to question 3; if no, go to question 2.)

2. Do you have children younger than six or older than 10?

   Yes _____   No _____

3. Mark the types of toys you have purchased for your child in the last year or so.

   • Puzzles _____
   • Kites _____
   • Push toys _____
   • Wagons _____
   • Other _____

4. Thank you. Have you found that your children prefer one kind of toy more than another? Please mark toys they seem to play with the most.

   • Puzzles _____
   • Kites _____
   • Push toys _____
   • Wagons _____
   • Other _____

(*continued*)

---

5. Where do you normally buy toys for your children? Please check one.

   - Toy store _____
   - Discount toy store _____
   - Drug store _____
   - Department store _____
   - Catalog _____

6. About toy packaging: do you find the box size, assembly instructions, or inside packaging materials to be any problem?

   Yes _____, No _____

7. If you checked yes, please mark which packaging element you find most troublesome.

   - Box size _____
   - Assembly instructions _____
   - Inside packaging _____

As with Susan's telephone interview, we must get some specific demographics of who we interviewed. The respondent has either thrown the survey form away or is open to offering some personal information. Here's the suggested form for asking mail survey respondents personal questions:

MAIL SURVEY (concluded)

You have been very helpful and we do appreciate your time. Just so we can group your opinions with other parents (and let us reinforce that any information you provide will not and cannot be identified with you), please answer the following questions:

A. What are the ages of your children? _____
B. How many are boys? _____ girls? _____

C. Your age is:
20 to 25 _____ 26 to 30 _____
31 to 35 _____ 36 to 40 _____
D. We find education important. Did you complete:
High school Yes _____ No _____,
College Yes _____ No _____,
Some college Yes _____ No _____
E. And the last question, what is your family income?
$15,000 to 20,000 _____ $20,001 to 25,000 _____
$25,001 to 50,000 _____ Over $50,000 _____

Thank you. Please insert the survey in the provided envelope and return it at your earliest convenience.

BILL

There don't seem to be any differences. The questions are the same.

Almost the same, but notice how I have changed the open-ended questions to multiple choice, and the introduction is phrased more like an application for a job or sending in for a free product sample.

Telephone interviews allow us to humanly communicate and build trust to create a flow of answers and reveal unguarded and true opinions. Over the phone there is meter and rhythm to the questioning and responses and the telephone interviewer has the discretion to move more quickly or slowly to match the respondent's pace. The mail survey respondent is not in a dialog with anyone and has to make a solitary decision to proceed. That's why the questionnaire must be constructed to convey trust and set up an answering rhythm. The questions must be phrased with clarity to obtain objective answers.

Analyzing Mail Survey Data

Now what's to be done with the returned questionnaire? There are four tools needed that can generate the respondent consensus. They are pencils, paper, and a calculator or personal computer. The procedure is quick and easy.

Paper, Pencils, and Calculators

We'll use paper and pencil to tally each yes, no, etc. The open-ended responses can be noted separately but should be marked to refer to the proper demographics. When a question asks for numeric answers, simply write down each number, separated by a comma. Here's how that would look: "Please tell me the ages of your children." *Answer*—6, 8, 4, 10, 12, 9, etc.

Here are a few tips to quickly and accurately tally answers:

- Take the original questionnaire to a photocopy center and have it blown up so there's plenty of room for tally marks or numbers beside or underneath each question.
- Go through each questionnaire and tally all the answers at one time; don't go through all the questionnaires just looking for question 1, then for question 2, etc.
- Place the tallied questionnaires face down to keep them in the analyzed order.
- Ask someone else to tally the questions in the same order that you did. Counting is very difficult and prone to mistakes; doing the tally at least twice is a good idea.

The averages and percentages for all respondents for each question and the demographics for the respondents are good information about total market or customer group. This is the first set of data. But we don't know the opinions of males and how they compare with the opinions of females, married people compared to singles, college graduates and nongraduates. Further analysis will bring into focus the opinions of each demographic characteristic. How do you suppose we can accomplish this kind of analysis?

PETER

Just repeat the process for each demographic characteristic.

BILL

I'd use a computer.

Using the paper and pencil process is easy. Just put the specific characteristic you want to analyze in a pile. Go through the slash or tally mark work to get the consensus opinion or answers for each characteristic. I'm a big proponent of using computers to do complex work, but realistically, it probably would take as long to set up and analyze 150 questionnaires in the computer as it would to complete the analysis by hand.

Let's talk more about using computers. Any commercially available spreadsheet or data base program will do the job. You can either build a spreadsheet or create a data base template of the actual questionnaire. In a spreadsheet, just assign each column a question, and each row represents a respondent. Summing answers and deriving percentages is a minor computer task.

Data base software uses a *template*, which is a replica of the actual survey form. The great advantage of the data base method is that cross-correlation formulas built into the software provide almost instant analysis. Another data base advantage is data entry. It's somewhat automatic as the computer moves the cursor to the next data entry point. There is less chance of losing your place. Summing, averaging, and creating percentages are also available in data base software. [*I prefer the data base software; it's faster and really lends itself to survey analysis.*] There are excellent references for market research analytical software in the appendix of Alan R. Andreasen's book, *Cheap but Good Marketing Research*, published by Business One Irwin.

Now all we have to do is interpret what the answers mean for our specific market intelligence project.

FOCUS PANELS

Have you ever been involved in a brainstorming session? Whenever a small group of 5 to 10 people who know something about a subject get together there are excitement, new ideas, and constructive disagreement. Focus groups are another tool for market intelligence gathering.

Why Use Focus Groups?

The focus panel exposes subjective reasons for what the customer wants. I find them most appropriate for:

- Defining products to supersede current competitive offerings.
- Refining a product or service to create a greater perceived value.
- Enhancing customer service to provide a competitive edge.
- Evaluating the sensitivity to changes in distribution as perceived by the end users or distribution channel participants.
- Designing product packaging for greatest ease of use and attractiveness.
- Creating advertisement layouts to attract the attention of the target reader.
- Locating field sales and service in more effective locations to satisfy customer demands.
- Training internal sales and service personnel to handle customer communications.
- Positioning prices and discounts to create higher perceived value in the customer's mind.
- Determining customer perceptions of competitive strengths and weaknesses for developing tactics and strategies to increase market share.

How the Focus Panel Works

The format and implementation of a focus panel are very straightforward. Here's how it works:

1. Panelists who represent end users, specifiers, buyers, or key individuals in the distribution chain are selected.

2. Invitations are sent for a meeting at a nonthreatening location. I like using a private dining room or conference room in a hotel or motel.

3. An independent moderator, not known to the panelists, has prepared a list of key questions that will be discussed by the group. These moderators need not be highly paid professionals. Local university or college professors are skilled in working with groups to probe for answers. They can be engaged for modest compensation.

4. A relaxed atmosphere is achieved by seating panelists at a round or U-shaped table arrangement. Their chairs should be comfortable. I prefer those that swivel and tip back.

5. The moderator:

   Sets the stage.

   Introduces all the panelists.

   States the purpose of the meeting.

   Sets the session time not to exceed two hours.

   Encourages panelists to get up and stretch, walk around the room, and get refreshments whenever they want.

   Identifies the session sponsor or withholds the sponsor's identity by claiming that anonymity will increase objective input.

   Assures participants that comments and opinions will not be used by anyone other than the sponsor.

   Asks permission to audio- or videotape the session so full attention can be directed at the job of moderating instead of taking notes, and so that the comments and suggestions can be reviewed later.

   Gives a background on the product or service, competitive offerings, and the general nature of the key questions to be addressed during the session.

6. Group dynamics usually result in stronger personalities trying to form a consensus around their own points of view via persuasion or intimidation. The moderator should

constantly coax opinions from all the panelists and should deftly provoke confrontation among panelists.

7. Key issues are probed to the deepest degree possible before the moderator allows a change in subject.

8. Check lists, vital points, and topic summaries are transferred to flip charts or a blackboard to assist opinion consensus.

9. Panelists are asked *not* to talk about the session with competitors and are offered some token compensation for taking the time to participate.

PETER

> I was once a panelist, and our group tore the product apart. We told them they should paint it a different color, change control knobs to shapes that fit our fingers, and agreed on a maximum price we thought people would pay. It was exciting. Do focus group sponsors really adopt what they learn?

No, not everything, but if the sample has been drawn correctly, the opinions of the panelists should carry a great deal of weight with the sponsor. In general, I would say that the output from focus groups is most always adopted.

JOHN

> You mean I could get a group of small business owners in a hotel and ask them to define the perfect accounting service? Find out what they would pay and why certain bookkeeping services have more value than others?

Sure! You could sponsor that event, but you shouldn't be the moderator. You have too many biases on what kinds of accounting services you like. Your strong personality would probably unconsciously lead them to a consensus you want to hear. Get an independent moderator for the session.

ANNE

> I think I'll try the focus group. It sounds inexpensive, fast, and objective.

It is, but remember it is just one way to validate all the information you gain from other intelligence gathering methods.

Analyzing the Focus Panel Information

There are no "yes" and "no" answers. There are no check marks to tally. There are only words, raised or lowered voices, and body language. Panelists, who have a common knowledge or perspective, are led through topics by a moderator in control of the group's dynamics. How then is information taken from this two-to three-hour collection of thoughts?

Simple. As the sponsor, client, or business owner who commissioned the focus panel, you just sit and listen to the information a minimum of three times. You take notes during each replay of the session and finally the messages will come together as answers to your key issues.

Here are some key analysis tips:

1. If the session was only audiotaped, then on the first listening train your ear to detect who is speaking. If the session was videotaped then you know exactly who has made a comment.

2. Match the voices and names with the information used to select the sample: company, title, consumer demographics.

3. During the first replay, make notes of the most important opinions following the outline the moderator used to lead the session.

4. During the second replay, make notes of the secondary points of view brought up during the "important opinion" discussions. Put the speaker's initials next to these comments. Listen for the tone and inflections in the panelist's voice. These may signal greater or lesser interest or concern about the topic.

5. The last review solidifies all the attitudes, concerns, excitement, and urgency the panelists have about the topics discussed.

Focus panels are also easy to organize and execute, and yield very valuable *qualitative* information.

OBSERVATION—THE INEXPENSIVE METHOD

The last significant primary data collection method is observation—the old-fashioned technique of just standing around watching people or events in a specific situation. When we observe what's taking place, we must consider the qualitative data of who, when, what, and where. To determine quantities of events, we observe how many, how often, and how much. Simple and straightforward observations of activities going on around us serve as the basis for validating other forms of surveys. They are the cornerstone of more extensive investigations into customer needs.

Here are a few questions that can be answered by just observing:

- Who enters Anne's bookstore—more men or more women?
- Who eats the pastries at Betsey's buffets—men or women, younger or older people?
- Who begins to play with Susan's wagons—little boys or girls?
- Which wall-scrubbing tools do Bill's maintenance customers most use: cloths, brushes, or steel wool?
- When is the peak time of day in the bookstore?
- What is the floor layout of high-traffic competitor bookstores?
- What competitors have signed in to see your customer's buyers?
- Who are the competitor's salespeople visiting your customers?
- What is the perceived difficulty people have reading the product instructions?
- How and for what purpose are Peter's scales used during a manufacturing or research process?
- Who are the coffee drinkers in Anne's bookstore—men or women?
- What kinds of cars are driven by people who attend Betsey's affairs—new or old, expensive or inexpensive?
- Which vendors are delivering goods to the competition?

- How much time does it take for the child or parent to get Susan's toys out of the box?
- How much time do the children typically spend playing with each kind of wooden toy?
- How often is the scrub water changed to clean floors?
- How many employees are going into your competitor's factory?
- How much time do bookstore browsers spend before buying or leaving?
- How many people enter a competitor's store per hour or per day?
- How much time does it take customers to assemble a product?

You get the idea—just simple observations that cannot be answered by any survey. Here are some key rules about observational data collection:

1. To objectively observe, whether to count or quantify, don't invade the zone where the activity is going on. If people see that you are watching them, they will unconsciously change their behavior and you will witness biased behavior.

2. To capture the most significant events by observation, stand, sit, or kneel to view the event from different vantage points. This tests the effectiveness and validity of the survey. Practice watching and determine the best procedure before inaugurating the observational survey.

3. To draw objective conclusions, create a survey agenda of specific events, colors, types of people, actions, or whatever. Observing should be as disciplined and structured as any of our other data collection methods.

4. To get the subjects at ease, particularly in an industrial or commercial setting where the subjects are in close quarters, ask their permission to just watch for a few minutes. At first they will act unnatural, but in a short period they will forget your presence and return to the way they usually work. It's just like having a camcorder turned on all the time at a party. Very quickly people adapt and act natural.

We're looking for the common threads or patterns to draw conclusions from observational surveys, just like the other data collection methods.

BETSEY

> I am far too busy during a party to stand around with a clipboard watching the guests. This doesn't seem very practical.

Before your next party, put together the survey agenda list with vital information you need to observe. Hire and instruct a high school student on how to take the data. Occasionally during the affair make sure the observations are being taken from vantage points that are not invasive or disturbing and make sure the data is being recorded accurately. Observational surveys do not take genius, but they do require thought and structure.

Observing is simple. It's fast and inexpensive. We take for granted all the market intelligence that can be gathered by just watching how people use our products, react to our services, enter and move through our stores, and convey their likes and dislikes with body language. Let me urge that you take watching seriously and treat it like any other primary data collection tool.

VITAL THOUGHTS

- Save time and gain market perspective—interview the gurus and experts first.
- Use all the survey tools to constantly validate answers.
- Do not interview too many people or too few—just enough to hear repetitious answers.
- Talk to anyone you want by using persistence and communications civility.
- Interviewing consumers, industrial, or commercial people employs the same methods and techniques to build respondent trust and openness.
- There are no indiscrete questions, only indiscrete answers!

CHAPTER 8

THE FINAL MARKETING
INTELLIGENCE REPORT

The phones are quiet, the mail surveys have been tallied, and the plane engines are shut down after your trekking to interview users and gurus. Now you have to write the report. Management wants to know what all these scraps of intelligence mean and how they will form a new set of marketing tactics and strategies.

Marketing intelligence is useful new market knowledge formed from fragmented facts, opinions, and observations. The final report is the objective, credible, and logical presentation of market conditions focused upon the *vital* questions that demanded answers. Its value will be to illuminate market-based alternatives for management decisions and actions to change the business.

We've talked about all forms of business decision makers— sole proprietors, partners, and product managers. Ultimately, market intelligence is converted, through decisions by those in authority, to changes in the business. Each of the business environments managed by these decision makers is different. Small business CEOs make decisions about facts that are presented in very informal ways. They usually process information from verbal communications or written summary statements, but in most cases will not need or take the time to fully understand market intelligence reports in the detail required by large corporate management. [*These entrepreneurs have extremely deep biases about their markets and should take the time to let an objective and realistic view reshape their views. Too often I hear, "I don't have the time to read all that detail," or, "I know what they need." In short, their minds are made up and they don't want to be confused with the facts.*]

I'm going to discuss structure and detail level typically required *by managers of a larger company*. Is it applicable for the entrepreneur or small company owner? Absolutely, but I know the vast majority of them will not take the time to construct the market intelligence report I'm suggesting for use by marketers in larger companies.

Here's what I've told these solo business owners. You don't have to write up a detailed report. I know you think your business is unique and that you know your business and customers better than anyone else does. Do yourself a favor—go out and objectively collect facts and opinions. Write down everything you hear; don't filter out anything. Find a quiet time and place to really analyze what you heard. Forget that the answers may conflict with your preconceived notions. Accept that the market wants change or that competition is forcing you to change. Ask your spouse, partner, or friend to read your notes, customer surveys, or the articles you've collected. Discuss what each of you learned from the market information, then make your decisions about what to offer and how to serve customers. Take this outline of a marketing intelligence report as a guide to doing your own data collection.

Here's the report format I find most useful in presenting the marketing intelligence results. It's constructed with these sections:

1. A Background Statement
2. Scope of Work and Mission
3. Methodology of the Work
4. Key Findings
5. Observations
6. Conclusions
7. Recommendations
8. Appendix   I—Industry Contacts and Demographics
9. Appendix   II—Market Investigators and Contractors
10. Appendix   III—Field Interviews and Tabulated Data
11. Appendix   IV—Detailed Findings

Let's discuss the content of each report section:

THE BACKGROUND STATEMENT

The marketing intelligence work was initiated because there are market conditions management doesn't fully understand. It could be competition encroachment, declining sales, or a need for new product ideas. The report writer refreshes the reader's memory with the history, importance, and urgency that caused the marketing intelligence effort to take place.

THE SCOPE OF WORK OR MISSION

We'll get the answers, but what are the questions? In this section, the prioritized market questions are displayed and linked to a potential marketing tactic or strategic change. This linking is crucial to reestablish the value or investment management has made to get the answers. In this section it is wise to restate the deliverables management was promised at the outset of the work. [*Managers have a habit of not remembering what they agreed to accept as a finished report product. I like to remind them.*]

METHODOLOGY OF THE WORK

This is a straightforward, brief discussion of how the work was accomplished. State where and how the secondary intelligence gathering was conducted. List the general kinds of resources that were used. Describe the primary research effort and rationalize the selection of the interview method, the number of interviewees, or the survey technique and sample size determination. Finish this section by describing how the information was sorted and analyzed and the conclusions drawn.

KEY FINDINGS

This is the executive summary that addresses the vital questions, more or less, as they appear in the *Scope of Work* section. You'll be detailing these findings in Appendix IV of the report, so it isn't necessary to mire management down at this point. If they're really interested in detail, they'll either stop your verbal presentation or move to the appendix. Keep the information here brief, using bulleted statements and a very matter-of-fact tone.

It's in this section that your credibility is on the line. Did you really grasp the essence of the mission? Did you really find just the right experts or talk to enough people to form the concrete finding? State your findings with the conviction you have developed from the collected information.

OBSERVATIONS

Market answers are not crystal clear. If we could interview 10,000 people about a subject, we would really be comfortable we had accurate opinions, but we don't have that luxury. The *Observations* section is the intuitive, not numeric, findings you have about the new market knowledge. These are the market conditions that cannot be supported by the collected evidence, but you believe they are the prevailing trends, undercurrents, and subliminal forces that must be factored into any tactical or strategic changes.

Typically, after management understands the *Key Findings* and *Conclusions* sections, it's ready to process a decision. That's why I always put *Observations* ahead of *Conclusions*—because it causes management to not jump to conclusions on just the facts.

CONCLUSIONS

Here's where all the marketing intelligence work comes together. Up to now, we've merged market facts and opinions into an objective report of the market knowledge as we see it. Now we tell management what we believe are the *vital* conclusions about the market environment. It's not the place or the time to pull any punches. This is risky, because managers don't usually want to hear either bad news or information that contradicts their perception of the business. But, believe it or not, these hard statements are what good managers want to hear. So tell them how it really is.

RECOMMENDATIONS

You've performed the marketing intelligence fieldwork, or at least monitored its collection. You now probably know more about the specifics of the market conditions than anyone. Management is open to your recommendations based upon your market knowledge. I think it's a good idea to give them your insights.

APPENDIX I—INDUSTRY CONTACTS AND DEMOGRAPHICS

The purpose of this section is to support the credibility of the findings. List all the experts, users, specifiers, buyers, and distribution managers interviewed during the study. Provide their names, titles, company affiliations, and relevant experience. Also detail the demographic mix of survey respondents.

APPENDIX II—MARKET INVESTIGATORS AND CONTRACTORS

Who performed the marketing intelligence work? These are the internal company people who did the interviews, put the questionnaires together, solicited interview candidates, and wrote the report. This isn't just to give people "screen credits"—you are reinforcing the professionalism and credibility of the staff who contributed to the key findings and conclusions.

If you hired outside contractors to perform part or all of the work, list who they are, who their clients are, why they were selected, and what their compensation was to complete the assignment.

APPENDIX III—FIELD INTERVIEWS AND TABULATED DATA

This section is critical from management's perspective because they want to "feel" the actual words that have driven the findings. Report the interview comments in their entirety. Quote the respondent as exactly as you can. This is not the place to editorialize what people said, or interpret what you thought they wanted to say.

There are two ways I use to detail field interviews: the *first* is to list each contact, and then detail the answers each provided for all the vital questions; the *second* is to list all the respondents' answers for each question under each question. I prefer the latter method because I feel it's more productive for management to see the composite of all responses to a particular question than to precisely know who said what about which question. Additionally, I have usually told all respondents that their answers would be melded for anonymity, and I want to honor that commitment.

The tabulations from surveys in some final format are included in the section so that management, if they are so inclined, can dig into the numbers to assure themselves of the findings' accuracy or completeness.

APPENDIX IV—DETAILED FINDINGS

In the *Key Findings* section, a general finding was stated for each *vital* question. There should not have been a deep background of support presented in that section. Management assumes you reached the finding after careful consideration of facts and opinions. The purpose of this section is to present those details that created the *Key Findings*. Under each vital question detail the how, who, how many, where, and why that led to the finding.

APPENDIX V—SECONDARY REFERENCES

This section merely presents a bibliography of the secondary source materials used during the study. I can also list individuals who provided the secondary research from their files. The more real people references, the more credible the data, and the more acceptance the report will gain from management.

APPENDIX VI—SUPPORTING DOCUMENTS

Every marketing intelligence project accumulates pounds of competitive brochures, outside reports, and supportive articles. Include only the most relevant materials in this section.

You've worked hard to understand the market; now work doubly hard to present new knowledge so that anybody can understand it.

VITAL THOUGHTS

- Convert marketing intelligence into management decisions through concise and coherent reports.
- Tell management: what you went to find, how and where you found it, what you heard, and what you believe it means to the business.
- Support your market work only with facts and credible opinions.
- Acknowledge what the market is saying, then apply your experienced bias.

CHAPTER 9

SOLVING REAL PROBLEMS

Now let's apply what we've learned. Here are the customer and competitor issues:

- The current total market size in units and dollars.
- The current buyers' value strata in units and dollars.
- The competitor's performance and share of market.
- The customers' new buying preferences.
- The customers' needs for technical and service support.
- The impacting market, technology, and service trends.

We've learned about getting answers using these intelligence collection methods:

- Secondary data sources: periodicals, reports, data bases, Yellow Pages, newspapers, government data and internal company information.
- Primary data sources: personal interviews, telephone surveys, mail surveys, focus panels, and observation.

We'll use these to solve your market intelligence needs. I'd say when we've discussed each of your businesses, you will have what you need to begin constructing new business and marketing strategies.

JOHN'S ACCOUNTING BUSINESS

John, earlier you wanted to know how to be perceived differently than your competition. We spent some time talking about changing the definition of your business from accounting and bookkeeping to a cash flow consultant.

You also were here to learn how to close more sales. I believe that researching the financial characteristics of your potential customers and then concentrating on marketing to these groups will automatically increase your closing rate. But you can't close sales if small companies have barriers to working with outside consultants, so we must identify those barriers and find ways to overcome them. [*This is not easy. Most small businesspeople don't like to open up as to why they like or dislike others intruding into their businesses, especially when it comes to money matters.*]

We have two vital questions: (1) what size companies have major cash flow problems? and (2) what are the key concerns that potential customers have about hiring consultants like you?

The cash question can be broken down into specific information requirements. First, you need cash flow profiles for your potential customers that include:

- What their typical dollar revenue is.
- How much cash is needed to support their future sales (cash for inventory, advertising, etc.).
- How long it typically takes for each business to collect receivables.
- How much money a bank usually allows each business to borrow.

Second, these cash related answers must be arranged by size of company and by type of firm (retail, manufacturing, service).

Now, where do we find the answers? When a business must borrow cash to support its growth, banks review the potential borrower's cash plans and evaluate the probability that a loan can be paid back in a reasonable time. Bankers make this evaluation by comparing what the businessperson says with an accumulated history of many other similar businesses that have borrowed money. These histories come from within the bank, or facts collected from bank cooperatives. The financial status and loan payback history of thousands of similar businesses are merged together into a report. Now, these financial facts would be a great source of cash flow and financial status information because they cover all types of businesses. They are also sorted into business size categories from the smallest to the largest. So,

John, your job is to get these composite reports. The leading sets of data are listed below.

What to Look for	Where to Find It
The Robert Morris Report	Your banker
U.S. Internal Revenue Service, Statistics of Income	Library
U.S. Bureau of Census, Census of Income	Library

These reports are not easily obtained, but be persistent. What you need next is the number of businesses in your locale, grouped by type of business, and by company size as measured by either sales revenue or number of employees. Finding this *is* easy. Let's see where we would look.

These demographics are collected annually by various levels of state, regional, and local governments. They use them for property and utility planning, taxation, and governmental services. The national government also collects the data as part of the census.

What to Look for	Where to Find it
State/local Census of Business	Library—government department
State/local sales tax data	Library, city hall, tax office
Business directories	Library, chamber of commerce

Now that you've secured the composite financial information and the number of businesses arranged by size, location, and type, here are my suggestions for processing the data.

Constructing Respondent Candidates

1. Select the sizes and types of businesses that fit your potential customer profile: small, medium, or large, and retail, service, or manufacturing. Now from the banking data, identify the company sizes and business activity types that appear to have a cash flow problem. As a screening tool, I would construct a ratio using sales revenue divided by current assets.

2. Find the information about these kinds of businesses from the appropriate columns, pages, or reports in the documents. Figure 9–1 is an example of the detail to look for in the government data.

3. Construct average cash flow ratios for each potential customer category using financial information obtained from banking and accounting sources.

4. Count the number of companies listed in the local business directories that meet the criteria. Then make a list of those candidates, including name, ZIP code, and telephone number.

Now, John, your next question was about smaller company attitudes toward using consultants. Let's list the specifics needed to get the right answers:

What types and sizes of business usually hire consultants?

How long do they typically engage a consultant to work on problems?

How much do they typically pay a consultant per hour or per day?

Why do they like or dislike using consultants?

What has been their past experience with consultants?

These answers can't be found in a book, but there could be a study on consultants to small business that would partially answer your questions. You'll validate any secondary findings on attitudes about cash management and general financial consulting by collecting primary market intelligence.

Here's a possible shortcut to understanding small business attitudes: consider whether it is reasonable to assume that attitudes about financial consultants are the same as attitudes about other professional service providers to your potential clients. Why? Customers generally will lump attitudes about services together. So, primary research involves asking other types of consultants, "How do your clients really feel about using outside consultants?" Get the idea?

JOHN

Sure, but where are these people or organizations? Why would they tell me about their clients? I might be a possible competitor.

FIGURE 9–1
Our City Firm Size and Worker Mix
Firm Size by Number of Employees

	Total Number of Firms	<5	<10	<20	<50	<100	<500	<999	<1,000	<10,000	10,000+
Agriculture	1,632	1,000	388	144	70	17	11	1	1	0	0
Mining	37	18	8	5	3	1	1	0	0	0	0
Construction	4,311	2,643	845	453	260	69	37	2	1	0	0
Manufacturing	2,427	779	567	422	363	148	119	13	11	2	2
Transportation, communication, utilities	1,102	467	271	175	120	37	26	3	3	0	1
Wholesale	2,599	1,227	704	371	207	56	31	2	2	0	0
Retail	7,991	4,257	2,002	911	562	166	81	7	5	1	1
Finance, insurance, real estate	4,106	2,309	824	457	306	104	84	10	9	2	1
Services	18,460	9,820	4,031	2,166	1,350	510	479	53	43	5	3
Total	42,665	22,520	9,640	5,140	3,241	1,108	869	91	75	10	8
Percent of Total Firms		53%	23%	12%	8%	3%	2%	—	—	—	—

Source: Adapted from U.S. Small Business Administration data.

Service Suppliers and Competitive Consultants

Good questions. Business consultants are all around us, either here locally or in a distant city or country. Surprisingly, they will be open to talk about customer attitudes if they don't perceive you as a competitor and you are too far away to be a threat. During the opening of the interview, you'll build a rapport because you both may have the same problems with customers' attitudes. It sounds a little strange, but it works. The key is to make them comfortable that you are not and will not be a competitor.

Surely these kinds of local consultants currently serve your potential customers:

- Insurance agents and brokers.
- Advertising and public relations firms.
- Printers and desktop publishing contractors.
- Temporary employee service companies.
- Bankers, credit unions, and loan companies.
- Major distributors.
- Painting, landscaping, and maintenance contractors.

In other words, any business serving your potential customer must have been in a consulting capacity *before* they could sell their goods or services. They had to establish trust, develop a rapport, and understand the customer's fears, apprehensions, motivations, and decision-making rationale. You need to know how they overcame your potential customer's resistance. Having those customer insights, you can sell your financial services.

Very well, we know who to talk with and what we want to learn. How do we proceed? Just ask these consultants how they did it through a combination of telephone and personal interviews. Here's how to approach it:

1. Consult the local Yellow Pages and look up three suppliers of insurance, painting, banking services, etc. Note the name of the owner, if it's in the ad, and the phone number.

2. Go to the library and find the Yellow Pages for a city or town at least 50 miles away. Look up two consultants that do *exactly* the same work you propose to do.
3. Construct a survey agenda and conduct the telephone or personal interviews.

Other sources include extensive studies of similar businesses. These surveys often become the basis for new government legislation, book or magazine articles, or the marketing rationale for promotions of goods or services to specific customers. These survey findings may not be exactly to the point of your questions but they usually are close enough to draw some observations and conclusions. Here are possible sources for these studies:

Government Agencies and Trade Associations

Governmental business-related agencies support legislative recommendations with survey data. This data is submitted as evidence during the deliberations and hearings. In addition, advocacy organizations dealing with matters of commerce, labor, environmental protection, and worker safety constantly poll large numbers of businesses for their attitudes. These reports are available to us, the public. Here are some techniques to locate and secure the material you want.

All government documents, except classified material, are available to the public, but they are sometimes tedious to find. A government repository library will have these publications, so that's a place to start. Before going to the library, list keywords about your interests (for example: business owner attitudes; consultant to business; costs for outside business counsel; financial management in business). Ask the librarian for help.

You and I are represented by elected officials at local, regional, state, and federal levels. The legislator's staff is usually helpful in directing you to exact government departments for the location of relevant surveys. The legislators and staff are public servants. You are their customer. The information is probably public information. Government personnel are there to assist your needs. Look in the front section of the telephone white pages, or call your local newspaper or library reference desk. They will quickly get you the correct telephone and mailing address for your government representative.

Trade associations and magazines serve similar businesses. For a nominal annual fee, members receive information on business sector trends, economic issues, and business attitudes of the general association membership. Associations survey their members and consolidate the results in periodically published journals or newsletters. The best way to get this information is to find a member of an organization and just ask to borrow the publication. Additionally, I have found these trade associations quite willing to provide parts of studies or at least the published conclusions. Most libraries have the publication *Encyclopedia of Associations*, published by Gale Research, Inc. Use it to look up insurance, bank, architect, etc. associations. Note the executive director's name, as well as the phone number, number of members, and purpose of the association. Find several pertinent trade magazines in the library. Locate the magazine masthead, usually four to 10 pages from the front cover. Find the researcher or librarian listed, and record his or her name. Be sure to also record the telephone number for the editorial offices, not the advertising department. Telephone interviews with these sources are the most efficient.

Ask the Customer

Lastly, get the information by asking potential customers, "What do you really think about using consultants in running your business?" Take a survey of their attitudes by asking only *vital* questions. Collect the data, arrange answers to make sense, and draw observations and conclusions. It's simple, direct, fast, and relevant.

You know where the customers are from local directories and the Yellow Pages. Business directories should also list the number of employees, the owner's or manager's name, and the type of business. If you are interested in businesses in specific areas or particular streets, go to the telephone company and use a backward directory. Conduct an observational survey by driving around the area you want to serve. Match business locations

with your potential customer profile or criteria. Note the business name and then find it in the telephone directory.
Let's condense what we've talked about:

What to Look for	Where to Find it
Existing consultants	Yellow Pages, directories
Directory of Trade Associations	Library, Yellow Pages
Trade magazines	Library
Government studies	Library, government offices
Direct surveys	Conducted by yourself

Well, John, now you know where and how to get the information to answer your questions. [*He sure is less negative than when he came in. My sense is that he realizes it's okay to not have all the answers.*]

JOHN

It seems too simple.

It really is simple. We make too much of finding data. It's all around us—we just don't recognize its value until we have the right questions in hand. Then these everyday tools make finding answers easy.

BETSEY'S CATERING BUSINESS

During our survey discussions we spent some time developing methods to answer Betsey's earlier questions about how to define new products and whether catering customers would buy items other than food. Now let's look at her data needs. The key catering business questions are:

1. How much do or would her customers pay for nonfood catered items? What nonfood items would they buy?
2. What are the franchisee potentials in other areas?

Let's start with question 1. What nonfood items are part of a catered party, and how much do customers pay for them? Who has these answers? Any ideas?

SUSAN

The customer does.

BILL

How about party or catering products distributors or dealers?

Good, anybody else have a suggestion?

ANNE

Sure. I think party planners would be a good source.

Alright, let's list your ideas:

• Customers and party givers.
• Party product distributors and dealers.
• Party planners and party rental firms.

Here are a few of my ideas:

• Other caterers.
• Florists and printers.
• Valet parking services.
• Public relations and advertising firms.

That's a good selection to get what we need. Remember, the best way to identify who has the answers is to stand in the customer's shoes. Look through their windows to identify which businesses may be important in making their event a success. This applies to all of your businesses—parties, bookstores, bookkeeping and cash management, wooden toys, etc. Once you have selected the vendors, suppliers, and services, it's simple to detail people to contact for answers.

What to Look for	*Where to Find it*
Customers	Your sales records, newspaper social pages
Planners, distributors, etc.	Yellow Pages
Caterers, valet parkers	Directories, Yellow Pages

BETSEY

> I don't understand why the newspaper social pages are a good source.

Think about the wedding announcement page. By the time you read about it, the reception is over. The guests have gone but the bills are just arriving. Right then, the parents usually know to the penny how much each item has cost. They know how many of each item they bought. They have definite opinions about catering services. It's an ideal time to contact them for objective and probably some emotional opinions. Scanning the newspaper is a great source of marketing intelligence contacts.

You have the contacts for other suppliers and recent catering users. Construct the interview guide and conduct some interviews. I suggest a telephone survey of vendors and users. You may want to validate the telephone results with personal interviews or maybe a focus panel to probe more deeply for new nonfood ideas.

Now for question 2, how to determine the potential for new franchisee sales volume. Let's imagine you have picked out some distant geographic area, a city or region. We will use San Diego as an example for a potential franchise site. Let's also suppose you know nothing about San Diego, its neighborhoods, business community, competitive catering climate, or attitudes about the use of caterers. Where do we start?

A reasonable first assumption is that your existing customer profile information is accurate. The second assumption is that these local profiles may be typical for San Diego. In other words, what works here will most likely apply there. If we accept these assumptions and begin, we need to answer these questions about San Diego:

1. How many homeowners and businesses have demographics comparable to your current customer base, including income for homeowners, and businesses grouped by number of employees.

2. How many existing competitors are there? Does the 80/20 rule apply?

3. What prices do caterers charge for food and nonfood items at catered affairs?

4. What's the referral and distribution process between party goods and service suppliers?
5. How difficult will it be for a new catering firm to penetrate the San Diego market?

If we can answer those five questions, we should know:

* The catering unit potential.
* The prices paid to determine the current total market.
* The current level of competition.
* The barriers to entry for a new supplier.
* The elements to develop a franchisee forecast.

What would your secondary and primary market intelligence plan include to get this information?

BETSEY

> I'd have to go all the way to the San Diego Library and look up the residential—

Wait a minute, it's right here in our library. I assume you're talking about U.S. census data.

BETSEY

> I forgot that most libraries have a complete set of the census data. I'll compare the San Diego household information with our city to determine the number of household units having similar demographics, particularly with respect to income. I'd do the same thing for businesses.

That's a great start, let me add to your analysis. We've got two sets of city data, here and in San Diego. The information is comparable because it was collected and reported by the same process. The first thing we do is see how much greater or smaller the residential unit potential is for San Diego. Next, from the *Sales and Marketing Management* data, we'll compare the buying power indexes of the two cities to estimate which city's householders are more or less affluent. Then we will derive a simple new index to estimate the San Diego unit potential. Let's get the information organized and display it in Figure 9–2.

FIGURE 9–2
Comparisons between San Diego and Our City

Column	D	E	F	G	H
Row					
8					
9					
10					
11	Number of	Food	Restaurants	EBI	Businesses
12	Households	Sales	& Bars	Index	over 20
13		(000, 000)			Employees
14					
15					
16	San Diego	906, 700	$ 3, 671	$ 2, 176	1.1084	3, 241
17					
18	Our City	561, 300	$ 2, 052	$ 1, 175	0.6271	2, 113
19					
20					
21	The data suggests San Diego has:				
22	– 61% more households than our city.				
23	– 53% more businesses with 20 employees.				
24	– 11% more spent for food.				
25	– 15% more spent for eating and drinking-out.				
26	– 77% more effective buying income per household.				
27					
28					
29					

} Observations

Source: Adapted from *Sales & Marketing Management Survey of Buying Power*, 1990, data.

BETSEY

From only two pieces of data we're able to get all that?

Sure. Remember we're deriving practical information. It's not 100 percent accurate, but it's probably close enough to make some decisions.

Now what about the second set of data needed, the number of competitors and their market share?

BETSEY

> Go to the library again, get the San Diego Yellow Pages and count the number of companies listing themselves under the heading *Caterers*.

Perfect. Incidentally, there is a very interesting way to calibrate or maybe validate the number of unit or dollar market potentials by using the Yellow Pages information in a different way. Count the number of caterers listed in our city's Yellow Pages and the caterers listed in San Diego. Now divide the number of caterers in each city into the total number of residences and businesses for each city. The results you will get are the potential residences or businesses each caterer in each city *could* have as customers. These specific customer unit numbers are meaningless and we won't use them. But we will compare the percentage differences between the numbers. Take our city's potential number and calculate the percentage difference from San Diego. If the percentage difference is too great, like 200 or 300 percent, more information is needed before you draw your conclusions about the markets. If the difference is minor, we've achieved some validation. Let's see if that works. Figure 9–3 illustrates the correlation between the two information sources.

So what we've done is to use counts from the Yellow Pages combined with census data to derive market opportunity. We know the level of competition in our city and when we know whether San Diego has more or fewer caterers to serve their potential residential or commercial customer base, we can make some decisions about how hard it may be to enter the San Diego market. In short, we know whether San Diego is oversupplied or undersupplied with caterers compared to our city.

Now what about the market share or 80/20 rule information? How are we going to get that?

BETSEY

> It seems to me that I should move to telephone interviews because there probably isn't secondary data that would be useful.

Not necessarily. Don't be too sure it doesn't exist. Always assume that what you need is available. I would make a few calls to the business section editors of San Diego newspapers and magazines and inquire whether they have run any articles on

FIGURE 9–3

Comparisons of Households and Caterers

Column	D	E	F
Row			
8			
9			
10			
11	Number of	Number of	Households per
12	Households	Caterers	Caterer
13			
14			
15			
16 San Diego	906, 700	275	3, 297
17			
18 Our City	561, 300	206	2, 721
19			
20			

21 The data suggests San Diego has:
22   – 61% more households than our city.
23   – 21% fewer caterers per household than our city.
24   – 31% more caterers than our city.
25
26
27
28
29

Source: Adapted from *Sales & Marketing Management Survey of Buying Power*, 1990, data and the Yellow Pages.

the San Diego catering industry. As a matter of fact, I just saw a roster of San Diego catering companies in their local business publication. Figure 9–4 displays summary results of a San Diego catering industry survey.

I want you to check my arithmetic, but here's what I learned from this data:

- Total sales represented by these ten caterers equal $9,834,000.
- Total number of events (units) catered equals 2,611.
- Total sales of firms also listing employees equal $9,134,000.
- Total number of employees in those firms equals 155.
- Total sales for firms reporting food sales equal $8,884,000.
- Total sales for food, of that group, equal $5,903,000.

Now here's the new information:

- Average sales for the Top 10 caterers equal $983,400.
- Average catering sales for an event equal $2,558.
- Average sales per catering firm employee equal $58,929.
- Food is 66 percent of total catering sales.
- Commercial events equal about 70 percent of sales, and private events, about 30 percent.

If we assume the 80/20 rule, then:

- Total market for catering equals $12,292,500 ($9,834,000/ .8).
- The number of caterers, similar to those reporting, is 50 (10/.2).
- Average sales for 80 percent of the caterers equal $61,462 [($12,292,500 − $9,834,000) ÷ (50 − 10)].

How do you feel about those market numbers, Betsey?

BETSEY

They're too low. If I looked at the San Diego Yellow Pages I would find hundreds of businesses claiming to be caterers. They would be restaurants, hotels, most delis, and some fast food chains. I don't think you can estimate the true total market from this little data.

FIGURE 9-4
The San Diego Catering Market—1991

Important → *Wouldn't tell*

Disregard →

Add (000)

Rank	Rank Last Year	Caterer Address Phone	Gross Catering Sales for Fiscal 1990 $ Thousands	Gross Food Sales for Fiscal 1990 $ Thousands	No. of Full-Service Events Catered in 1991	No. of Full-time Employees	% Gross Sales '90 Commercial	Private
1.	1	Picnic People and Festivities Catering 8395 Camino Santa Fe, Suite C San Diego 92121 587-1717	3,156	1,552	wnd	46	90	10
2.	7	Tony Kopas & Associates/Tastes P.O. Box 8657 La Jolla 92038 277-8822	1,500	1,500	658	31	35	65
3.	4	Carriage Trade Catering 4660 La Jolla Village Drive, Suite 650 San Diego 92122 455-0400	1,314	845	262	16	70	30
4.	Not On List	Continental Catering 6062 Lake Murray Blvd. La Mesa 92042 698-3500	900	700	550	35	25	75
5.	Not On List	Art Bolic Catering 8360 Clairemont Mesa Blvd., Suite 112 San Diego 92111 292-6944	700	700	300	wnd	75	25
6.	9	Culinary Associates 13163 Portofino Del Mar 92014 481-7227	672	209	85	5	70	30
7.	Not On List	A Catered Affair 9265 Activity Road, Suite 108 San Diego 92126 271-8180	542	322	311	8	70	30
8.	Not On List	Party Pro's 5567 Kearny Villa Road San Diego 92123 292-5247	500	wnd	120	8	95	5
9.	10	At Your Service Catering 3636 Ashford St. San Diego 92111 482-9797	450	wnd	250	3	80	20
10.	Not On List	Mavis & Cyn's Catering and Sweet Co. 7353 El Cajon Blvd. La Mesa 91941 236-1312	100	75	75	3	75	25

Total = $9,834

Source: The caterers.
It is not the intent of this list to endorse the participants nor to imply that a caterer's size or numerical rank indicates its quality of service.

Researched by Susan Beel

Source: *San Diego Business Journal*, September 1991.

I agree, we don't have enough or good enough information. However, I am comfortable that we know something about the businesses shown in Figure 9-4.

Remember, use others' market intelligence results before spending the time and money to generate your own primary data. But question any conclusions you reach.

Back to the idea of a telephone survey. It's a good one, but who are your target respondents?

BETSEY

> I would call the food, rental furniture, music, tent, and florist suppliers. I'd introduce myself, and say that I'm developing a report on catering in various cities around the country. I'd mention that they should not tell me anything they think is confidential. Some of my questions would be:
>
> * Approximately how many catered parties do you think are held in San Diego each month, week, or year?
> * Would you say there are more residential or more business catering activities?
> * Could you make an estimate as to what percent is residential?
> * Could you give me, off the top of your head, who you think are the top three caterers in the city?
> * I know some caterers are more expensive than others, but of those caterers you named, which ones have you heard are the most expensive?
> * I noticed a great many caterers listed in your current Yellow Pages and I compared that to the Yellow Pages of a few years ago. It looks like you are enjoying a catering business growth. What's your opinion about the catering market?
>
> I used an open-ended question so I would be able to talk about a lot of topics.

The answers to those questions should reveal much about the market share and also give you real insights into the dynamics of the San Diego market. After talking with 8 to 10 suppliers, you should know about San Diego's referral network, opinions about competitors, and other elements to develop a market penetration strategy. One topic not understood from those telephone calls is the price for catering and the nonfood items market.

BETSEY

> I thought I would take your suggestion about the wedding an-
> nouncements in the local newspaper. I can get the parents' names
> from the paper, look up the addresses in the phone book, and de-
> velop my sampling base. I don't think a telephone interview would
> be good because the respondents wouldn't have all those prices at
> their fingertips. I think a mail survey would be better. We have a
> "party planner guide" and I'll offer that as an incentive to send
> back the questionnaire.

Won't there be a great deal of bias in your answers by only using
wedding receptions?

BETSEY

> I thought about that, but my experience is that prices quoted for
> food, bands, tents, and so forth are the same for most catered par-
> ties, regardless of the type of celebration.

You may want to validate your pricing experience by reviewing
your historic fees for different types of parties. You also wanted
to know if there was a possibility of using existing caterers, in
your city or elsewhere, to distribute your line of nonfood items.
What are you going to do about that?

BETSEY

> I just have to ask them directly. The calls I just talked about were
> all to San Diego, not our city. Any new business idea should start
> locally, where I can control the situation. My local competitors
> don't like me, so I'm sure I would get very biased answers if I
> called them. I'll assume the nonfood answers I get from San Diego
> will apply to our city.

My suggestion is that you personally not make those calls. Hire
a graduate student from a local university business school. But
you develop the interview agenda because you're a caterer and
know the sensitivities of how you would respond to the questions. Here are the steps I'd suggest:

1. Create the introduction along these lines: "I'm a graduate student hired to conduct a survey for a leading catering products company. We're collecting opinions from
   other caterers like yourself about how receptive you

would be to buying nonfood products or services from a firm that is also in your business and possibly operating in the market area you serve." Then go on to ask specific questions about items, price, and delivery.

2. Have the student practice by calling you. Have the student also call a caterer in a nearby city.

3. Adjust the question sequence and wording until it is smooth.

4. Monitor the first several calls to judge the respondents' resistance. Then readjust the questionnaire.

I'll add only a few more suggestions to validate your market intelligence plan, which is a good one. They are:

• Call the San Diego caterers who have the largest Yellow Page ads for quotes for specific items to serve small and large groups. Identifying who you are will take finesse and I'll leave that to you. I might say that I was a professional party planner for businesses and that a national company has retained me to organize an event for their local office.

• Call the editors of two catering trade magazines or associations requesting recent articles on regional market size.

You're going to have a great set of data to base new decisions on.

PETER'S SCALES BUSINESS

Peter's marketing needs are to expand his business through new international distribution channels and to keep a closer eye on his competition. Customers and markets are served differently around the globe. American industry has unique reseller channels and marketing policies that do *not* conform to other countries' traditions. My observation is, as we move towards worldwide consolidation, international distribution strategies will be homogeneous. Goods and services moving between nations will mandate standard distribution discounts regardless of locale.

Peter, you're trying to establish new distribution in foreign countries, but what specific questions do you need answered?

PETER

> My impression is that barriers exist that deter acceptance of American scales in the Far East and parts of Europe. I have visited these countries and cannot get a clear picture of how distribution works; nor can I determine which instrument distributors in each country would be best suited to handle our scale line.

Let's take the first problem of characterizing distribution patterns. Do you have some feel for where we should start?

PETER

> Yes. I know there are directories of importers and sales representatives for most countries and regions. But I don't know how to access the bureaucracy to get the specifics. I also know that the U.S. Commerce Department assists American manufacturers in locating potential business contacts in foreign countries.

Remember I said to sit back and try to imagine who has the information you want? Also think what kind of a report or book might exist that has all the answers to your questions? This exercise permits considering nontraditional sources and marketing intelligence techniques. The secondary data collection techniques we will use should apply to any country.

Foreign Secondary Information Sources

We're looking for a foreign marketing model of the value-added chain, the chart showing users, dealers, distributors, etc. (See Figure 4–2.) Here are the sources and sequence to follow:

1. Foreign country Yellow Pages are not exactly like ours but the information is grouped in a similar fashion. Go to the page headings for *instruments, scales, weights and measures*, and *scientific apparatus* to find suppliers.

2. Trade directories for all industrialized regions are available and list addresses, phone numbers and key individuals for similar product manufacturers, distributors, importers, and manufacturer's representatives.

3. Foreign embassies all have trade and industry officers responsible for facilitating working relationships between their country's firms and American suppliers or buyers.
4. Importer/exporter directories are available from the U.S. Commerce Department and foreign embassies.
5. Foreign trade publications cover quality assurance, measurement and testing, and good manufacturing or research practices.
6. Foreign newspapers and business magazines covering international commerce often run special supplements listing local agencies that facilitate partnering opportunities. Distribution channel partner information may be included. I'll mention the *Financial Times* of London and the *Economist* as two publications that regularly have these supplements.

Here's a summary:

What to Look for	Where to Find it
Yellow Pages	Library and embassies
Trade directories	Library, U.S. Trade Association
Foreign embassies	Major cities or Washington, D.C.
Importer/exporter directory	Major U.S. exporters
Trade publications	Library or corporate libraries
Newspapers and magazines	Major libraries

What are you going to do with that information?

Foreign Primary Techniques

PETER

Make lists of potential respondents for either a mail or telephone survey.

Absolutely. Also, these articles are especially helpful to identify gurus or experts. Reporters usually reference experts by name and affiliation. These are your prime interview targets. When you call the gurus, you'll be able to set them at ease by referring to the article and matters of interest to them. The content of these articles is an excellent catalyst to frame questions.

PETER

> You mentioned getting the names of companies that manufacture or sell products similar to mine. Do you mean other scale manufacturers?

Yes! Competitors should really understand how scale distribution works in their country. One phone call and a well executed interview could produce all the information you need. But I'm going to suggest that you concentrate on companies making other kinds of instruments and let me tell you why.

Let's assume the distribution channels used for scales are the same as those used for micrometers, spectrometers, gauges, or any measuring instrument. You've somehow obtained the product or marketing manager's name at a company supplying these types of products. After your introduction, he should not perceive you as a competitor because his company doesn't make scales. The product manager doesn't take a risk by talking to you, and has a potential reward by getting U.S. distribution information for measuring devices. These contacts should be open to discuss how distribution of scales could be accomplished.

My message is, don't be reluctant to call anyone, whether a competitor or a supplier of products serving a mutual customer for similar applications. Everyone likes to trade information, provided they perceive low risk in the exchange.

PETER

> You really think the direct approach would work?

I know it does. Here are my suggestions to develop your next steps in primary market data collection:

1. Primary validation: After absorbing the secondary information, telephone surveys or open-ended interviews are my preferred methods to determine distribution trends, attitudes, and identification of sales representatives.
2. Foreign information sources: Arrange the call sequence to talk to and get information from the most knowledgeable to the least knowledgeable in instrument distribution. I'd say the contacting order should be like this:

- Gurus and experts.
- Foreign marketing and sales managers of similar products.
- Trade magazine editors and reporters.
- Foreign importers.
- Potential foreign customer purchasing agents.
- Foreign country distributors and resellers.
- Foreign embassy trade officers.
- U.S. exporters.
- U.S. Commerce Department officials.

To get you started, look at Figure 9–5. Here are specific foreign business office telephone numbers at the U.S. Department of Commerce. I took these from the 1989 Edition of the *Business and Investment Almanac*, published by Dow Jones-Irwin. Peter, over time government office numbers may change, but, in my experience, you will always be directed to the new telephone extension.

3. Setting appointments: Foreign business cultures are more formalized than we are in setting appointments. So, send a letter or fax introducing yourself, a brief description of why you want to talk specifically with them, and the general nature of the topics to be covered. State that you would like to call them at some convenient time. Ask for a prompt return communication to set a telephone appointment time. Make very certain that you are punctual.

4. Conducting interviews: Listen for the common elements related to policies, names of distributors, pricing and discount practices, and general distribution traditions. This qualitative information is the most important and will become the foundation for tactical and strategic planning to penetrate a foreign market.

5. Focus panels: Validate the telephone interviews by staging at least two focus group sessions with foreign distributors and potential customers. These meetings should be arranged by a local executive of your company. The panel sessions should be facilitated by a foreign national. Perhaps the leading local university or one of the local interpreter service companies could provide facilitator special-

FIGURE 9–5
Access to Foreign Market Information: Select Department of Commerce Offices That Will Assist You

U.S. and Foreign Commercial Service (US&FCS)

The U.S. and Foreign Commercial Service (US&FCS), the only federal agency with a global network of international trade professionals, is charged with the nuts-and-bolts work of improving the ability of U.S. business to compete overseas. US&FCS collects marketing information at overseas posts and makes it available to U.S. companies at district offices and branch offices.

The US&FCS emphasizes practical advice and information help U.S. exporters in very specific ways. A company can find out which countries have the best market potential for its products and can then find out who to contact overseas.

Useful US&FCS Telephone Numbers:

Headquarters	(202) 377-5777
Caribbean Basin Business Information Center	377-0703
Domestic Operations	377-4767
Export Counseling	377-5551
Export Promotion Services:	377-8220
Marketing Programs Division	377-4231
Trade Event Programs	377-8220
Foreign Operations	377-8300
Public Affairs	377-3808

International Economic Policy (IEP)

International Economic Policy (IEP) identifies and analyzes foreign commercial barriers and opportunities, offers a range of counseling services to U.S. businesses, and participates in bilateral and multilateral consultations and negotiations.

Call here first.

Useful IEP Telephone Numbers

Headquarters	(202) 377-3022
GATT Division	377-3681
International Organizations	377-3227
U.S. Trade by Region	
Africa	377-2175
Canada	377-3101
Caribbean Basin & Mexico	377-5327
Eastern Europe	377-2645
European Community	377-5276
Israel Information Center	377-4652
Japan	377-4527
Near East	377-4441
Pacific Basin	377-4008
Peoples Republic of China and Hong Kong.................	377-3583
South America	377-2436
South Asia	377-2954
U.S.S.R.	377-4655
Western Europe	377-5341

Call here first

Source: Sumner R. Levine, *Business and Investment Handbook* (Homewood, Ill.: Dow Jones-Irwin, 1989), p. 677.

ists. Coach the facilitator on the vital issues requiring deep probing. You can be in attendance, but only participate if the facilitator fails to cover the vital questions.

PETER

When will I know if I have *enough* information and whether what I learn in one country really applies to other areas?

Good question. You start by building a comprehensive data base in one or two countries to get the feel for a region. For example, a German and French focus panel may begin to represent Europe. You'll know you have enough information when answers on the same subjects become repetitive. You're just validating the information. Then, you need only make a few select calls into the Netherlands, the United Kingdom, or Italy to see whether the focus panel distribution patterns are comparable.

PETER

> That's foreign distribution, but my domestic competition is another matter. We have some confidence in our market share position. We know which competitor is strong in each region, as well as what they are doing in the major accounts. I'm more interested in setting up a monitoring system to pick up early signals of competitive change.

Here are some strategic and tactical changes that competitors make:

- Pricing changes that reflect anticipated or actual reduced costs in manufacturing; or an internal policy to acquire more market share with a price move.
- Product line changes that reflect profit concentration by dropping low volume or unprofitable products from their line; or by upward product positioning to the higher perceived value strata; or by offering a systems solution.
- Sales representation changes that emphasize more customer service effort; or additions or deletions in field sales customer coverage.
- Management changes that reflect internal morale issues; or repositioning the company by depending on different management expertise.

PETER

> Now I need to know where and how this information can be accessed and then monitored.

Let's start with secondary information. Companies operate as private corporations, partnerships, or proprietorships, and as public corporations. We need to build an information base: (1) for the public company competitors; (2) for private company competitors; and (3) for both business structures.

Public Company Competitors

The law requires public companies to publish critical information to inform their shareholders. Matters of finance, sales, research and development, competitive threats, and new products are detailed in annual reports, press releases, talks before the security analysts, and periodic mandatory federal filings. Product pricing, distributional changes, and nonofficer management changes are not required to be reported, but investigative Wall Street and trade industry reporters usually publish these changes.

Tracking Public Company Change

The sources to monitor are:

- Annual and quarterly shareholder reports.
- SEC mandatory document filings: the 10K (an expanded and quantitative annual review of company operations); the 10Q (covers quarterly activity); and the 8K (reports any significant company management changes, lawsuits, and loss of large customers).
- Press releases issued by the company cover significant events that shareholders should know about immediately, including pending mergers; acquisitions; contracts that could influence potential earnings; law suits or major violations related to environmental or employee issues; and management changes that could be perceived as impacting their business.
- Transactions or verbatim reports of company presentations to the stock brokerage community. The leading publication reporting these meetings is the *Wall Street Transcript*. Usually the transcript of the management's remarks to the analysts is available directly from the company by calling and asking the shareholder relations manager for a copy. I have learned much from management's answers to questions posed by the security analysts attending these sessions. Management's goal is to convince Wall Street that either: (1) everything is going very well (they back these assertions with detailed charts and inter-

nally generated market data); or (2) things aren't going that well. In the second case, the audience discussions dwell on market problems and how the management in- tends to correct the situation. The correcting strategies contain the most useful information. Management's re- sponses illuminate new marketing tactics, low-cost manu- facturing strategies, overseas expansionary plans, and ac- quisition plans. To repeat, it is an excellent source.

Monitoring Methods and Sources for Public Company Information

Historic public company data resides in several traditional ref- erence guides: the *Standard & Poors Corporate Directory; Moody's Manuals*; and *Value Line Investment Survey*. These guides dis- play stock prices, sales and earnings information, operating ra- tios, trends, and relative financial performance of companies and industry groups. Begin building competitor files from these historic information sources.

What about some more timely facts? Three daily and one weekly newspaper cover public companies. They are *The Wall Street Journal, The Financial Times*, and the weekly *Barron's*. Business periodicals I find most useful are *Business Week, Forbes*, and *The Economist.*

Private or nonpublic companies are often referenced in these publications as part of industry-specific articles. They're normally cited in the context of marketing, technology, and product issues.

Do we need whole departments of people scanning stacks of newspapers and magazines in search of this information? There still remain clipping service firms that browse the world's busi- ness publications, snip out articles, and send them to clients. My belief is that electronic data base service companies will replace that older physical clipping technology. Now, monitoring compe- tition can be done simply and quickly. You can obtain the entire article on competition, or at least specific publication references. I find the two most comprehensive business data bases are Dow Jones Retrieval Service for American markets and companies, and Data Star for the European markets.

What are some primary methods to keep track of competition?

JOHN

Can't you just call public company competitors and ask them what they are doing?

Sometimes, but with care. Here are ways that I've suggested clients penetrate the information barriers of a public company competitor:

1. Own the competitor's stock.
   a. Buy one share of each competitor's publicly traded stock. You'll receive all of the mandatory shareholder reports, including the annual report and the more expansive 10K.
   b. Read these documents very thoroughly and note comments about your markets, distribution changes, new products, etc.
   c. Call the competitor's main office and ask for the top official in shareholder relations; or ask to be directed to the best person to answer a shareholder's question.
   d. Introduce yourself as a shareholder and request the annual report or 10K. Amazingly, because you are a shareholder in need of additional information, this office will usually refer you to the marketing or product department related to your question. Larger firms are very guarded about answering questions and may just take your name and later respond by mail or telephone. Remember, you are the customer and they want to give you what you want.
2. Obtain and study Wall Street analysts' reports.
   a. Ask your stockbroker to provide the institutional reports on your competitors.
   b. Ask your company financial officer to request the firm's investment banker to send analyses they have done for each competitor. Again, your company is the investment banker's customer. They should provide that extra service.
   c. Call each competitor's financial officer and tell them you are considering becoming a shareholder. In order to more

fully understand the company's potential, you would like to receive their current annual report and 10K, as well as any current Wall Street reports on the company's future. I've rarely been turned down for this request.

d. Find a library that subscribes to the *Wall Street Transcript*. Look in the annual and quarterly index for a listing of brokerage firms that have done reports on your competitors. Locate the analyst who wrote the competitor report. Call and probe for reasons for their bullish or bearish outlook, and ask what reasons the competitors have to support their future outlook.

3. Lawsuits and government violations: We overlook the availability of public information. Should the competitor's 10K reveal pending lawsuits relating to municipal, state, or federal actions, the proceedings of these investigations or trials are usually public information. As citizens, we have a right to access that data. Ask your corporate attorney to coach you with the jargon or legalese to expedite your request for the legal documents. Now contact the entity engaged in the legal action. Request the charges brought against the competitor (this includes a background of why the plaintiff believes there is a violation); the evidence to support the charges; the competitor's answer to the charges and the evidence to support the answer; the trial transcripts, particularly witness testimony; and the routine competitor filings to the agency engaged in the lawsuit or inquiry. Here are some government-based intelligence activities that can yield valuable insight into a competitor's business:

a. The Federal Trade Commission (FTC) can legally stop company operations for trade practice violations related to pricing, distribution, dumping, and package labeling.

b. At all government levels, environmental agencies can interfere with company operations and file lawsuits on manufacturing waste discharge violations. The legal documents and testimony can contain production volume, cost data, raw material composition of the violating products, and the anticipated correction methods, costs, and timetables.

c. The Securities and Exchange Commission (SEC), while only a quasi-governmental agency, is charged to protect the rights of public company shareholders. Their legal actions involve matters of stock value misrepresentations and full disclosure, and violations on the sale of company stock. The SEC is also the cognizant agency for a competitor's foreign operations, usually reported through an entity such as a domestic international sales corporation (DISC). All company filings are available from electronic data bases.

d. The labor departments of local, state, and federal governments usually engage in matters of worker safety, employee benefits, hiring practices, and skill training. You can discover information on employee counts, wages, productivity, manufacturing capital improvements, and your competitor's general cost of doing business.

PETER

I'll really have to become a detective as well as a legal eagle.

This is not an everyday marketing intelligence activity. If you're imaginative, persistent, and creative, you'll find unique clues to the competitor's business activity.

The Private Company Competitor

These closely held firms are not as visible or accessible, but getting competitive intelligence is possible. Here are several techniques I've used to discover what the private firms are up to.

Local newspaper business editors are always eager to use and publish company press releases. Electronic data base publishers are increasingly picking up these smaller, nonpublic company stories. So this combination of specific local newspaper sources and data bases provides some information access to these companies. To deeply monitor competitive activity, I search the local or regional newspapers where the competition is headquartered. If electronic data base services do not have the full text, I will call the local business editor and request copies of the cited articles. Editors and their staffs are most helpful.

Local "Help Wanted" advertisements are an excellent way to monitor the competitor's hiring patterns. Pay careful attention to the qualifications required for the job candidate. A recruiting composite often signals change in technology, expansion of sales coverage, greater management information systems, transaction volume, and the perceived level of management experience needed to manage the company's future.

Observing operational activity is easy. Just sit in your car near the front office entrance or in back at the shipping dock. Now observe and note who the vendors are and their delivery frequency. Over time the employee car count in the parking lot may signal increases or decreases in the number of employees not reported in the paper or to shareholders. The time of day people arrive for and leave work can signal general morale levels. And the car value driven by the executives may signal management's feelings of a bullish or bearish future.

Talk to the competitors' switchboard operators. They really know what's going on inside a company. I try to get them talking about any subject and then say, "I guess you'll be busy when they hire more people because the company just got that big order," or, "About how many new people is the company expecting to hire?" or, "How does everybody feel about the layoff?" or, "Are all the salespeople in for a big meeting?" and then, "Where are they staying?" This only works if the operator is not too busy and you establish the telephone interviewing rapport. Don't rely on this information channel too heavily. Validate it with primary data gathering.

Visit after-hours spots where employees gather. You'll be surprised at the amount of unsolicited information that comes your way about morale, big orders gained or lost, pay raises or layoffs, new products, and management changes.

Local or state sales tax data is generally available. Resellers collect sales tax from you and me. They pay and file these taxes using their unique identification number. Reseller taxes become public information and the amount of tax paid by an individual company can be obtained. Getting the tax information takes work and persistence. Here are the steps:

- Find out the competitor's tax ID number.
- Call the taxing authority and request the information.

- Calculate the competitor's total sales revenue by dividing the sales tax rate into the taxes paid.

Peter, these competitor monitoring techniques should serve you well. Let's summarize the key marketing intelligence tasks to answer your vital questions:

1. Foreign distribution participants can be discovered through the secondary data sources of Yellow Pages, directories, data bases, and foreign publications.
2. The reseller cultures and patterns can be discovered through telephone interviews with similar, noncompeting foreign companies.
3. Focus panel interviews conducted by a foreign national will validate the barriers for a new market entrant.
4. Private and public competitors can be monitored through current business publications, corporate communications to shareholders, personal observation techniques, and mandatory reporting and lawsuit channels.

BILL'S MAINTENANCE PRODUCTS DISTRIBUTION BUSINESS

As I remember, Bill, you need to know the total market for maintenance products so that you can expand your business. You also need to know how many of your existing customers the competition has stolen away from you. Let me ask, what are your annual sales and what percent would you say is attributable to your number one product?

BILL

We're a private company and don't usually disclose sales figures, but confidentially they'll run $2,500,000 this year. As far as the key product, I'd say it accounts for about 35 percent of our total sales. Now, when I find answers to my major questions, I'll be able to put together new sales and marketing programs to increase those revenues and recapture my customers.

Here's the marketing intelligence to help you do that. To find the total market, I suggest the following steps. Start the process with internal secondary research. Let's assume that customer sales data for at least two years is in the company computer and that each customer record has: customer name, ZIP code, sales by month and year to date, and specific product sales in both units and dollars.

Right here, let's dig into your second question, lost customers. Once you have the customer information for two years available, simply look for those customers who bought last year but have not purchased anything this year. Now you can see if all the lost customers purchased similar products, were in the same geographic territory, or bought in similar quantities. In other words, look for commonalities that might explain the cause for losing their business. The next task is to survey all these lost customers, as well as your new ones, to determine why they switched to or from competitors.

Now here's how you would manipulate the information to understand your customer and sales base:

1. Set up a spreadsheet with the following columns:
   D for customer name or code number.
   E for customer ZIP code.
   F for the cumulative percent of all customers.
   G for sales to each customer.
   H for each customer's percent of your total sales.
   I for the cumulative sales to all customers.
   J for the cumulative percent of sales to all customers.
   K for key product sales to each customer.
   L for the customer's percent of total key product sales.
   M for the cumulative percent of key product sales.

2. Enter customer information for columns *D*, *E*, *G*, and *K*. Also enter your total sales in column *G*, row 29 and your total "Key Product Sales" in column *K*, row 29. [**Exact formulae for columns and rows is found in Appendix IV, page 257.**]

3. Sort by customer sales, column *G*, from the highest to lowest. The percent each customer represents of your total sales is calculated in column *H*, and the cumulative percent is shown in column *I*.

FIGURE 9–6
Bill's Sales Analysis

Column legend:
"D" = Customer name or code   "T" = Cumulative customer sales
"E" = ZIP code (last 3 digits)   "J" = Cumulative percent of sales
"F" = Cumulative percent of customers   "K" = Key product #1 sales to date
"G" = Customer sales (000)   "L" = Percent of total #1 sales
"H" = Customer percent of total sales   "M" = Cumulative percent of #1 sales

Column	D	E	F	G	H	I	J	K	L	M
Row		ZIP	%	$	%	$	%	$	%	%
8	BRAD	103	1	322	12.9	322	12.9	98	11.2	11
9	BUD	100	2	259	10.4	581	23.2	76	8.7	20
10	SID	103	2	144	5.8	725	29.0	42	4.8	25
11	MOE	104	3	103	4.1	828	33.1	21	2.4	27
12	FRANK	100	4	102	4.1	930	37.2	19	2.2	29
13	SALLY	102	5	97	3.9	1027	41.1	39	4.5	34
15	HARRY	102	6	97	3.9	1124	45.0	23	2.6	36
16	JACK	105	6	95	3.8	1219	48.8	22	2.5	39
17	MIKE	101	7	88	3.5	1307	52.3	33	3.8	43
18	ALICE	101	8	88	3.5	1395	55.8	12	1.4	44
19	FRED	105	9	87	3.5	1482	59.3	25	2.9	47
20	HARRY	103	10	72	2.9	1554	62.2	17	1.9	49
21	LOU	101	10	68	2.7	1622	64.9	48	5.5	54
22	MANNY	100	11	66	2.6	1688	67.5	29	3.3	58
23	DICK	102	12	52	2.1	1740	69.6	23	2.6	60
24	JOE	101	13	48	1.9	1788	71.5	16	1.8	62
25	IRMA	101	14	34	1.4	1822	72.9	22	2.5	65
26	TED	104	14	29	1.2	1851	74.0	13	1.5	66
27	BOB	102	15	22	0.9	1873	74.9	9	1.0	67
28	MARY	104	16	15	0.6	1888	75.5	7	0.6	68
29	Company Totals			$2,500				$875		
30										

4. Looking at the cumulative sales percentage, column *I*,
find the approximate 80 percent point and draw a line
under that row. Now look across to cumulative percent of
customers, column *F*, and find that percent. Figure 9–6
shows what the spreadsheet should look like. (The formula for each column is located in Appendix IV. This ar-
ray and sorting will indicate whether the 80/20 rule applies to your business.

FIGURE 9–7
Bill's ZIP Code Analysis

Column legend:
"D" = Customer name or code   "T" = Cumulative customer sales
"E" = ZIP code (last 3 digits)   "J" = Cumulative percent of sales
"F" = Cumulative percent of customers   "K" = Key product #1 sales to date
"G" = Customer sales (000)   "L" = Percent of total #1 sales
"H" = Customer percent of total sales   "M" = Cumulative percent of #1 sales

Column	D	E	F	G	H	I	J	K	L	M
Row		ZIP	%	$	%	$	%	$	%	%
8	MANNY	100	1	66	2.6	66	2.6	29	3.3	3
9	FRANK	100	2	102	4.1	168	6.7	19	2.2	5
10	BUD	100	2	259	10.4	427	17.1	76	8.7	14
11	ALICE	101	3	88	3.5	515	20.6	12	1.4	16
12	MIKE	101	4	88	3.5	603	24.1	33	3.8	19
13	LOU	101	5	68	2.7	671	26.8	48	5.5	25
15	JOE	101	6	48	1.9	719	28.8	16	1.8	27
16	IRMA	101	6	34	1.4	753	30.1	22	2.5	29
17	SALLY	102	7	97	3.9	850	34.0	39	4.5	34
18	DICK	102	8	52	2.1	902	36.1	23	2.6	36
19	BOB	102	9	22	0.9	924	37.0	9	1.0	37
20	HARRY	102	10	97	3.9	1021	40.8	23	2.6	40
21	SID	103	10	144	5.8	1165	46.6	42	4.8	45
22	BRAD	103	11	322	12.9	1487	59.5	98	11.2	58
23	HARRY	103	12	72	2.9	1559	62.4	17	1.9	58
24	TED	104	13	29	1.2	1588	63.5	13	1.5	59
25	MARY	104	14	15	0.6	1603	64.1	7	0.8	60
26	MOE	104	14	103	4.1	1706	68.2	21	2.4	63
27	JACK	105	15	95	3.8	1801	72.0	22	2.5	65
28	FRED	105	16	87	3.5	1888	75.5	25	2.9	68
29	Company Totals			$2,500				$875		
30										

5. Now re-sort using the primary key set to ZIP code (column *E*). You'll calculate the total sales in each ZIP code, which is the difference between the last cumulating sales figure for the ZIP code and the last cumulating sales figure for the preceding ZIP code. Now count the number of companies in that area. To calculate the average of all customers within each ZIP code, divide the summed sales

for the ZIP code by the number of customers in the ZIP code. Figure 9–7 separates your customers into ZIP codes and shows a different perspective about your market.

6. Next put the primary key on Product No. 1, column *K*, sales volume, and sort using the descending order (highest to lowest). See if the 80/20 rule applies. Also look for customers that buy a lot of your key product, but not of your other products. Maybe competition gets most of their other business.

7. You can repeat this process for all the major products in your line.

Bill, another important measure is looking at the number of customers you've lost or gained over the past few years. Determine what the customer profiles were for those you lost to the competition. Try to understand, account by account, why they were lost. Do the same for all the new customers. There are probably consistent themes or causes for the gained or lost groups and you can consider fixing the problems to lose less or gain more.

There's a wealth of information about the importance of customers to your total sales, ZIP code contribution to total sales, averages, and contributions of products to total business. Now we're ready to match what you're doing with some estimates of potentials in your total market area.

External secondary research can be overlaid to estimate a total market. Here are the information pieces needed to do that:

1. Customer size by number of employees, which is not usually part of the internal sales information, can be collected directly from the customer, from local business directories, or from the city license department. A little known fact is that many cities or locales base their annual business license fee on the number of employees. This is public information and a visit to the city or county hall will surface an alphabetical printout of business licensees showing the employee count.

2. The number and demographics of area businesses can be collected from chambers of commerce, economic development agencies, the local newspaper, state departments of commerce or trade, and a special source, the local public utility's marketing department. The utility is unique be-

cause it has no competitors and is typically open to sharing information. We're particularly looking for the total number of companies by employee size and ZIP code. Refer to Figure 1–1; this is how the information should be arrayed. Let's use the spreadsheet again. Now when you collect the utility or other secondary business employee numbers, enter them into a new column titled *Number of Employees*, next to *Customer Name*, column D. Set the primary sort key on *Number of Employees* and sort in ascending order. When the sort is complete find the row where the company sizes approximately match Figure 1–1. Insert a row in the spreadsheet and average the sales for each company size category. Now determine the average number of employees in each size. Finally, to derive the average employees per company in each size category, divide the employee average into the sales average.

3. Sales for your city, region, or state, broken down by SIC codes, are usually available from the business data sources we've already mentioned. Getting the total market may be as easy as finding the reported sales in a SIC breakdown. Bill, your SIC is 5087, janitorial supplies wholesaler (refer to page 93).

4. Janitorial work involves cleaning square footage, so another helpful, but not vital, data set is the square footage for your customers and all businesses in your area. Good sources for this information are city or county property departments, major industrial and commercial real estate firms, and business directories. Insert two new columns in the spreadsheet labeled *Square Footage* and *Average Square Footage*. Enter the company data into the *Square Footage* column, and sort to the primary key *Sales Revenue* in descending order. Now insert another new column, *Sales Revenue per Square Foot*, and determine the average sales revenue per square foot by dividing average sales by average square footage.

That's all the external data you need to get a reasonable estimate of the total market.

BILL

How do I put all that together? It's just pieces and parts and I don't see how it fits.

We've constructed the total market model using secondary data. Now let's validate that with your *internal* data. Here's how to do it:

1. Find the total number of employees working for your customers.
2. Divide your total sales by the total employee figure to get the average dollar sale per employee.
3. Total the sales for customers in a ZIP code and divide the total by the number of customers in the ZIP code. Now you have the average sale per company for each specific ZIP code.

Bill, you told us that your company had a major share of the market you serve. So, the *first* assumption I will make is that the mix of pails, mops, and chemicals your customers buy from you is representative of what your competition sells to their customers.

BILL

Yes, that's reasonable.

Now, the *second* assumption is that dollar sales to any customer are directly proportional to the number of employees working at the customer company.

BILL

I don't understand.

Whether a buyer is a service, retail, or manufacturing business, the number of pails, mops, and chemicals purchased will depend on the number of employees at that firm. One employee equals the purchase of one gallon of cleaning chemicals; 50 employees equal the purchase of 50 gallons. Bill, the *third* assumption is that cleaning problems are solved by mops, pails, and brooms. You and your competitor probably carry the same quality and priced items. Are you comfortable with these assumptions?

BILL

I'm comfortable.

Alright, the next internal or secondary source information is the average number of employees that work for all companies in your trade area. Our *fourth* assumption will be that characteristics of firms in Bill's geographic area are similar to the national average business characteristics. So, if that assumption is acceptable, then we can compare national business establishment and employee data with the market Bill serves.

Now, let's look at this national data for establishments (businesses with payrolls). Figure 9–8 displays a page from the *Statistical Abstract*.

This is the 1990 Edition, but in the tables the most current available data is from 1986. Remember I said that published information usually lags by a few years? Here's the data we'll use:

- There are 5,807,000 establishments with paid employees.
- There were 83,380,000 people employed in those firms.
- The average employees per firm (83,380,000 divided by 5,807,000) equals 14.36 employees per company

To keep the record straight, let me comment on the 5,807,000 establishments found in the *Abstract* and the 19,000,000 detailed in Figure 1–1. The difference is that some 13,000,000 do not have employees.

The national average of 14.36 employees per firm is the key number to estimate total sales in your market area. Bill, I described the methodology to derive the average sale per customer employee. Do you happen to known what that is? I also want to know your estimate for the total number of businesses in your area.

BILL

We figured out the number of employees working for customers when we wanted to send holiday cards to each one. So, dividing our sales by the number of customer employees, the average sale per employee is about $4. That's the answer to your first question.

For total businesses in the area, I'd want to verify my guess by analyzing local directories and governmental data, but I believe

FIGURE 9-8
Employee Data Determine a Total Market

Business Enterprise   *This is the number we want to use*

No. 870. EMPLOYEES AND PAYROLL, BY EMPLOYMENT-SIZE CLASS: 1975 TO 1986

EMPLOYMENT-SIZE CLASS	Unit	1975	1979	1980	1981	1982	1983	1984	1985	1986
Employees, total [1]	1,000	60,519	75,411	74,844	74,848	74,287	72,974	78,021	81,111	83,380
Under 20 employees	1,000	16,393	19,406	19,423	19,515	19,898	20,136	21,171	21,810	22,296
20 to 99 employees	1,000	16,272	20,992	21,168	21,231	21,143	20,806	22,449	23,539	24,311
100 to 499 employees	1,000	13,713	17,527	17,840	17,977	17,444	16,794	18,348	19,410	20,260
500 to 999 employees	1,000	4,872	5,780	5,689	5,497	5,436	5,186	5,614	5,716	5,780
1,000 or more employees	1,000	9,315	10,976	10,716	10,630	10,376	10,050	10,413	10,645	10,734
Annual payroll [1]	Bil. dol	596	952	1,035	1,076	1,198	1,269	1,339	1,514	1,609
Under 20 employees	Bil. dol	138	210	231	254	272	298	326	352	375
20 to 99 employees	Bil. dol	147	239	261	288	303	319	358	388	414
100 to 499 employees	Bil. dol	135	224	249	279	286	297	334	362	391
500 to 999 employees	Bil. dol	53	84	91	99	104	107	120	126	132
1,000 or more employees	Bil. dol	123	196	208	229	234	248	269	286	298

[1] Prior to 1986, totals for employees and annual payroll have been revised. Detail may not add to totals because revisions for size class are not available.

Source: U.S. Bureau of the Census, County Business Patterns, annual.

Very specific and detailed for your area

This is another number for our calculations.

No. 871. ESTABLISHMENTS, EMPLOYEES, AND PAYROLL, BY INDUSTRY: 1975 TO 1986

INDUSTRY	ESTABLISHMENTS (1,000)				EMPLOYEES (1,000)				PAYROLL (bil. dol.)			
	1975	1980	1985	1986	1975	1980	1985	1986	1975	1980	1985	1986
All Industries [1]	4,114	4,543	5,701	5,807	60,519	74,844	81,111	83,380	596	1,035	1,514	1,609
Agricultural services [2]	40	46	64	68	195	290	380	412	2	3	5	6
Mining	24	30	37	35	720	994	943	847	10	22	28	24
Contract construction	364	418	476	492	3,322	4,473	4,480	4,659	44	75	98	104
Manufacturing	306	319	358	355	18,372	21,165	19,429	19,142	213	355	458	468
Transportation [3]	147	168	203	210	3,908	4,623	4,809	4,884	51	88	123	128
Wholesale trade	350	385	438	440	4,332	5,211	5,624	5,725	52	89	130	138
Retail trade	1,190	1,223	1,407	1,441	12,271	15,047	16,852	17,550	76	124	179	193
Finance and insurance [4]	372	421	488	504	4,247	5,295	6,004	6,371	42	77	132	151
Services	1,118	1,278	1,712	1,811	12,655	17,186	21,549	22,878	102	197	346	381

[1] Includes nonclassifiable establishments, not shown separately. [2] Includes forestry and fisheries. [3] Includes other public utilities. [4] Includes real estate.

Source: U.S. Bureau of the Census, County Business Patterns, annual.

Source: U.S. Dept. of Commerce, Bureau of the Census, *Statistical Abstract of the United States* (Washington, D.C.: Government Printing Office, 1990), p. 527.

there are 45,000 to 60,000 companies with employees in my market area.

Good. Let's use 52,500 area companies and a $4 sale per employee. Here's how to forecast your total market:

1. Total number of employees in your market is 753,900, which is 52,500 firms multiplied by 14.36 employees per firm.

2. Therefore, the total sales potential in your market area is $3,015,600 which is 753,900 employees multiplied by the $4.00 average sale figure you derived.

How does that square with your annual sales?

BILL

> Interesting, our sales are about $2,500,000 and I figure we have about an 80 percent share of the market.

To validate these derived numbers, we'll use another set of secondary data and your internal data on sales per employee. I happen to have the U. S. Dept. of Commerce's *Census of Wholesale Trade* for 1987, which lists the establishments and sales for SIC 5087. It shows that in 1987 there were 106 janitorial wholesalers. Their combined sales were $268,429,000. The average sales revenue for janitorial wholesalers calculates to $2,532,349. You're right on the national average, Bill.

To attempt validation of your $4 average sale per employee, we'll again use national data. There'll be a risk of inaccuracy because we must mix data sets to get an answer. Let me explain. The county business pattern information, from the census, allowed us to determine there were an average of 14.36 employees in a single firm. We developed that using the 5.8 million firms with a payroll (see Figure 9–8). The census data shows some 13 million companies are without a payroll. However, these 13 million companies must buy and use janitorial supplies. Bill sells supplies to large and small firms, some with and some without employees. So, I'll assume his customer base reflects a national janitorial buyer profile. To be consistent, let's divide national total janitorial sales by total U.S. payrolled employees.

Here's the data:

- Total 1987 janitorial wholesale sales equals $268,420,000.
- Total 1987 payrolled employees equals 83,380,000.
- Average sale per employee equals $3.22.

Let's now correlate Bill's customer employee average of $4 with the national average of $3.22. The yearly price inflation between 1987 and 1990 should account for the difference. To test that assumption we'll use a 6 percent inflation increase per year:

1987, $3.22 × 1.06 = $3.41; 1988, $3.41 × 1.06 = 3.62; 1989, $3.62 × 1.06 = $3.84; and 1990, $3.84 × 1.06 = $4.07. So the inflated 1990 sales per employee was $4.07, compared to your $4.00. What do think, Bill?

BILL

It's close enough, but I'm going to work for more accuracy now that I understand the methodology.

That's the answer to your question, what's the total market? Let's look at your next marketing intelligence need—how to expand your business and get new customers.

It appears the difference between the total area potential of $3,015,600 and your current annual sales offers you a $540,000 expansion opportunity. However, my experience suggests it's difficult to extend market share beyond 80 percent. Customers want supplier choices and will work hard to keep competitors available to assure competitive pricing and service. Here's what I would do to determine whether customers will allow you to increase your share.

Draw an interview candidate sample of 15 to 25 buyers from various types and sizes of firms. Half the sample should be from existing customers and the other half should be from potential customers now buying from competitors. Conduct personal interviews with their purchasing and upper management. The key information to obtain is:

1. Why do they buy from the competitor?
2. What internal purchasing policies exist that prohibit buying from only one supplier?
3. What services would they prefer that you or the competition are not currently offering?
4. What percent of janitorial supplies are they buying at large warehouse stores like the Price Club and Home Depot?
5. What other distribution methods would they prefer, for example catalog or mail order?

That's about all I can suggest, Bill. Ask the customers; they have the answers to market share questions.

SUSAN'S WOODEN TOY BUSINESS

You need to determine new product features and the highest prices customers will pay for your wooden toy products. Where would you start?

SUSAN

How about a focus panel of parents?

Yes, that's a great primary data source. But first, here's some secondary sources that will provide background opinions and help to prepare for the focus panel:

1. Attend national trade shows and listen to the product features the competition is promoting. They've worked to differentiate their products, so you might as well capitalize on their marketing intelligence effort to identify product features they believe customers want.

2. Go on-line to electronic data bases and search the current toy trade periodicals and government documents sections to look for articles, reports, and bibliographic references. Key words I would use are: *toys* and *wooden*; *toys* and *safety*; *children* and *safety* or *education*; *regulations* and *toys*, and so on.

3. Contact industry trade associations to inquire about new or pending legislation that may affect product materials, designs, or other consumer-related safety issues. Have them provide the names of the government staff people working on the regulation changes or industry practice investigations. Call these people for copies of draft legislation materials.

4. Call the U.S. Federal Trade Commission (FTC) or the comparable state agency. Ask the operator to put you through to the department responsible for children's toy safety or the consumer protection department. Now after introducing yourself, ask to be directed to the most recent report on complaints or findings on children's toys. It may take a while, but chances are a relevant document will surface. Request that they send you the information

directly. Sometimes you'll be referred to a document distribution department.

5. Obtain and read government hearings of any agency's proposals to change consumer protection laws. This source is very important because agency staffs must prepare extensive background material as evidence to support new legislation. Advocates for and against the proposed changes in the law appear before congressional hearings to persuade the lawmakers on their points of view. They also offer materials into the hearing record which become public information. The complete transcript of testimony, evidence, and support material is, after a period of time, found at the nearest government repository library. Again, the government document librarians are very helpful. A request to your elected representative for the hearing documents may speed the process. [*I can't stress the importance of this secondary source enough. Published government hearings are, in my experience, the most comprehensive and focused collection of information. With the political cast of characters, I usually find hearings easy to read and often more humorous than a good comedy.*]

6. Analyze domestic and foreign competitor advertisements and brochures. Extract the unique product feature claims they are making. You're looking for product elements not related to the fundamental performance of the toy. Find the "sizzle," not the "steak." Build a competitive matrix to identify new product feature opportunities not offered by the competition. Constructing the matrix is rather simple. Use a flip-chart-sized piece of paper. Across the top, enter all your competitors' names. Along the left margin list all the performance features offered for the product class. Under each competitor, fill in its performance claims. Now sit back and try to identify feature gaps in the matrix that you could bring to the market.

7. Talk with industry trade publication editors to locate gurus and experts. I'd try to find people who understand the psychology of children's play, ways to improve manual dexterity, and so on. Remember to introduce yourself

and state that industry executives said they were the experts.

Now let's use the focus panel to validate the secondary source information. Parents are perfect panelists, but I'd add two other kinds of participants: toy store owners and preschool teachers.

Susan, you mentioned that your toys are priced in the *best* value stratum and that your toys are bought by the more affluent. I'd be comfortable making the following sweeping assumptions: (1) that any child's reaction to your toys would represent the reaction any other child would have anywhere in the world, regardless of the parents' affluence; (2) product opinions of any group of toy store owners mirror all toy buyer opinions; and (3) attitudes about the use of toys by any group of preschool teachers represent the attitudes of their specialty. If these are reasonable assumptions, then panel members can be drawn from a local sample base. Here's what to do next:

1. Locate the local ZIP codes where affluent families live.
2. Drive around those neighborhoods on a Saturday and identify streets heavily populated by children.
3. Find a backward phone directory and pull a list of names and phone numbers of families living on these streets.
4. Call the sample, introduce yourself, describe what the panel hopes to accomplish, motivate the respondents to participate by offering free toys for their children, and secure their commitment to attend.
5. Look in the Yellow Pages for preschools and toy stores, call the principals and owners, and gain their commitment to participate.
6. Prepare a list of questions for the moderator, who could be a preschool teacher.
7. Ask permission to tape the proceedings.

SUSAN

I would think observing children playing with the toys would be useful too.

Yes, observation will show preferences for different colors and surface textures, as well as attention spans or playing times, but you may not be able to get any specific insights into product features. My experience is that children can't articulate what you may be looking for, unless they are over seven to nine years old.

Earlier you had another question, how to find the highest price that customers will pay for your toys? The focus panel is an excellent forum to get that kind of an answer. Divide the panel session time in half—one for product ideas, the other to probe for the highest price point. Here's how to get at the price question:

1. Bring unbranded toys, each with a different functional performance, to the focus panel.
2. Select a toy currently marketed in the better value category. Tell the panelists what the price is, what basic performance they get for that price, and describe the product's "sizzle" features.
3. Demonstrate successively increasing value products and ask, "If this were available in your toy store, what price do you think it should sell for?" Don't ask what they would pay for it just yet. Keep working up the value strata, each time asking about price/value perceptions and also ask why or how they rationalize their price opinions.

These are efficient techniques to secure your base marketing intelligence. Then plan new product and pricing strategies.

ANNE'S BOOKSTORE

Well, Anne, your objectives are to build store traffic, know what subjects to inventory, and make more profit. Easy to say, but not always easy to do. The marketing challenge is to get more people into your bookstore. You believe when more people enter your store and browse the shelves stocked with the right subjects, book sales will go up. That's a valid and reasonable assumption.

Location, location, location is the rule for retail success. Increasing sales can sometime be as simple as verifying whether too much competition has moved into your trading area or whether your store is not located in the right place to satisfy customer book buying needs. Here's a simple way to check on your location.

Take a street map of your area. Get out the Yellow Pages and find the listings for retail bookstores. Put a big X on the map where your store is, and then put a C where all the competitive stores are located. Now find the distance scale on the map. Get a piece of string or a drawing compass and measure off 2.5 miles. Now place the end of the string or compass where your store is located. Draw a 2.5-mile-radius circle. This is your trading area. See how many competitors are located in the circle and think about whether this is too many, too few, or just about right. [*All people thinking about a retail or consumer service business should do this before they rent space.*] Alright, now look at the census data for the area you serve and determine whether the education and income fit the profiles of book buyers. This may sound like a simple exercise, but it can be very influential in your location or relocation decision process.

Let's see how your bookstore revenues compare to the competition. We begin the secondary research by consulting the *Statistical Abstract*. Figure 9–9 displays, from the *Abstract*, Table 384, taken from the annual Book Industry Study Group, Inc., *Book Industry Trends*. The table details unit and dollar book sales through a variety of distribution channels. Preliminary 1988 data shows 1.155 billion combined hardback and softback units were sold through general retailers, and that's your type of store. The total dollar sale (at consumer prices) was $8.572 billion. Now we have the unit and dollar facts.

Here's how to determine the 1988 average general retailer book price. Divide the total consumer list price sales, $8.572 billion, by total units sold to derive an average price of $12.37. Accounting for inflation over the past few years I'd estimate today's average price at $14. Does that selling price feel about right?

ANNE

Well yes, but to be competitive we do have to cut the prices from suggested list. I'd say that's a reasonable selling price range.

Another interesting calculation from Table 384 data is that 63 percent of the book units sold are softback and 37 percent are

FIGURE 9–9
How Many Books Were Sold, on What Subjects, at What Price?

Unit ratio, hard to softback ↗ *Units* *Dollars*

No. 384. QUANTITY OF BOOKS SOLD AND VALUE OF U.S. DOMESTIC CONSUMER EXPENDITURES, BY TYPE OF PUBLICATION AND MARKET AREA: 1975 TO 1988

[Includes all titles released by publishers in the U.S. and imports which appear under the imprints of American publishers. Multi-volume sets, such as encyclopedias, are counted as one unit]

TYPE OF PUBLICATION AND MARKET AREA	UNITS SOLD (mil.)						CONSUMER EXPENDITURES (mil. dol.)					
	1975	1980	1985	1986	1987	1988, prel	1975	1980	1985	1986	1987	1988, prel
Total [1]	1,541	1,856	2,044	2,071	2,122	2,195	4,969	8,854	14,072	15,052	16,653	18,416
Hardbound, total [2]	526	638	724	745	775	814	3,276	5,536	8,603	9,268	10,263	11,405
Softbound, total [2]	1,015	1,218	1,320	1,327	1,347	1,381	1,693	3,318	5,469	5,784	6,390	7,011
Trade	272	487	666	702	737	773	1,092	2,349	4,488	4,936	5,810	6,742
Adult	182	369	455	465	486	509	866	1,954	3,669	3,979	4,670	5,429
Juvenile	90	118	210	237	251	264	226	395	818	958	1,140	1,313
Religious	96	152	144	142	130	124	358	687	1,130	1,177	1,242	1,320
Professional	51	103	140	156	165	173	590	1,453	2,415	2,705	2,910	3,163
Bookclubs	195	127	107	103	104	104	336	473	544	557	627	708
Elhi text	257	217	238	231	210	205	683	880	1,420	1,522	1,621	1,744
College text	84	118	110	108	113	117	635	1,138	1,707	1,803	1,952	2,097
Mail order publications	85	145	111	111	115	118	321	592	597	599	606	618
Mass market paperbacks	491	495	519	509	540	571	651	987	1,479	1,458	1,580	1,712
General retailers	595	841	1,023	1,051	1,101	1,155	1,565	3,341	6,159	6,636	7,543	8,572
College stores	195	242	258	257	265	272	895	1,603	2,615	2,769	3,026	3,261
Libraries and institutions	73	93	94	98	99	101	452	846	1,227	1,338	1,453	1,578
Schools	309	271	270	264	245	242	845	1,176	1,709	1,829	1,956	2,105
Direct to consumers	286	328	285	282	290	298	1,118	1,764	2,113	2,211	2,373	2,563
Other	83	80	115	118	121	127	94	124	249	269	302	338

[1] Types of publications include university press publications and subscription reference works, not shown separately.
[2] Beginning 1980, revised since originally published.

Source: Book Industry Study Group, Inc., New York, NY, *Book Industry Trends*, annual. (Copyright.)

This would be a good study to get

hardback. However, the softback dollar revenue only accounts for 38 percent of publishers' total sales. Hardback sales account for 62 percent of the dollars. Looks like we almost have the 80/20 rule here.

Look at Figure 9–10 (Table 1357, "Retail Trade Establishments").

It lists 11,000 retail bookstore establishments doing business in 1987. The table also shows that in 1982 there were 10,000 bookstores. This data indicates that total bookstore population only grew 10 percent from 1982 to 1987.

ANNE

There in the left margin is my SIC—5942. I'll use it to find more in-depth industry statistics.

FIGURE 9–10
How Many Bookstores Are There and How Much Did They Sell?

Retail Trade Establishments

NO. 1357. RETAIL TRADE ESTABLISHMENTS WITH PAYROLL—NUMBER, SALES, PAYROLL, AND EMPLOYEES, BY KIND OF BUSINESS: 1982 AND 1987

[Each kind-of-business classification includes leased departments classified in that kind of business as if they were separate establishments. See *Historical Statistics, Colonial Times to 1970*, series T 79–196 for similar but not comparable data]

1972 SIC code [1]	KIND OF BUSINESS	ESTABLISH-MENTS [2] (1,000)		SALES (mil. dol.)		ANNUAL PAYROLL (mil. dol.)		PAID EMPLOYEES [3] (1,000)	
		1982	1987	1982	1987	1982	1987	1982	1987
	Retail trade, total............	1,425	1,506	1,039,029	1,494,112	123,619	177,708	14,468	17,793
52	Building materials and garden supplies stores............	70	74	49,939	81,487	6,221	9,760	504	668
521, 3	Building materials, supply stores.........	36	38	34,827	60,525	4,179	6,929	307	432
525	Hardware stores...........	21	20	8,335	10,535	1,250	1,564	127	138
526	Retail nurseries, lawn and garden supply stores............	8	11	2,872	5,444	450	822	47	71
527	Mobile home dealers.........	5						24	27
53	General merchandise stores......								
531	Department stores	37	35	102,207	139,440	13,150	18,754	1,470	
			35	17,340	18,597	1,310	1,454	167	15,
	...pping goods stores.........	19	18	3,798	4,305	730	823	80	81
5941	Sporting goods stores and bicycle shops.........	108	123	32,524	49,460	4,623	6,481	566	706
		20	22	6,718	10,077	844	1,218	98	121
5942	Book stores............	10	11	3,133	5,116	401	581	58	72
5943	Stationery stores........	5	5	1,495	1,814	257	287	28	27
5944	Jewelry stores............	24	28	8,352	11,994	1,433	1,921	132	163
5945	Hobby, toy, and game shops...........	8	10	3,238	7,031	325	614	46	76
5946	Camera, photographic supply stores...........	4	4	1,884	2,294	225	276	21	21
5947	Gift, novelty, souvenir shops...........	24	32	4,620	7,459	694	1,055	110	151
5948	Luggage, leather goods stores...........	2	2	589	839	94	122	11	11
5949	Sewing, needlework, and piece goods stores...........	10	10	2,495	2,836	350	406	62	65
596	Nonstore retailers...........	23	23	20,155	33,894	2,942	4,523	274	318
5961	Catalog and mail-order houses...........	8	7	11,254	20,347	1,194	1,932	103	123
5962	Merchandising machine operators....	6	5	4,727	5,692	935	1,090	84	74
5963	Direct selling establishments...........	9	11	4,175	7,855	813	1,501	88	121
598	Fuel and ice dealers...........	13	13	16,818	14,250	1,405	1,834	95	100
5992	Florists...........	24	27	3,416	4,810	711	1,019	104	125
5993	Tobacco stores and stands...........	2	2	576	518	68	57	9	7
5994	News dealers and newsstands...........	2	2	500	703	60	90	9	10
5999	Miscellaneous retail stores, n.e.c.[6] [7]...	35	44	7,078	12,902	1,301	2,472	127	191
5999 pt.	Optical goods stores...........	11	14	1,729	3,415	404	811	34	54

NA Not available. [1] Based on 1972 Standard Industrial Classification; see text, section 13. [2] Represents the number of establishments in business at any time during year. [3] For pay period including March 12. [4] Includes sales from catalog order desks. [5] Establishments defined as department stores with 25 employees or more. [6] Includes other kinds of businesses, not shown separately. [7] N.e.c. means not elsewhere classified.

Source: U.S. Bureau of the Census, *1987 Census of Retail Trade*, RC87-A-52.

Much more detail here — *Doesn't apply to Anne's bookstores data except this*

Source: U.S. Dept. of Commerce, Bureau of the Census, *Statistical Abstract of the United States* (Washington, D.C.: Government Printing Office, 1990), p. 769.

Excellent. When you inquire at the library or government commerce departments, the SIC reference will speed you to the right data. Let's continue. To derive the average annual individual bookstore sales revenue, I'm going to use 1988 total list priced sales and 1987 bookstore establishments. We're mixing annual statistics again but it's reasonable to do so because the bookstore population growth in that one year between 1987 and 1988 is insignificant and really does not impact the calculated accuracy.

Using 1988 total list price sales of $8.6 billion divided by 11,000 stores, the calculated average annual bookstore revenue equals $781,818. Again, accounting for inflation, I'd say the average annual sales today are approximately $890,000. Anne, you now have an average to measure whether your store is above, below, or equal to the competition. You also know that $14 is an average suggested retail book price. But how much discount do you offer customers from the suggested list price? Here are my analysis suggestions:

1. Calculate your average sale price by totaling the units you sold and the dollars received last year and this year to-date. Here's the process:

   a. Use your cash register rolls, receipt pads, reported IRS sales, or data on the store computer to determine net book sales.

   b. Sum the units purchased from supplier invoices.

   c. Divide the total sales dollars by units to get *your* average book sales price.

   d. Compare your price to the national average.

2. To determine the amount you are discounting from the suggested list price of the books you actually bought:

   a. Add all supplier invoiced dollars and divide that total by 60 percent, the reciprocal of a 40 percent discount (I'll assume this is an average discount for booksellers), to get the total "publisher suggested" list price dollar revenue for books you actually bought.

   b. Divide the suggested list price dollar revenue by the total book units you bought over a comparable sales period. That amount is *your* average book suggested list price.

   c. Compare your actual average book price with the suggested book price. The percentage difference is how much, on average, you are discounting or overpricing books.

3. Compare your annual sales with the industry average of $890,000, calculating the percent you exceeded or undersold

the average bookstore. This only has value to increase or decrease your urgency to find out more about the customer.

ANNE

My annual sales are under that average.

The key word is *average*. Looking at national averages includes big and small cities and more or less affluent consumer buying locations. But knowing how you compare does prompt marketing questions. To find more specific information that may more closely relate to your buyer demographics, I'd contact bookselling trade associations and ask for their current business survey data. It may detail sales dollars by bookstore square footages, bookstore specialties, and urban versus rural locations. Visit the library to locate detailed references at the end of pertinent articles. Just dig deeper!

Building Traffic

Getting people in your store depends on store location, window displays, advertising, interior attractiveness, and in-store service. No one technique can increase store traffic except a going-out-of-business notice, and that's only used once.

Let's use an observational technique to see whether your store is getting its fair share of traffic. Hire someone to count the people going into your store and the stores on either side of your store. (As an alternative, you could get three mechanical counters to tally the people entering each store.) Have this done in 30-minute increments, three times a day. The time of day is not that important, but I'd say between 9:30 A.M. and 10:00 A.M., 12:30 P.M. and 1:00 P.M., and 4:30 P.M. and 5:00 P.M. Keep a log for several weeks during holiday and nonholiday periods. Compare, at week's end, whether your traffic counts are comparable to your neighbors'. What we're looking for are major differences between stores because each store has equal access to shoppers. You may find the merchandising that attracts shoppers to enter your neighbor's store useful to you. Wide differences in counts signal you are not getting your fair share. The question is, why not?

My next suggestion is to conduct a simple personal shopper survey. Develop several questions that ask:

- How often do you buy books?
- Where do you usually buy books?
- Can you recall how you heard about that particular bookstore or what caused you to go there?
- Would you tell me one feature that you like or dislike about that bookstore?
- If you had all the money you needed to design the perfect interior in a bookstore, what would it look like?
- Do you normally shop in this mall or area?
- Do your prefer hardback books or softback?
- Do you buy hardback books?

Hire someone who is well groomed and personable to conduct the survey of 75 to 100 shoppers. I'd position the interviewer just out of sight of your store—for example, at the opposite end of the strip retail center. Develop a similar questionnaire to interview the traffic coming out of your store. Be sure to ask these additional open-ended questions:

- How would you characterize this store's selection of book subjects? Are there any subject areas that you would like to see expanded?
- You went into this bookstore for some reason. Could you tell me what that was?

Try to see if serving coffee is a preference. You'll also learn about coffee in the shopper survey through the question that asks about likes and dislikes.

In summary, here's what you will learn:

1. The percent of shoppers who often buy books.
2. The share of all shoppers that prefer your bookstore over the local competition.
3. The advertising medium or store merchandising that attracts customers.
4. The preference that frequent shoppers in your store location have for competitive bookstores.

5. What shoppers like and dislike about your store and the competitor's.

I would also suggest consulting with mall management. They frequently conduct traffic surveys to support leasing sales programs. Local business groups also commission surveys to develop retail area traffic-building strategies. Anne, when you study these opinions and shopper facts you'll find new directions and ideas to explore to build store traffic.

Let's see how marketing intelligence can boost your profits. Anne, what do you mean by increasing profit? Are you talking about percent profit margin, or more profit dollars?

ANNE

> I need more money to cover my expenses after paying the suppliers for my books. I need profit dollars.

Okay, let's work on dollars. Profit percent is a very important way to measure management performance and to compare your management results with a competitor's. But profit dollars, not percents, pay the bills.

Your average book price is $14. You determined that price through internal sales figures and supplier invoices. The profit-impacting elements are: units sold, unit price, and cost. There are three possible ways you can increase profits: sell more book units, raise book prices, or lower book and operating costs. [*I want to emphasize two other marketing words that cause confusion:* cost *and* price. Cost *is what you pay to a supplier, plus the additional money you spend to prepare to sell*; price *is the amount at which you agree to sell the customer a product or service. There's a big difference.*]

Building in-store traffic may lead to more book unit sales, and lowering prices may also increase unit sales volume. But the lower price strategy reduces profits if the unit costs stay the same. Costs can be lowered if suppliers offer greater discounts for substantial increases in unit volume. My experience suggests that particular strategy will not work for a business your size. The only alternative left is to execute pricing strategies. Increasing profit dollars using price alternatives can be done by:

1. Selling all units at a higher price.

2. Selling more of the higher-priced units currently in stock.
3. Selling a new inventory of high-priced books.
4. Selling a combination of all of the alternatives.

Let's construct a higher-priced inventory alternative. Let's look at Figure 9–11, from the *Abstract*, tables 385 and 386, "New Books and New Editions Published" and "Books and Periodicals—Average Retail Prices," respectively.

Look at the book topics listed on the left. [*These tables really demonstrate the value of consulting secondary data before doing any primary work.*] No need to survey thousands of consumers to ask what subjects they would like to read. The tables detail what the publishing industry believes customers want, so we'll use these to construct an inventory profile.

Table 385 covers several years. We'll focus on the 1988 unit volume of published subjects. I'm going to assume that many subjects listed are not appropriate for a consumer bookstore. I'll delete as inappropriate inventory in the following subject areas: agriculture, law, medicine, music, socioeconomics, science, and technology. We'll build a spreadsheet from the *Abstract* data, excluding the subject deletions. Figure 9–12 illustrates a spreadsheet of the subjects we assume retail bookstore customers prefer. (The details for column and row formulas are found in Appendix IV.)

Column *D* lists the subjects to be inventoried; in column *E* are the total units published in 1988 for each subject and the total of all these selections; column *F* lists the computed percent each subject's unit volume represents of the total units published; and column *G* is the average hardcover retail price for each subject book from Table 386 in Figure 9–11. Everyone with me?

Now, we can see that some subjects have an average price higher than others. Likewise, some subjects have more units published than others. Column *H* is the weighted average price, which is a combination of price and the percent of each subject's unit volume (multiply column *F* by column *G*). Pay no attention to the fractional price figure in column *H* or whether it matches the price in the *Abstract*. The weighted average price for all the selected books in the unit volumes indicated is $24.95.

FIGURE 9-11
How Many New Books Were Published and What Were the Retail Prices?

Books and Periodicals

NO. 385. NEW BOOKS AND NEW EDITIONS PUBLISHED, AND IMPORTS, BY SUBJECT: 1980 TO 1988

[Covers listings in Bowker's *Weekly Record* in year shown, plus titles issued in that year which were listed in following six months. Comprises new books (published for first time) and new editions (with changes in text or format). Excludes government publications; books sold only by subscription; dissertations; periodicals and quarterlies; and pamphlets under 49 pages. See also *Historical Statistics, Colonial Times to 1970,* series R 191–216]

More units published not sold

SUBJECT	NEW BOOKS AND NEW EDITIONS							IMPORTS				
	1980	1983	1984	1985	1986	1987	1988, prel.	1980	1984	1985	1986	1987	1988, prel.
Total	42,377	53,380	51,058	50,070	52,637	56,057	47,489	5,390	6,337	7,304	7,749	8,229	7,077
Agriculture	461	572	507	536	564	652	575	104	103	118	124	135	114
Biography	1,691	1,896	1,836	1,545	1,697	1,693	1,338	157	61	166	168	128	109
Business	1,891	2,135	2,098	1,953	2,152	2,259	1,994	126	240	216	188	173	163
Education	1,185	1,636	1,696	1,518	1,604	1,462	1,375	74	140	196	159	154	173
Fiction	1,011	1,059	1,052	1,085	1,029	1,081	979	133	190	201	220	276	208
General works	2,835	5,470	5,413	5,105	5,578	6,298	5,144	71	164	171	247	291	256
History	1,643	2,767	3,021	2,905	2,484	2,620	2,083	132	268	329	346	382	294
Home econom- ics	2,220	2,296	2,257	2,327	2,471	2,882	2,550	296	324	395	384	482	434
Juvenile	879	1,325	1,306	1,228	1,103	1,168	929	40	41	41	42	39	28
Language	2,859	3,197	3,128	3,801	4,516	4,642	4,212	58	69	92	112	109	77
Law	529	669	670	632	668	699	534	134	174	216	334	201	185
Literature	1,102	1,756	1,406	1,349	1,385	1,544	1,129	112	158	170	190	225	169
Medicine	1,686	1,957	2,006	1,964	2,145	2,358	1,982	183	238	267	261	295	286
Music	3,292	4,002	3,654	3,579	3,445	3,995	3,376	671	508	598	665	757	599
Philosophy, psychol- ogy	357	417	387	364	356	352	273	35	54	70	66	66	61
Poetry and drama	1,429	1,578	1,554	1,559	1,669	1,845	1,656	218	211	267	263	331	320
Religion	1,179	1,164	1,164	1,166	1,278	1,236	1,106	120	174	220	216	180	183
Science	2,055	2,433	2,482	2,564	2,788	2,850	2,306	94	160	173	141	163	139
Sociology, econom- ics	3,109	3,620	3,236	3,304	3,360	3,658	3,118	1,069	1,032	1,242	1,214	1,302	1,099
Sports, recreation	7,152	8,470	7,794	7,441	7,912	8,115	7,119	1,050	1,373	1,559	1,635	1,736	1,519
Technology	971	1,335	1,299	1,154	1,192	1,263	941	85	137	107	110	97	70
Travel	2,337	2,994	2,639	2,526	2,698	2,756	2,216	373	454	419	618	651	549
	504	562	551	465	543	629	554	55	61	61	46	56	42

[1] Increase is due largely to a major improvement in the recording of paperbound books.   [2] Revised since originally published.

Source: R. R. Bowker Co., New York, NY. *Publishers Weekly* (Copyright by Reed Publishing.)

NO. 386. BOOKS AND PERIODICALS--AVERAGE RETAIL PRICES: 1980 TO 1988

Here's our price

Here's where I deleted subject

Got ratio of hardback to softback from here

SUBJECT	BOOKS (per vol.)				SUBJECT	PERIODICALS [2]			
	1980	1985	1987	1988, prel.		1980	1985	1987	1988
Hardcover [1]	**$24.64**	**$31.46**	**$36.28**	**$38.39**	**Total**	**$34.54**	**$59.70**	**$71.41**	**$77.93**
Agriculture	27.55	36.77	46.24	46.86	Agriculture	15.24	26.05	31 14	33 56
Art	27.70	35.15	37.71	39.84	Business and economics	25.42	44.41	50.39	53.89
Biography	19.77	22.20	25.04	25.81	Chemistry and physics	137.45	238.43	294.05	329.99
Business	22.45	28.84	33.31	37.60	Children's periodicals	7.85	13.31	15.19	16.39
Education	17.01	27.28	31.58	33.52	Engineering	49.15	84.38	103.49	114.83
Fiction	12.46	15.29	18.19	17.84	Fine and applied arts	18.67	27.03	30.58	32.43
General reference	29.84	37.91	43.81	49.29	History	15.77	25.55	27.54	30.16
History	22.78	27.02	31.74	33.24	Home economics	24.63	41.04	48.67	54.73
Juvenile	13.31	17.50	20.13	21.57	Industrial arts	20.70	35.09	41.45	44.20
Language	8.16	9.95	11.48	11.92	Journalism, communications	27.34	44.08	50.66	53.39
Language	22.16	28.68	37.80	39.12	Labor and industrial relations	18.84	34.75	38.65	44.06
Law	33.25	41.70	49.65	49.94	Law	20.00	35.15	39.82	43.33
Literature	18.70	24.53	28.70	30.81					
Medicine	34.28	44.36	57.68	64.69	Library and information science	23.25	40.66	48.42	51.61
Music	21.79	28.79	35.82	36.76	Literature and languages	15.30	24.18	26.21	28.04
Philosophy, psychology	21.70	28.11	33.31	35.10	Mathematics, botany, geology, and general science	67.54	116.93	146.08	159.33
Poetry and drama	17.85	22.14	28.46	27.19	Medicine	73.37	137.92	169.36	180.67
Religion	17.61	19.13	24.51	26.90	Philosophy and religion	14.73	24.30	25.60	27.09
Science	37.45	51.19	62.16	66.46	Physical education and recreation	23.45	37.81	43.30	47.95
Sociology, economics	31.76	33.33	34.38	36.44	Political science	13.83	23.72	26.67	28.60
Sports, recreation	15.92	23.43	23.96	25.55	Psychology	19.30	32.27	36.93	41.55
Technology	33.64	50.37	60.24	63.29	Sociology and anthropology	41.95	76.34	92.05	100.57
Travel	16.80	24.66	26.07	26.74	Zoology	27.56	50.87	60.29	64.27
Paperbacks:					General interest periodicals	44.58	90.75	112.91	127.33
Mass market [3]	(NA)	3.63	3.98	4.58		19.87	26.41	27.79	28.29
Trade or other [3]	8.60	13.98	14.55	14.67					

Here's our price

Annual subscription price

More detail on the book industry

NA Not available.   [1] Excludes publications of U.S. and other governmental units, books sold only by subscription, and dissertations.   [2] "Pocket-sized" books sold primarily through magazine and news outlets, supermarkets, variety stores, etc.   [3] Average annual subscription prices.

Source: R. R. Bowker Co., New York, NY. Books, *Publishers Weekly,* March 1989; (*The Bowker Annual of Library and Book Trade Information;* Periodicals, *Library Journal,* April 15, 1988, and earlier issues. (Copyright by Reed Publishing.)

Source: U.S. Dept. of Commerce, Bureau of the Census, *Statistical Abstract of the United States* (Washington, D.C.: Government Printing Office, 1990), p. 227.

Anne, this begins to answer two of your questions. You now know the percentage of units each subject should represent in your inventory, column *F*. Now I'm going to call column *I* "Anne's Percent." In the computer, column *I* is changeable to

FIGURE 9–12
1988 Book Subject Preferences Base Data

Column	D	E	F	G	H
Row					
8					
9					
10		Units	Percent of	Retail	Weighted
11	Subject	(000)	Publ. Books	Price	Price
12					
13	Art	1,338	4.7%	$ 39.84	$ 1.89
14	Biography	1,994	7.1%	25.81	1.83
15	Business	1,375	4.9%	37.60	1.84
16	Fiction	5,144	18.3%	17.84	3.26
17	Reference	2,083	7.4%	49.29	3.64
18	History	2,550	9.1%	33.24	3.01
19	Home Econ.	929	3.3%	21.57	0.71
20	Juvenile	4,212	15.0%	11.92	1.78
21	Literature	1,982	7.0%	30.81	2.17
22	Philosophy	1,656	5.9%	35.10	2.06
23	Poetry	1,106	3.9%	27.19	1.07
24	Religion	2,306	8.2%	26.90	2.20
25	Sports	941	3.3%	25.55	0.85
26	Travel	554	2.0%	26.74	0.53
27		28,170	100.0%	$ 26.40	$ 24.95
28					
29					

reflect what your interview sample wants to read. I'll now use column J, called "Anne's Price," to compute a new total weighted average price for "Anne's Percent" selections shown in column J, row 27. Adopting the right book subject mix should increase sales volume or your average price. Figure 9–13 is the complete book inventory and price spreadsheet.

FIGURE 9–13
Anne's Adjusted Percent of Subjects to Inventory and Anne's New Average Price

Column Row	D Subject	E Units (000)	F Percent of Total	G Retail Price	H Weighted Price	I Anne's Percent	J Anne's Price
Art		1,338	4.7	$ 39.84	$ 1.89	4.0	$ 1.59
Biography		1,994	7.1	25.81	1.83	7.5	1.94
Business		1,375	4.9	37.60	1.84	4.5	1.69
Fiction		5,144	18.3	17.84	3.26	18.0	3.21
Reference		2,083	7.4	49.29	3.64	8.2	4.04
History		2,550	9.1	33.24	3.01	10.0	3.32
Home Ec.		929	3.3	21.57	0.71	3.0	0.65
Juvenile		4,212	15.0	11.92	1.78	13.0	1.55
Literature		1,982	7.0	30.81	2.17	7.0	2.16
Philosophy		1,856	5.9	35.10	2.06	6.0	2.11
Poetry		1,106	3.9	27.19	1.07	3.3	0.90
Religion		2,306	8.2	26.90	2.20	7.5	2.02
Sports		941	3.3	25.55	0.85	3.5	0.89
Travel		554	2.0	26.74	0.53	4.5	1.20
		28,170 Total	100.0	$ 26.40 Average	$ 24.95 Total	100 %	$ 24.47 Total

Another profit increase opportunity, regardless of subject, depends on the sales mix of hardback and softback books. The derived 1988 hardback weighted average price was $24.95, but the average for all paperback "mass market" books was only $4.58 (see Figure 9–11, Table 386). The average price for hardbacks is far higher than for softbacks, so we can assume there is an opportunity for more profit dollars if more hardbacks can be sold. You must do more research on whether sales of hardbacks to your existing customer base can be increased; or find and attract new customers who prefer hardbacks.

The surveys of passersby and your customers should surface hardback and subject preferences. Also, it looks like managing the sales mix of hardback and softback books increasing your in-store traffic flow to areas featuring the more expensive hardbacks, like coffee-table books, may maximize the average price.

Anne, these marketing intelligence ideas are easy to implement. When you've collected and looked at the data, you'll be comfortable in repositioning your bookstore for growth.

In the time we have left, let's review the key messages I've presented to all of you.

WHERE WE'VE BEEN AND WHAT WE'VE LEARNED

We've covered a lot of material, from what is a customer to Anne resetting the price of her books. Let's review our journey.

We learned to think in new ways about:

- The customer's perception of product and service value.
- The multi-levels of performance the customer will buy.
- The distribution methods and costs to satisfy the customer.
- The real threats of competition.
- The priorities of information.
- Unique methods and techniques to find information.

Then we explored how to apply marketing intelligence tools by:

- Going to the library and using everyday articles and reports.
- Talking with government officials, users, and our competitors.
- Traveling to foreign lands and trying to access new markets by telephone and electronic database.
- Eating bad restaurant food, trying to crack a butcher shop sale, and introducing computer tape to customers who didn't know who we were.
- Browsing a bookstore shelf to find more profit, and dissecting the San Diego catering market.

- Selecting the right interview candidates and talking with them in person or on the phone, and by conducting mail surveys.
- Using and asking vital unbiased questions.
- Counting mops, employees, shoppers, and cars.
- Negotiating our way into the offices of key people who held the answers we needed.
- Manipulating simple spreadsheets to uncover new marketing ideas.
- Adding new words to our marketing vocabulary.

It was fun, and I really enjoyed it. You're all bright people. Now go out and use these new tools to discover what your customer really wants, and what your competitor is up to. Good luck!

APPENDIX I

THE VITAL QUESTIONS—HOW, WHAT, WHEN, WHERE, WHICH, WHO, AND WHY?

The "How" Questions

- How do I tell where people want to buy new products?
- How do the new competitors know what the customer really wants?
- How do you find the right price to charge?
- How do customers decide about shopping in a certain store?
- How do I change the business and build in-store traffic?
- How do I communicate my business story?
- How do I continually monitor the marketplace?
- How do I create potential customer traffic and sales leads?
- How do I define after-sale service needs?
- How do I define products and services my customers will buy?
- How do I determine available market potential?
- How do I differentiate my business?
- How do I expand my business and locate new customers?
- How do I find and attract new customers?
- How do I find new distribution and track competition?
- How do I find out what else people want to drink, besides coffee?
- How do I identify competitive technologies or services that may replace mine?
- How do I identify new product features?

- How do I learn about and track competition?
- How do I locate import or export opportunities?
- How do I secure new products and set sales forecasts?
- How do I select the best method of distribution to reach customers?
- How do I set prices according to what customers will pay?
- How do the customers want after-sale service changed?
- How are products used in the manufacturing or research process?
- How high a price will end users pay?
- How long do customers typically engage a consultant to work on problems?
- How long does it typically take for the business to collect receivables?
- How many of the customer's employees help make the purchasing decision?
- How many dollars are spent to buy all the units?
- How many employees are going into your competitor's factory?
- How many people enter a competitor's store per hour or per day?
- How many revenue and profit dollars are my competitors getting?
- How many sales calls does it take to get an order?
- How many sizes, shapes, or colors should be offered customers?
- How many times do customers expect me to visit them in a month?
- How many units are each of my major competitors selling?
- How many units do customers usually buy at one time?
- How many units does the total market buy?
- How much does a bank usually allow the business to borrow?
- How much cash is needed to support the customer's future sales, such as cash for inventory or advertising?

- How much change has the customer demanded in quality?
- How much detail is needed in customer price or work proposals?
- How much will distribution cost?
- How much do customers typically pay a consultant per hour or per day?
- How much margin does the distribution channel expect?
- How much of the interviewee's valued time will the questions take?
- How much space is needed to store my product?
- How much will the customer pay for change?
- How much time do retail browsers spend before buying or leaving?
- How much time does it take customers to assemble a product?
- How much time does it take for the customer to get the product unpackaged?
- How much will low-cost suppliers drive prices down?
- How often do customers buy my type product or use my service?
- How quickly do customers want product or service delivery?
- How can I be perceived differently than the competition?
- How do I build store traffic?
- How should I change the business?
- How do I close more sales?
- How do I determine the total market potential?
- How can I expand the business and find new resellers?
- How do I find the highest price customers will pay?
- How do I get information that will define new products for our company?
- How do I get new product definitions?
- How do I identify new distribution channels?
- How do I inventory best sellers?
- How do I locate new distribution?

The "What" Questions

- What advertising is the most effective to pull customers into the reseller outlets?
- What after-sale service and training do customers expect?
- What are the barriers to entry for a new supplier?
- What are the elements to develop a franchisee forecast and entry strategy?
- What are the major trade or consumer shows customers go to?
- What are the perceived good and bad points of the competition?
- What are the periodicals that potential customers read?
- What are the prices that should be used to calculate the current total market?
- What attitudes allow people to throw away a book, give it to charity, or just leave it where they finished the last chapter?
- What business am I really in, and how can I appear differently to my customers than my competitors?
- What changes in product reliability are customers expecting?
- What competitors have signed in to see my customer's buyers?
- What distribution will the competition use?
- What do customers like or dislike about my store or service?
- What does the customer expect in after-sale support?
- What does the customer really think about the competitors?
- What does the customer really think about my products/service?
- What has been the customer's past experience with consultants?
- What information am I trying to get?
- What internal purchasing policies are there about buying from only one supplier?

- What is currently performing to meet customer preferences?
- What is the catering unit potential?
- What is the competitive technology or service to replace me?
- What is the current distribution channel for products/services?
- What is the current level of competition?
- What are the customer's criteria to make a buying decision?
- What is the perceived difficulty people have reading the product instructions?
- What is the typical warranty for products/services like mine?
- What is the typical dollar revenue of a store like mine?
- What new perceptions do book buyers have about the value of owning a good book?
- What other distribution method would customers prefer, for example, catalog or mail order?
- What percent of products like those I sell are customers buying at large warehouse stores?
- What price and performance approach will make my product or service attractive?
- What product/service is needed to replace what the customer uses?
- What products/services give me the most revenue and profit?
- What services would the customer prefer that my competition or I am not now offering?
- What share of all shoppers prefer my store compared to the local competition?
- What is the competition doing?
- What do the customers like and dislike about my store and the competitor's store?
- What should I change?
- What types and sizes of business usually hire consultants?

- What should my secondary and primary market intelligence plan include to get the needed information?
- What's the next technology that will change my product performance?
- What, if any, distribution changes for my products will be required to assure my company the same profit?

The "When" Questions

- When must change be available?
- When does product/service performance have to pay back the price?
- When does the customer usually buy products/services like mine?
- When is product/service training and maintenance expected?
- When is the normal payment period for invoices?
- When is the peak traffic time of day in my store?
- When is delivery of the product/service typically expected?
- When will a replacement technology or service be available?
- When will new technology for products that perform better than mine become more widely available?
- When will pricing become too eroded to support some levels of distribution?
- When will I have to do business differently because of new technology?
- When will your customers begin to buy similar products from large warehouse-type stores at lower prices?

The "Where" Questions

- Where and from whom do customers want to hear my selling proposition?
- Where, how, and by whom will the information be used?
- Where are the customers?
- Where are the major and minor customers located?

- Where do customers buy products/services similar to mine?
- Where do customers go first to buy products/services like mine?
- Where do customers learn how to use or fix my product?
- Where do customers normally do most of their shopping in this mall or area?
- Where do customers want to buy products that I sell?
- Where or how does the customer gain value from my services?
- Where is the customer using my product or the competitor's?
- Where does the customer want to buy a new value?

The "Which" Questions

- Which advertising medium or store merchandising attracts customers?
- Which do customers prefer, best quality or better quality?
- Which service companies, like banks or insurance firms, provide basic accounting as part of their service package to the customer?
- Which vendors are delivering goods to the competition?

The "Who" Questions

- Who are the competitive salesmen visiting my customers?
- Who are the competitor's major customers?
- Who are the industry opinion leaders and gurus?
- Who is the buyer?
- Who is the reseller closest to the customer?
- Who is the current competition?
- Who is the end user?
- Who is the potential competition?
- Who is the specifier of product/service performance?
- Who wants change, and why do they want it?
- Who am I?

The "Why" Questions

- Why do customers buy from my competitors?
- Why do customers just look around the store and not buy?
- Why do my ads create so few or so many worthless sales leads?
- Why does the competition use the distribution channels it does?
- Why does the customer need more than one supplier?
- Why aren't people collecting books anymore?
- Why do customers still prefer wood?
- Why do customers like or dislike using consultants?
- Why have paperbacks not replaced hardback books?
- Why should resellers buy, stock, demonstrate, and sell my goods and services?
- Why do customers buy from the competition?
- Why won't businesses do their own business tasks with off-the-shelf solutions, instead of hiring service providers?

THE VITAL QUESTIONS ARRANGED BY KEY BUSINESS ELEMENTS

Performance

- How do I define products and services my customers will buy?
- How do I identify new product features?
- How do I secure new products and set sales forecasts?
- How are my products used in the manufacturing or research process?
- How many sizes, shapes, or colors should be offered customers?
- How much change has the customer demanded in quality?
- How much time does it take customers to assemble a product?
- How much time does it take for the customer to get my product out of the packaging?

- How do I define new products?
- How do I get information that will define new products for my company?
- How do I get new product definitions?
- What changes in product reliability are customers expecting?
- What is currently performing to meet customer preferences?
- What products/services give me the most revenue and profit?
- What services would the customer prefer that the competition and I are not now offering?
- What should I change?
- When is product/service training and maintenance expected?
- Where or how does the customer gain value from my services?
- Which do customers prefer, best quality or better quality?
- Why hasn't new technology or methods replaced the old?

Price

- How do I set prices according to what customers will pay?
- How do I find the right price to charge?
- How high a price will end users pay?
- How many dollars are spent to buy all the units?
- How much detail is needed in customer price or work proposals?
- How much will the customer pay for change?
- How do I find the highest price customers will pay?
- How do I inventory best sellers?
- What prices should be used to calculate the current total market?
- What is the catering unit potential?
- What is the typical warranty for products/services like mine?
- What is competitors' typical dollar revenue?

- What price and performance approach will make my product or service competitive?
- When does product/service performance have to pay back the price?
- When will pricing become too eroded to support some levels of distribution?

Distribution

- How do I change the business and build in-store traffic?
- How do I expand my business and locate new customers?
- How do I find new distribution and track competition?
- How do I select the best distribution to reach customers?
- How do customers want after-sale service changed?
- How do I tell where people want to buy new products?
- How many units do customers usually buy at one time?
- How many units does the total market buy?
- How much will distribution cost to reach customers?
- How much margin does the distribution channel expect?
- How can I build store traffic?
- How do I expand the business and find new resellers?
- How do I identify new distribution channels?
- How do I locate new distribution?
- What after-sale service and training do customers expect?
- What do customers like or dislike about my store or service?
- What is the current distribution channel for products/ services?
- What other distribution method would customers prefer, for example, catalog or mail order?
- What, if any, distribution changes for my products will be required to assure my company the same profit?
- When is the peak traffic time of day in the bookstore?
- Where are the major and minor customers located?
- Where do customers go first to buy products/services like mine?

- Where do customers learn how to use or fix my product?
- Where do customers normally do most of their shopping in this mall or area?
- Where do customers usually buy products that I sell?
- Where does the customer want to buy a new value?
- Who is the reseller closest to the customer?
- Why should resellers buy, stock, demonstrate, and sell my goods and services?

Customers

- How do I define after-sale service needs?
- How do I determine available market potential?
- How do I find and attract new customers?
- How do I find out what else customers want to buy from me?
- How do customers decide about shopping in a certain store?
- How many of my customer's employees help make the purchasing decision?
- How much does a bank usually allow the business to borrow?
- How much cash is needed to support the customer's future sales, such as cash for inventory, advertising, etc.?
- How much of the interviewee's valued time will the questions take?
- How much space does the customer need to store my product?
- How much time do retail store browsers spend before buying or leaving?
- How often do customers repeat a buy of what I sell?
- How quickly do customers want product or service delivery?
- What are the major trade or consumer shows customers go to?
- What are the periodicals that potential customers read?

- What attitudes allow people to dispose of a product, give it to charity, or just leave it where they finished using it?
- What does the customer expect in after-sale support?
- What does the customer really think about my products/ services?
- What has been the customer's past experience with consultants?
- What information am I trying to get?
- What are the customer's criteria to make a buying decision?
- What is the perceived difficulty people have reading the product instructions?
- What new perceptions do buyers have about the value of owning a product in the "best value" category?
- What percent of shoppers are high volume, the 20 percent, buyers?
- What types and sizes of business usually hire consultants?
- When must change be available?
- When does the customer usually buy products/services like mine?
- When is delivery of the product/service typically expected?
- Where and how will product or service information be used by the customer?
- Where is the customer using my product or the competitor's?
- Where are the customers?
- Which advertising medium or store merchandising attracts customers?
- Which service companies, like banks or insurance firms, provide basic accounting as part of their service package to the customer?
- Who is the buyer?
- Who is the end user?
- Who is the specifier of product/service performance?
- Who wants change, and why do they want it?

- Who am I?
- Why do customers just look around the store and not buy?
- Why won't businesses do their own tasks with off-the-shelf tools, instead of hiring outside service providers?

Competition

- How do I identify competitive technologies or services that may replace mine?
- How do I learn about and track competition?
- How do the new competitors know what the customer really wants?
- How many employees are going into your competitor's factory?
- How many people enter a competitor's store per hour or per day?
- How many revenue and profit dollars are my competitors getting?
- How many units are each of my major competitors selling?
- How much will low-cost suppliers drive prices down?
- How can I be perceived differently than the competition?
- How do I track the competition?
- What are the barriers to entry for a new supplier?
- What are the perceived good and bad points of the competition?
- What competitors have signed in to see my customer's buyers?
- What distribution system will the competition use?
- What does the customer really think about the competitors?
- What internal purchasing policies are there about buying from only one supplier?
- What is the competitive technology or service to replace me?
- What is the current level of competition?

- What product/service is needed to replace what the customer uses?
- What share of all shoppers prefer my store to the local competition's?
- What is the competition doing?
- What do customers like and dislike about my store and the competitor's store?
- What's the next technology that will change my product's performance?
- When will a replacement technology or service be available?
- When will I have to do business differently because of new technology?
- When will my customers begin to buy products from large warehouse-type stores at lower prices?
- Where do customers buy products/services similar to mine?
- Which vendors are delivering goods to the competition?
- Who are the competitive salespeople visiting my customers?
- Who are the competitor's major customers?
- Who is the current competition?
- Who is the potential competition?
- Why do customers buy from my competitors?
- Why does the competition use the distribution channels it does?
- Why does the customer need more than one supplier?
- Why do customers buy from the competition?

Other Marketing Functions

- How do I communicate my business story?
- How do I create potential customer traffic and sales leads?
- How do I differentiate my business?
- How do I locate import or export opportunities?
- How long do customers typically engage a consultant to work on problems?

- How long does it typically take for the business to collect receivables?
- How many sales calls does it take to get an order?
- How many times do customers expect me to visit them in a month?
- How much do customers typically pay a consultant per hour or per day?
- How should I change the business?
- How do I close more sales?
- How do I determine the total market potential?
- What advertising is the most effective to pull customers into the reseller outlets?
- What are the elements to develop a franchisee forecast?
- What business am I really in, and how can I appear differently to my customers than my competitors?
- What should my secondary and primary market intelligence plan include to get to the information I need?
- When is the normal payment period for invoices?
- Where and from whom do customers want to hear my selling proposition?
- Who are the industry opinion leaders and gurus?
- Why do my ads create so few or so many worthless sales leads?
- Why do customers like or dislike using consultants?

Monitoring

- How do I continually monitor the marketplace?

APPENDIX II

SECONDARY INFORMATION SOURCES

By now you've determined that I am a great advocate of the telephone to quickly find information. We can now add the facsimile to the arsenal of marketing intelligence tools to speed information flow. People with expertise will usually offer addresses, names, and phone and fax numbers for contacts at data sources. So rather than a detailed list of secondary information references you've found in the book, I'm just going to list the key sources under the appropriate category, give the phone and/or the fax number, and in some cases the title of the individual you should ask for to begin the searches.

Use the local information operators by dialing (area code)-555-1212, and always inquire whether these sources have toll-free numbers by dialing (800)-555-1212.

Newspapers and Magazines

- *The New York Times*: Tel. (212)556-1234, Fax (212) 556-4603.
- *Los Angeles Times*: Tel. (213)237-7000.
- *The Wall Street Journal*: Tel. (212)416-2676, Fax (212) 416-3299.
- *Barron's*: Tel. (212)808-6600.
- *Financial Times* (U.S. Office): Tel. (212)628-8088.
- The local or regional newspaper: Tel. 1-(area code) 555-1212.
- *Business Week*: Tel. (212)512-2000, Fax (212)512-6875.
- *Fortune*: Tel. (212)522-1212, Fax (242)522-0907.
- *Forbes*: Tel. (212)620-2000, Fax (212)620-2417.
- *Inc.*: Tel. (617)248-8000.

- *Sales & Marketing Management*: Tel. (212)986-4800, Fax (212)986-3727.

Directories and Annuals

- Dun & Bradstreet: Tel. (212)593-6800.
- Moody's—Investors Service: Tel. (212)553-0300.
- Standard & Poors: Tel. (212)208-8000, Fax (212)208-8423.
- The Thomas Register: Tel. (212)695-0500.
- Encyclopedia of American Associations: Tel. (800)877-4253.
- Washington Information Directory, Congressional Quarterly: (202)887-8500.
- White & Yellow telephone pages: Dial 411 for local telephone company.
- Elected officials—local, regional, national: Dial 411 for number.
- U.S. Industrial Outlook—Commerce Dept.: Tel. (301) 763-4040.
- Annual Reports of Fortune 100: Tel. (212)522-1212, Fax (242)522-0907.
- *Hoover's Handbook of American Business*: Tel. (512) 454-7778.
- Local chamber of commerce membership lists: Dial 411 for number.
- Import-Export & Foreign Trade—directories: Tel. (202) 377-2000.

Government Sources and Publications

- Superintendent of Documents—local government bookstores: (202)783-3238.
- The Commerce Department—main information: Tel. (202) 377-2000.
  - Bureau of the Census—main information: Tel. (301) 763-7662.
    - Deputy Director's Office: Tel. (301)763-5192.
    - Statistical Abstract—Data User Division: (301) 763-7662.

- Public Information Office: (301)763-4051.
- Data requests: (301)763-4040.
- Center for Demographic Studies: Tel. (301)763-7720.
- Center for Economic Studies: (301)763-2337.
- Center for International Research: Tel. (301) 763-2870.
- Center for International Statistics: (301)763-2832.
- Office of Economics and Statistics Administration—Undersecretary: (202)377-3737.
- Travel and Tourism Administration—Undersecretary: (202)377-0140.
- The Patent Office—main information: Tel. (703) 557-3158.
- Federal Drug Administration: Tel. (301)443-1544.
- Environmental Protection Agency—main information: (202)260-2090.
- IRS—Statistics of Income—Public Affairs: Tel. (202) 566-4743.
- Department of Defense—main information: Tel. (703) 545-6700.
- Federal Trade Commission: Tel. (202)326-2000.
- Hearings before the state and federal legislatures: 411 for local representative.
- United Nations Information Center: Tel. (202)289-8670.

Electronic Data Bases

- Dialog Information Services, Inc.: Tel. (800)334-2564.
- Knowledge Index: Tel. (800)334-2564.
- Dow-Jones News Retrieval: Tel. (609)452-1511, Fax (609) 520-4775.
- Data-Star of Radio Suisse: Tel. (215)687-6777.

For a more comprehensive listing of documents, electronic data bases, and survey software, consult the appendixes of Alan R. Andreasen's book, *Cheap But Good Marketing Research*, published by Business One Irwin.

APPENDIX III

MARKETING INTELLIGENCE TRAINING AND PRACTICE

The following questions and suggestions will prepare you to launch a marketing intelligence program for your own business. They are based on the chapter contents of this book.

Chapter One

1. Describe four conditions that qualify your customer.
2. Prepare a list of questions that focus on potential changes in your business.

Chapter Two

1. Complete the who, what, where, when, and how worksheet on pages 28–30.

Chapter Three

1. Identify and write down your key business questions.
2. Draw your business in a good, better, and best triangle (see Figure 3–3). Now put in your competition. Your price. Your competitor's price. What can you assume from this information?

Chapter Four

1. Describe your business as an OEM.
2. List how manufacturer's reps, resellers, or VARs play a part in your business. Now list who they are or could be.
3. Calculate the percentage mark-up or discount you offer your customers.
4. Complete the competition questionnaire on pages 65–66.

Chapter Five

1. Complete the vital questions found in Figure 5–1.
2. Identify and list the elements of your business that increase your perceived value with the customer. Evaluate and describe whether or why your pricing is competitive.
3. List what new elements can be offered or communicated to your customer to add value.
4. Form and write down two unbiased questions for a specific customer, user, specifier, buyer, and distribution decision maker with whom you currently conduct business.

Chapter Six

1. Go to the library and find the demographics for your ZIP code or census tract.
2. Find the SIC code for your business and your major customers.
3. Write the keywords to conduct an electronic data base search. With your computer, or a friend's, enter an electronic data base and find current articles about your business.
4. Locate your business records for the past two years that will give you customer sales and product or service cost information.

Chapter Seven

1. Find the name of a guru in your industry, business activity, or area of special interest. Get a name and phone number, and cite where or how the person was referred to you.
2. Call a government office to obtain information about the current economic conditions and future trends for your business sector.
3. Put together an agenda and a short questionnaire to get answers to two of your vital questions.
4. Select a sample of five local telephone interview contacts and conduct a survey. You can practice on fellow employees or outside business friends.

5. Conduct one personal interview. Take only a few notes during the session, and then later write down all you learned.
6. Construct a simple spreadsheet to tabulate and analyze the survey information.

Chapter Eight

1. Locate and study a completed marketing intelligence report.
2. Critique the format, depth of information, and supporting evidence.
3. Write down how you would improve the report.

APPENDIX IV

BILL'S AND ANNE'S SPREADSHEET FORMULAS

Here are the ways to use the following formulas that are in the spreadsheets we built for Bill's business as shown in Figure 9–6, and Anne's book inventory and price problem in Figure 9–13.

1. Where the column and row intersect is the cell "address." Each line in the following sets of formula correspond to a specific cell address. Enter the information exactly as it appears after the cell address, for example, D8: — 'MANNY.

2. The lines and shading you see in the Figures are not included. You'll have to do that on your own.

Okay, get started. Just use your own business information to get new perspectives about your market.

Bill's Sales Analysis	Anne's Price–Volume Analysis
Spreadsheet Cells	Spreadsheet Cells
D8: 'MANNY	E10: "Art
E8: 100	F10: "% of
F8: @COUNT($E$8..E8)/$F$28	G10: "Retail
G8: 66	H10: "Weighted
H8: +G8/$G$28	I10: "Anne's
I8: +I7+G8	J10: "Anne's
J8: +J7+H8	D11: "Subject
K8: 29	E11: "(000)
L8: +K8/$K$28	F11: "Total
M8: +M7+L8	G11: "Price
D9: 'FRANK	H11: "Price
E9: 100	I11: "Percent
F9: @COUNT($E$8..E9)/$F$28	J11: "Price
G9: 102	D13: 'Art
H9: +G9/$G$28	E13: 1338
I9: +I8+G9	F13: +E13/$E$27

J9: +J8+H9
K9: 19
L9: +K9/$K$28
M9: +M8+L9

—Now "COPY FROM": D9 to M9
               to D10 to D28
AND, fill—in column D, E, G
                  and K
D29: 'Company
F29: 125 (My guess)
G29: 2500
K29: 875

G13: 39.84
H13: +G13*F13
I13: 0.04
J13: +I13*G13
D14: 'Biography
E14: 1994
F14: +E14/$E$27
G14: 25.81
H14: +G14*F14
I14: 0.075
J14: +I14*G14
—Now "COPY FROM": D14 to M14
                to D15 to D26
AND, fill—in column D, E, G and I
E27: @SUM(E13..E26)
F27: @SUM(F13..F26)
G27: @AVG(G13..G26)
H27: @SUM(H13..H26)
I27: @SUM(I13..I26)
J27: @SUM(J13..J25)

INDEX

Also Available from Business One Irwin . . .

AFTERMARKETING
How to Keep Customers for Life through Relationship Marketing
Terry G. Vavra

Aftermarketing shows you how relationship marketing is the new imperative to keep your company ahead of the competition. You'll discover how to identify your customers and build a customer information file, measure customers' satisfaction levels to constantly strive for improvement, analyze informal customer feedback, and manage formal customer communication programs, plus much more!
ISBN: 1-55623-605-0

TARGETING THE TRENDSETTING CONSUMER
How to Market Your Product or Service to Influential Buyers
Irma Zandl and Richard Leonard

Make your product a success with those who determine what's hot and what's not! Drawing on examples from a broad range of businesses—from Harley-Davidson to Chanel—the authors show you how to develop a unified, multichanneled strategy that will attract trendsetting consumers.
ISBN: 1-55623-478-3

THE COMPLETE GUIDE TO REGIONAL MARKETING
Shawn McKenna

Discover how you can stimulate new business and satisfy existing customer and consumer demand more efficiently. Using McKenna's unique Marketing Assessment Process, you can "customer-ize" your marketing effort and use your marketing budget more effectively.
ISBN: 1-55623-422-8

CREATING DEMAND
Powerful Tips and Tactics for Marketing Your Product or Service
Richard Ott

Double the effectiveness of your advertising at no additional cost! Ott gives you new ways to stimulate demand for your products or services so you can allocate precious resources to maximize appreciable return.
ISBN: 1-55623-560-7

MEGABRANDS
How to Build Them/How to Beat Them
John Loden

Leverage the strength of existing brand leaders and build market share, customer loyalty, and sales. Even if you're not currently working for the number one brand, Loden shows you how to use guerrilla tactics to overcome a leader's superior resources and prosper in the face of intense competition.
ISBN: 1-55623-469-4